Shannon Lush is a fine-arts restorer and artist who uses a range of tools, adhesives and solvents to repair items. She has a deep passion for household handy hints, with knowledge passed down through her family. For the past decade, she's been solving other people's domestic disasters through regular media appearances on radio, TV and newspapers and the bestselling *Spotless* series of books with Jennifer, *Kids Can Clean* with Erin Lush and *Stainless* with Trent Hayes. She's never been stumped with a 'how to' question about the home and loves finding creative solutions to everyday domestic problems.

Jennifer Fleming is a long-time producer and presenter at ABC Radio working across a range of popular programs. She's also a bestselling writer of seven books, including the #1 selling non-fiction title of 2006, *Spotless: Room-by-room solutions to domestic disasters* (with Shannon). Her other books include *The Feel Good Body: 7 steps to easing aches and looking great*, with Anna-Louise Bouvier and *The Advertising Effect: How to change behaviour,* with Adam Ferrier.

Titles by
Shannon Lush and Jennifer Fleming
Spotless
Spotless 2
Speedcleaning
How to be Comfy
Save
Completely Spotless

Title by
Shannon and Erin Lush
Kids Can Clean

Title by
Shannon Lush and Trent Hayes
Stainless

Title by
Jennifer Fleming and Anna-Louise Bouvier
The Feel Good Body

SPOTLESS A-Z

The Ultimate Guide to Stain Removal

Shannon Lush & Jennifer Fleming

First published in Australia in 2014
by HarperCollins*Publishers* Australia Pty Limited
ABN 36 009 913 517
harpercollins.com.au

HarperCollins *Publishers*
Macken House,
39/40 Mayor Street Upper
Dublin 1, D01 C9W8, Ireland

National Library of Australia Cataloguing-in-Publication data:

Lush, Shannon, author.
Spotless A–Z / Shannon Lush and Jennifer Fleming.
978 0 7333 3340 8 (pbk.)
978 1 4607 0279 6 (ebook)
House cleaning – Handbooks, manuals, etc.
Spotting (cleaning) – Handbooks, manuals, etc.
Other Authors/Contributors: Fleming, Jennifer, author.
Australian Broadcasting Corporation.
648.5

Cover design by Hazel Lam, HarperCollins Design Studio
Cover images by shutterstock.com
Typeset in 10/13pt Georgia Regular by Kirby Jones
The papers used by HarperCollins in the manufacture of this book are a natural, recyclable product made from wood grown in sustainable plantation forests. The fibre source and manufacturing processes meet recognised international environmental standards, and carry certification.
Printed and bound in Australia by McPherson's Printing Group

Contents

Introduction

Welcome to *Spotless A–Z* – your one-stop shop for stain removal. Now, solutions are even easier to find in this A–Z guide. Not only that, it also features brand-new stains, surfaces and solutions – from pesto to pomegranate, fake tan to faux fur, hoisin sauce to hummus – as well as old favourites – from red wine to rust, banana to butter, moths to mayonnaise.

It's almost a decade since *Spotless: Room-by-room solutions to domestic disasters* became a must-have staple in homes across Australia – and the world. Its tried-and-true remedies have rescued many an accidental stain maker. The solutions are based on basic chemistry with an emphasis on low-toxicity stain removal. Mix an acid, such as white vinegar, with an alkali, such as bicarbonate of soda, and you get a cleaning reaction.

As mentioned in previous books, there are a couple of tricks with stain removal. First, don't panic and put something on the stain that could make it worse. Instead, work out what the stain is made of – protein, carbohydrate, fats, dye, resins or glue – and apply its solvent. If the stain has multiple components, first remove proteins – these have a dark ring around their edge – using pH neutral soap and cold water. Then remove carbohydrates – which are dark in the centre and feel stiff – using pH neutral soap and blood-heat (body temperature) water. Next come fats that feel greasy between your fingers. These are removed by emulsifying the stain with dishwashing liquid. Dyes, glues and resins need specific solvents, such as acetone, methylated spirits and white spirits. If you're unsure, test an inconspicuous part of the stain by applying the solvent on a cotton bud and see what works.

The other rules of stain removal include:

- The sooner you get to the stain, the easier it is to remove.
- More is not better. Use the least amount of solvent possible.
- Oils ain't oils. Darker coloured oils, such as engine grease, are removed with baby oil first then dishwashing liquid. Lighter coloured oils, such as olive oil, are removed with dishwashing liquid.
- It's best to dry most clothing in sunshine because it's a natural disinfectant and gentler on the fibres than a dryer. Some items must be dried in sunshine to remove stains. Remove items from the clothesline as soon as they dry – don't leave them hanging for days or they will deteriorate and fade. Dry silk and wool in the shade. Ensure silk is dried away from the wind so the fibres don't tangle and leave a dusty look. If you don't have a clothesline outside, use a clothes airer inside. Make sure enough air can circulate around the items. If you must use a dryer, add a dry tea towel to speed the drying time.
- Blood-heat water is water at body temperature – 37°C. Test the temperature on your inside wrist as you would a baby's bottle.
- Use pure acetone, not nail polish remover.
- Consult care labels.
- If in doubt, test first on an inconspicuous area using a cotton bud.

We've tried to include every stain imaginable but new ones pop up all the time. If you have a stain that isn't featured, consult 'Mystery Stains' to help you work out the solution. We wish you well in your stain removal.

Useful Ingredients

ACETONE is a volatile, flammable ketone. It's a liquid solvent for resins, primers, nail polish, superglue, acrylics and heavy plastics. Available at the supermarket and hardware stores.

BABY OIL is also known as mineral oil. It's a lubricant and skin ointment and dilutes dark oils. Available from the supermarket or chemist.

BATHROOM SOAP is a regular white cake of soap (not laundry soap). The less fragrance it has, the better it is to clean with. Use to remove protein stains. It's available at the supermarket.

BAY LEAVES are a moth and weevil deterrent available from the greengrocer or supermarket.

BEESWAX is the wax produced by bees when making honeycomb and is used as a polishing, lubricating and sealing agent. It's available at hardware stores, chemists, some supermarkets or your local apiarist.

BICARB (BICARBONATE OF SODA OR BAKING SODA) is a salt and alkaline that neutralises acid. When added to an acid (such as white vinegar), it releases carbon dioxide and water. It penetrates stains and dissolves grease. Available at the supermarket.

BLOOD-HEAT WATER is water at body temperature or 37°C.

BORAX is crystalline sodium borate and is used as a fungicide, insecticide and detergent booster. It's mildly toxic and should be used with care. Avoid contact with skin and avoid ingestion. Available from the supermarket.

BRAN – see 'Unprocessed wheat bran'.

BRASSO is a proprietary abrasive product that partially melts polyurethane. It's available at the supermarket.

BROOMS come in many sizes and varieties. Available from the supermarket and hardware store.

BUCKETS come in various sizes – 9 litres is most common – and are available at the supermarket and hardware store.

CAMPHOR is a ketone from the camphor laurel tree. It's flammable and has a strong vapour that deters many insects, particularly moths, as well as cats and possums. It's found in mothballs, naphthalene flakes and *Vicks VapoRub* and is available from the supermarket. Do not use mothballs or naphthalene flakes if you have children under 3 years of age. Any children's clothes that have been exposed to these should be aired outdoors to remove odour and washed before use.

CARNAUBA WAX is a hard, fine wax used in furniture and timber polish. It's available from the hardware store.

CARPET CLEANER comes in many varieties. They can be soap-based, bicarb-based, detergent-based or alcohol-based.

CEDAR CHIPS are a moth deterrent. Available from the supermarket.

CERA WAX is a component of liquid wax polish used on marble and natural stone. Brands include *Tenax CeraFluida Natural Stone Liquid Wax* and *Surie Liquid Wax Polish.* Source it online.

CHALK STICKS are very absorbent and are also useful to mark around urine stains. Available from the supermarket, craft store, newsagent and toy store.

CIGARETTE ASH removes smoke and soot stains. Get some from your local club or hotel.

CITRIC ACID POWDER is a white crystalline powder derived from lemons, oranges and some berries. Available at the supermarket.

CLOTH is any lint-free, cotton-based cloth used to blot or wipe over stains. Old cotton T-shirts make great cloths.

CLOVES are a spice from the dried flower bud of the clove tree. They deter silverfish. Clove oil is extracted from the clove flower bud and is used to inhibit mould. Available from the chemist. (See also 'Oil of Cloves'.)

CLR stands for Calcium, Lime and Rust. It removes calcium deposits from glass and kettles, lime scale from coffee machines, toilets and sinks, and rust from cement, porcelain, chrome and fabric. It can burn, so wear protective gloves when using it and don't get it on your skin. Available from the supermarket and hardware store.

COLD WATER is the coldest possible tap water and is used when removing protein stains.

COLOUR RUN REMOVER (formerly called *Runaway*) comes in two varieties – *Colour Run Remover: Whites* and *SOS Colour Run*. It removes colour run in fabrics and carpet. Available from the supermarket in the laundry aisle. Other colour run remover products are available online.

COPPER SULPHATE is a fungicide. It's available at the hardware store and gardening suppliers.

CORNFLOUR is a starch of maize, rice and other grains. It's absorbent and a very fine abrasive. Available from the supermarket.

COTTON BALL is a round fluffy ball made of cotton. Use to absorb stains. It's available from the supermarket.

COTTON BUD is fluffy cotton wrapped over the ends of a plastic tube. Use to absorb stains. It's available from the supermarket.

DAMP CLOTH is a cloth that's been run under water and then tightly wrung so it doesn't drip. It could also be a cloth dabbed with water.

DENTURE TABLETS are used to clean dentures but also whiten porcelain and ceramic surfaces. Available from the supermarket and chemist.

DISHWASHING LIQUID removes grease. Add a couple of drops to your fingertips and massage into oil and grease stains. It's available at the supermarket.

DISPOSABLE RUBBER GLOVES protect your skin from harsh chemicals and heat. Available from the supermarket.

EPSOM SALTS are a hydrated magnesium sulphate named because they were first found at Epsom in the UK. Use as a bath soaker and also to unshrink jumpers and other woollens. Available from the supermarket and chemist.

ERASER (pencil or biro) is made of rubber and removes lead pencil or biro marks on some surfaces. It's available from the supermarket or newsagency.

EUCALYPTUS OIL is an essential oil distilled from certain eucalyptus tree leaves. It's a paint and dye stripper and a solvent for adhesives and some resins, and it releases vapours that inhibit some insects. Available at the supermarket and chemist.

FULLER'S EARTH is a calcium clay with a bleaching agent and is very absorbent. It's a wool relaxant. Use to shrink and unshrink woollens. Available at the chemist or from cosmetic manufacturing companies.

GLYCERINE is a clear liquid used as an agent in cosmetics, toothpaste and shampoos. It's water- and alcohol-soluble. Glycerine helps to loosen stains, particularly tannin stains. Available at the supermarket or chemist.

GROUT RAKE is a handheld device with a flat tungsten tip that's run against grout to remove it by making it powdery. Grout rakes are available at the hardware store.

GUMPTION is a greyish cleaning paste with many uses. It contains a mild bleaching agent and is an abrasive. Available at the supermarket.

HAIR CONDITIONER (CHEAP) has fewer perfumes and additives than more expensive ones. Use to rinse and soften woollens. Available at the supermarket or chemist.
HAIR DRYER speeds drying time and helps melt wax and crayon stains. It's available from department stores.
HYDROGEN PEROXIDE (3 PER CENT) is an oxidising liquid. Use as an antiseptic and bleaching agent. It's available at the supermarket and chemist.
IRON is a household clothes iron. It's available from department stores.
JEWELLERS ROUGE removes fine scratches in glass. Available at the hardware store or online.
KEROSENE is a combustible liquid hydrocarbon. Use as a solvent. It's available at the hardware store and some supermarkets.
LAUNDRY DETERGENT is used in the washing machine to lift dirt and stains from fabric. It's available at the supermarket.
LAVENDER OIL is from lavender flowers and is used in many ways, including as a pollen remover, insect repellent, dog inhibitor and air freshener. Available at the supermarket, chemist and health food store.
LEATHER CONDITIONER is used to treat leather. It's available at shoe repair stores and hardware stores. Or make your own – see **Household formulas.**
LEMON JUICE is used to remove rust stains and to lighten or bleach colour. Lemons and lemon juice are available at the supermarket and greengrocer.
LEMON OIL is the oil in lemon peel. Use to deter spiders, polish pale timbers and provide a fresh fragrance. Available at the health store, or make your own – see under 'Spiders'.
METAL COMB is used to remove nail polish from carpet. It's available at chemists.

METHYL ETHYL KETONE (MEK) is a solvent. It's very toxic and should only be applied wearing gloves and a mask in a well-ventilated area. Available at the hardware store.

METHYLATED SPIRITS is a raw alcohol with menthol. It's a solvent for some paint and marker inks, and helps release stains and smells from synthetic materials. Available from the supermarket and hardware store.

***NO-FIL* SANDPAPER** is a lightweight sanding sheet made of silicon carbide abrasive. Available at the hardware store.

NYLON BRUSH is a dishwashing brush. It's available at the supermarket.

OIL OF CLOVES is cold-pressed oil from the dried flower bud of the clove tree. It's a mould inhibitor, insecticide, toothache soother and ingredient in cooking. Available at the chemist.

OIL OF PENNYROYAL is oil from a small-leafed mint. It deters moths, bed bugs and fleas, but is **harmful to pregnant women and pregnant pets**. Use with care. Remember 1 drop means 1 drop. Available at the chemist or online.

PANTYHOSE/STOCKINGS have a weave and fibre that make them a great scrubber and polisher. Available at the supermarket and chemist.

PAPER TOWEL is used to polish glass, and absorb stains and excess moisture. It's available at the supermarket.

PETROLEUM JELLY (*VASELINE*) is a mixture of mineral oils, paraffin and microcrystalline waxes. It acts as a water barrier and inhibits snails. Available at the supermarket and chemist.

PILLOWCASE can be used to hold items and protect delicates in the washing machine. Available at department stores.

PLASTIC COMB is ideal for picking up spills and stains

from carpet and upholstery. It's available at the supermarket or chemist.

PLASTIC WRAP is cling wrap. Available from the supermarket.

PLASTER OF PARIS is white powder made of calcium sulphate, which forms a paste when mixed with water. It has absorbent properties. Available from art suppliers and hardware stores.

POTTER'S PLASTER is very similar to plaster of Paris, but is higher in lime. It also has absorbent properties. Available from art suppliers and hardware stores.

RANEX removes calcium, lime and rust. It can burn, so wear protective gloves when using it and don't get it on your skin. It's available at hardware stores.

ROTTEN MILK is full cream milk left to rot in the sun until it forms solids. It absorbs ink stains. Buy milk from the supermarket.

RUST CONVERTER is a product that converts iron oxide rust into metal that protects the surface from corrosion. Available at hardware stores.

SADDLE SOAP cleans leather. It's available at shoe repair stores and some supermarkets.

SHAMPOO (CHEAP) has fewer fragrances and is better for cleaning than more expensive shampoos. Use to wash woollens. Available at the supermarket or chemist.

SHELLAC is a varnish made of a resinous substance secreted through the pores of the *Coccus lacca* scale insect. This substance is then dissolved in alcohol or a similar solvent. Used for making varnish, polish and sealing wax. Available at the hardware store.

SILICONE is a liquid gel that hardens once applied. It's used as a join sealant and is water-impermeable. Available at the hardware store.

SPRAY PACK is a plastic bottle with a removable nozzle head. It's available at the supermarket or hardware store.
SQUEEGEE is an implement with a rubber blade on one side. Use to wipe moisture from surfaces. It's available at the supermarket or hardware store.
STIFF BRUSH is a brush with strong bristles. Available from the supermarket.
SUGAR SOAP is a highly caustic soap. It comes in powder or liquid form. The powder has a mild abrasive. It's available at the supermarket and hardware store.
SWEET ALMOND OIL is the oil from almond nuts. Use to clean bone, glass, ivory, *Bakelite* and plastics. It's available from the supermarket or chemist.
TALCUM POWDER is a mineral powder. It's a superfine abrasive and lubricant, and is also absorbent. Available at the supermarket and chemist.
TEA BAG is used after you've finished your cup of tea to clean timber and aluminium and to restore tannins. Available at the supermarket.
TEA TREE OIL is oil extracted from the tea tree bush. It's an antibacterial and removes glues and resins, including chewing gum. Available at the supermarket and chemist.
TISSUES can be used to absorb stains and moisture, and protect surfaces. Available at the supermarket and chemist.
TOOTHBRUSH makes a great mini scrubbing brush. Keep old ones to clean difficult-to-reach areas and grout. Available at the supermarket and chemist.
TURPENTINE is a volatile oil and resin distilled from trees and is a solvent for oil-based paints. It's available at hardware stores.
ULTRAVIOLET (UV) LIGHT is used to fade stains. (If using ultraviolet light, protect areas around the stain with

cardboard.) UV light doesn't dry stains and you will need to absorb remaining moisture with paper towel. Available from electronics stores, lighting stores or online.

UNIODISED SALT is salt that doesn't contain iodine. The iodine in salt can stain some fabrics. Available at the supermarket.

UNPROCESSED WHEAT BRAN is the ground husk of wheat. It is absorbent and can be used as a scourer and to clean fabrics and furs. Don't substitute another type of bran. Available at the supermarket.

VACUUM CLEANER sucks up dirt. It's available at department stores and specialist vacuum cleaning stores.

VANILLA ESSENCE is extract from vanilla beans combined with alcohol. It offers fragrance and flavour to food and is a deodoriser. Available from the supermarket.

VANISH NAPISAN OXI ACTION has an active ingredient of sodium percarbonate, and is a detergent and bleaching agent that removes some stains. Available at the supermarket and some chemists.

VANISH PREEN OXI ACTION CARPET STAIN REMOVER is a proprietary product designed to remove a range of carpet stains. Available from the supermarket.

VINEGAR is an acid. It's also a preservative, condiment, beverage and, for our purposes, cleaner and sanitiser. White vinegar is best for cleaning but not on marble surfaces. Available from the supermarket.

WHITE SPIRITS is a mixture of petroleum hydrocarbons and a solvent. It's also known as dry-cleaning fluid, *Shellite* or *Murlex*. Available at hardware stores.

WHITE VINEGAR is an acid that cleans and sanitises. Available at the supermarket.

WHITING is a powder used in cleaning and polishing glass. Available from leadlight stores.

WITCH-HAZEL is extracted from the bark and leaves of the shrub *Hamamelis virginiana*. It's a soothing and mildly astringent lotion. Available at the supermarket and chemist.
ZIP-LOCK BAG is a plastic bag with a resealable top. Available at the supermarket.

Other basic household items not listed here may be called for in methods from time to time.

ABALONE

Abalone is high in protein, fat and zinc. Remove as soon as possible because it will smell and attract maggots and flies.

On carpet/upholstery

- Remove excess by lifting with a plastic comb or by blotting with paper towel.
- Scribble with a cake of bathroom soap run under cold water.
- Place equal parts talcum powder and tea tree oil over the stain until it dries.
- Remove with a stiff brush. Vacuum as you brush.

On cotton/fabric

- Remove excess under the tap using cold water.
- Scribble with a cake of bathroom soap run under cold water. Rub the fabric against itself using your hands.
- Place equal parts talcum powder and tea tree oil over the stain until it dries.
- Brush off and wash according to the fabric. Dry in sunshine.

ACNE CREAM

Acne cream can leave bleach marks. Remove immediately.

On carpet/upholstery

- Remove excess by lifting with a plastic comb or by blotting with paper towel.
- Place white vinegar on a cloth and wring tightly so it's damp but not wet. Blot over the mark.

- Place the vinegar cloth in one hand and a dry cloth in the other and wipe hand over hand, as though stroking a cat, until the stain is removed.
- Absorb moisture by covering the area with paper towel. Place a book on top of the paper towel to assist with absorption.

On cotton/fabric

- Remove excess under the tap using cold water.
- Blot with or soak in white vinegar until the stain is removed.
- Wash according to the fabric. Dry on the clothesline or clothes airer.

On stone/tiles

- Remove excess by blotting with paper towel.
- If a mark remains, mix plaster of Paris and water to the consistency of peanut butter.
- To each cup of mixture, add 1 teaspoon of dishwashing liquid.
- Spread 5 mm to 1 cm thick over the stain.
- Allow to dry completely. If it feels cold on the back of your hand, it's not dry.
- Crack with a wooden spoon or with the back of a broom.
- Sweep away.

ADHESIVE STAINS

(see 'Glue' or 'Sticky Tape Residue')

AFTERSHAVE COLOGNE

On carpet/upholstery

- Remove excess by blotting with paper towel.
- Lightly brush over the surface of the stain with 2 drops of glycerine on a toothbrush or cloth. Leave for 90 minutes.
- Tightly wring a cloth in white vinegar, fold the cloth flat and polish out the glycerine without pushing it into the back of the carpet or upholstery.
- Absorb moisture by covering the area with paper towel. Place a book on top of the paper towel to assist with absorption.

On cotton/fabric (not silk/wool)

- Soak in ½ lid of *Vanish NapiSan Oxi Action* in a 9-litre bucket of cold water for 30 minutes. Don't use on wool or silk.
- Wash according to the fabric. Dry on the clothesline or clothes airer.

On silk/wool

- Wash in 1 teaspoon of cheap shampoo and blood-heat (body temperature) water.
- Rinse in blood-heat water.
- Gently wring and dry flat on a towel in the shade. Ensure silk is dried away from the wind so the fibres don't tangle and leave a dusty look.

On timber

- Remove excess by blotting with paper towel.
- Wipe with a paste of bicarb and water on a cloth.

- Wipe with a damp cloth.
- If bleached, leave a damp tea bag over the timber.

AIOLI

(see 'Mayonnaise')

ALCOHOL

(Clear)

On carpet/upholstery

- Remove excess by blotting with paper towel.
- Place white vinegar on a cloth and wring tightly so it's damp but not wet. Blot over the mark.
- Place the vinegar cloth in one hand and a dry cloth in the other and wipe hand over hand, as though stroking a cat, until the stain is removed.
- Absorb moisture by covering the area with paper towel. Place a book on top of the paper towel to assist with absorption.

On cotton/fabric

- Remove excess under the tap using cold water.
- Rub with white vinegar until removed.
- Wash according to the fabric. Dry in sunshine.

ALGAE

On canvas/pavers/vinyl

- Mix 2 tablespoons of copper sulphate solution in a 9-litre bucket of hot or cold water.
- Sweep the mixture over the surface with a brush or broom.

- Allow to dry. It will blow away in a couple of days.
- For vinyl, wipe with 2 drops of glycerine on a cloth. Leave for 24 hours. Then follow instructions above.

TIP

To deter algae in birdbaths and water features, add a pinch of salt to each litre of clean water.

ALUMINIUM

On mesh filter in range hood

- Remove the mesh filter from the range hood.
- Mix 2 cups of black tea and 1 teaspoon of dishwashing liquid in a sink of hot water.
- Wash with a nylon brush.
- Rinse with clean water and allow to dry.

To clean

- Wipe with a damp black tea bag placed in the toe of pantyhose.
- Alternatively, dip pantyhose into a cup of cold black tea and wipe over the area. The tannins in tea dissolve aluminium oxide.

TIP

To prevent corrosion, store aluminium on baking paper.

ANCHOVY

On carpet/upholstery

- Remove excess by lifting with a plastic comb or by blotting with paper towel.
- Scribble with a cake of bathroom soap run under cold water.
- If stubborn, massage with a couple of drops of dishwashing liquid on your fingertips until the liquid feels like jelly. Wipe with a damp cloth until the dishwashing liquid is removed.
- In all cases, absorb moisture by covering the area with paper towel. Place a book on top of the paper towel to assist with absorption.

On cotton/fabric

- Remove excess under the tap using cold water.
- Scribble with a cake of bathroom soap under cold water.
- If stubborn, massage with a couple of drops of dishwashing liquid on your fingertips until the liquid feels like jelly. Rinse with blood-heat (body temperature) water.
- Wash according to the fabric. If the stain has disappeared, dry in sunshine. If not, repeat.

On stone

- Scribble with a cake of bathroom soap run under cold water.
- If stubborn, mix plaster of Paris and water to the consistency of peanut butter.
- To each cup of mixture, add 1 teaspoon of dishwashing liquid.

- Spread 5 mm to 1 cm thick over the stain.
- Allow to dry completely. If it feels cold on the back of your hand, it's not dry.
- Brush away.

ANGORA

For shedding

- Place item in a plastic bag and remove as much air as possible.
- Place in the freezer for 20 minutes to 1 hour.
- Remove from the freezer and allow the item to come to room temperature.

ANTS

To deter

- Place a little eucalyptus oil or garlic along their path.

To eradicate

- Some ants favour sweet while others favour savoury food.
- To eradicate sweet eaters, mix ½ teaspoon of borax and ¼ teaspoon of icing sugar and place along the ant trail.
- To eradicate savoury eaters, mix equal parts borax and parmesan cheese and place along the ant trail.
- The ants will take the mixture back to the nest and die.
- Alternatively, find the nest and pour boiling water down it.

⚠ WARNING

Borax is mildly toxic and should not be placed where children or pets could eat it.

APPLE

On carpet/upholstery

- Remove excess by lifting with a plastic comb or by blotting with paper towel.
- Wipe with 2 drops of glycerine on a cotton ball or toothbrush. Leave for 90 minutes.
- Sprinkle with talcum powder.
- When dry, vacuum.
- Alternatively, mix *Vanish NapiSan Oxi Action* and water to form a paste the consistency of spreadable butter.
- Place over the stain for a few minutes.
- Remove and wipe stain with a damp cloth.
- Absorb moisture by covering the area with paper towel. Place a book on top of the paper towel to assist with absorption.
- Allow the carpet to dry, then vacuum.

On cotton/fabric

- Remove excess under the tap using cold water.
- Wipe with 2 drops of glycerine. Leave for 90 minutes.
- Wash according to the fabric. If the stain has disappeared, dry in sunshine. If not, repeat.

APPLE JUICE

On carpet/upholstery

- Remove excess by blotting with paper towel.
- Wipe with 2 drops of glycerine on a cotton ball or toothbrush. Leave for 90 minutes.
- Sprinkle with talcum powder.
- When dry, vacuum.

On cotton/fabric

- Remove excess under the tap using blood-heat (body temperature) water.
- Rub with 2 drops of glycerine. Leave for 90 minutes.
- Wash according to the fabric. If the stain has disappeared, dry in sunshine. If not, repeat.

On juicer

- Pour ½ teaspoon of glycerine and 1 cup of warm water into the juicer.
- Turn the machine on for 1 minute.
- In some cases the staining will have penetrated into the plastic and can't be removed. The juicer will still be safe to use.

APRICOT

On carpet/upholstery

- Remove excess by lifting with a plastic comb or by blotting with paper towel.
- Wipe with 2 drops of glycerine on a cotton ball or toothbrush. Leave for 90 minutes.
- Sprinkle with talcum powder.
- When dry, vacuum.
- Alternatively, mix *Vanish NapiSan Oxi Action* and water to form a paste the consistency of spreadable butter.
- Place over the stain for a few minutes.
- Remove and wipe stain with a damp cloth.
- Absorb moisture by covering the area with paper towel. Place a book on top of the paper towel to assist with absorption.
- When dry, vacuum.

On cotton/fabric

- Remove excess under the tap using blood-heat (body temperature) water.
- Rub with 2 drops of glycerine. Leave for 90 minutes.
- Wash according to the fabric. Dry on the clothesline or clothes airer.

ASH

On carpet/upholstery

- Vacuum as much ash as possible.
- Sprinkle residue with bicarb. Leave for 90 minutes.
- Scrub with a brush and vacuum at the same time.
- If staining remains, wipe with white spirits on a cloth.
- Sprinkle with talcum powder.
- When dry, vacuum.

On hard surfaces/walls

- Put on rubber gloves and mix equal parts cigarette ash, bicarb and white vinegar. Let the mixture stand for 5 minutes.
- Wipe the mixture over the ash with rolled up pantyhose.
- Remove with damp pantyhose.

AVOCADO

(see also 'Guacamole')

This is high in fat and can leave a greasy mark.

On carpet/upholstery

- Remove excess by lifting with a plastic comb or by blotting with paper towel.

- Massage with a couple of drops of dishwashing liquid on your fingertips until the liquid feels like jelly.
- Rub with a damp pair of loosely rolled pantyhose.
- Wipe with a damp cloth until the dishwashing liquid is removed.
- Absorb moisture by covering the area with paper towel. Place a book on top of the paper towel to assist with absorption.

On cotton/fabric

- Remove excess under the tap using blood-heat (body temperature) water.
- Massage with a couple of drops of dishwashing liquid on your fingertips until the liquid feels like jelly.
- Rinse using blood-heat water.
- Wash according to the fabric. Dry on the clothesline or clothes airer.

B

BABY FOOD

On carpet/upholstery

- Remove excess by lifting with a plastic comb or by blotting with paper towel.
- Scribble with a cake of bathroom soap run under cold water.
- Wipe with a cold damp cloth.
- Absorb moisture by covering the area with paper towel. Place a book on top of the paper towel to assist with absorption.

On cotton/fabric

- Remove excess under the tap using cold water.
- Scribble with a cake of bathroom soap. Rub the fabric against itself using your hands.
- Rinse using cold water.
- Wash according to the fabric. Dry on the clothesline or clothes airer.

BABY FORMULA

On carpet/upholstery

- Remove excess by lifting with a plastic comb or by blotting with paper towel.
- Scribble with a cake of bathroom soap run under cold water.
- Scrub with a toothbrush in every direction – north, south, east and west.
- Wipe with a damp cloth.
- Absorb moisture by covering the area with paper towel. Place a book on top of the paper towel to assist with absorption.

On cotton/fabric (not wool)

- Remove excess under the tap using cold water.
- Scribble with a cake of bathroom soap. Rub the fabric against itself using your hands.
- Rinse using cold water.
- Wash according to the fabric. Dry on the clothesline or clothes airer.

On wool

- Remove excess under the tap using cold water.
- Scribble with a cake of bathroom soap. Gently rub the wool against itself using your hands.
- Wash in 1 teaspoon of cheap shampoo and blood-heat (body temperature) water.
- Rinse in blood-heat water.
- Gently wring and dry flat on a towel in the shade.

BABY OIL

On carpet/upholstery

- Remove excess by blotting with paper towel.
- Massage with a couple of drops of dishwashing liquid on your fingertips until the liquid feels like jelly.
- Wipe with a damp cloth until the dishwashing liquid is removed.
- Absorb moisture by covering the area with paper towel. Place a book on top of the paper towel to assist with absorption.

On cotton/fabric

- Massage with a couple of drops of dishwashing liquid on your fingertips until the liquid feels like jelly.

- Rinse using blood-heat (body temperature) water.
- Wash according to the fabric. Dry on the clothesline or clothes airer.

BACON

The main stain will be from oil.

On carpet/upholstery

- Remove excess by lifting with a plastic comb or by blotting with paper towel.
- Massage with a couple of drops of dishwashing liquid on your fingertips until the liquid feels like jelly.
- Wipe with a damp cloth until the dishwashing liquid is removed.
- Absorb moisture by covering the area with paper towel. Place a book on top of the paper towel to assist with absorption.

On cotton/fabric (not wool)

- Remove excess under the tap using cold water.
- Massage with a couple of drops of dishwashing liquid on your fingertips until the liquid feels like jelly.
- Rinse using blood-heat (body temperature) water.
- Wash according to the fabric. Dry on the clothesline or clothes airer.

On wool

- Massage with a couple of drops of cheap shampoo on your fingertips.
- Rinse in blood-heat (body temperature) water.

- Rinse in 1 teaspoon of cheap hair conditioner and blood-heat water.
- Gently wring and dry flat on a towel in the shade.

BAKED BEANS

On carpet/upholstery

- Remove excess by lifting with a plastic comb or by blotting with paper towel.
- Place white vinegar on a cloth and wring tightly so it's damp but not wet. Blot over the mark.
- If there's a pink mark, follow previous instructions, then expose to sunlight or ultraviolet light. (If using ultraviolet light, protect areas around the stain with cardboard.) Check every 2 hours.
- In all cases, absorb moisture by covering the area with paper towel. Place a book on top of the paper towel to assist with absorption.

On cotton/fabric

- Remove excess under the tap using cold water.
- Blot with or soak in white vinegar.
- If there's a pink mark, wipe with white vinegar and hang in sunshine before washing.
- Wash according to the fabric. Dry in sunshine.

BALLPOINT PEN

(see 'Pen')

BALSAMIC VINEGAR

On carpet/upholstery

- Remove excess by blotting with paper towel.
- Place white vinegar on a cloth and wring tightly so it's damp but not wet. Blot over the mark.
- Absorb moisture by covering the area with paper towel. Place a book on top of the paper towel to assist with absorption.

On cotton/fabric

- Remove excess under the tap using cold water.
- Blot with or soak in white vinegar until the stain is removed.
- Wash according to the fabric. Dry on the clothesline or clothes airer.

BANANA

On carpet/upholstery

- Remove excess by lifting with a plastic comb or by blotting with paper towel.
- Wipe with 2 drops of glycerine on a cotton ball or toothbrush.
- Sprinkle with talcum powder.
- When dry, vacuum.
- Alternatively, mix *Vanish NapiSan Oxi Action* and water to form a paste the consistency of spreadable butter and place on the stain for a few minutes.
- Remove and wipe stain with a damp cloth.

- Absorb moisture by covering the area with paper towel. Place a book on top of the paper towel to assist with absorption.
- When dry, vacuum.

On cotton/fabric

- Remove excess under the tap using cold water.
- Wipe with 2 drops of glycerine on a cloth.
- Wash according to the fabric. Dry on the clothesline or clothes airer.

On granite/marble/stone

- Remove excess by lifting with a plastic comb or by blotting with paper towel.
- Mix plaster of Paris and water to the consistency of peanut butter.
- To each cup of mixture, add 1 teaspoon of glycerine.
- Spread 5 mm to 1 cm thick over the stain.
- Allow to dry completely. If it feels cold on the back of your hand, it's not dry.
- When dry, brush off.

TIP

To ripen soft fruits, place them in a brown paper bag with a banana and leave in a cupboard. Bananas give off ripening chemicals called ethylene. Never keep bananas in the fridge or they'll go black.

BANANA PEEL/SAP

On carpet/upholstery

- Remove excess by lifting with a plastic comb or by blotting with paper towel.
- Scrub with 2 drops of tea tree oil on a toothbrush.
- Wipe with a damp cloth.
- Absorb moisture by covering the area with paper towel. Place a book on top of the paper towel to assist with absorption.

On cotton/fabric

- Wipe with 2 drops of tea tree oil.
- Alternatively, wipe with 2 drops of glycerine on a cotton ball. Then wipe with white spirits on a cotton ball.
- Wash according to the fabric. Dry on the clothesline or clothes airer.

On pavers

- Scrub with 2 drops of tea tree oil on a toothbrush.
- For an old stain, wipe with 2 drops of tea tree oil and leave for 5 minutes before scrubbing with a toothbrush.
- Rinse using blood-heat (body temperature) water. Repeat, if needed.

BARBECUE

To clean

- Heat the barbecue for a few minutes.
- Turn the heat to low and use a scraper to remove food residue.
- Stand clear of the hotplates and spray with white vinegar.

⚠ WARNING

White vinegar is flammable so be careful when spraying it on hot surfaces.

- When the hotplates are cool, wipe with paper towel.
- If stains are very stubborn, sprinkle equal parts sugar and white vinegar over a heated hotplate until the vinegar evaporates. It will look like toffee. Remove the toffeed sugar with a scraper.
- For all levels of staining, when clean, wipe the hotplates in cooking oil and heat until they fume to season and prevent rust.

BARBECUE SAUCE

(see also 'Steak Sauce')

On carpet/upholstery

- Remove excess by lifting with a plastic comb or by blotting with paper towel.
- Place white vinegar on a cloth and wring tightly so it's damp but not wet. Blot over the mark.
- Place the vinegar cloth in one hand and a dry cloth in the other and wipe hand over hand, as though stroking a cat, until the stain is removed.
- In all cases, absorb moisture by covering the area with paper towel. Place a book on top of the paper towel to assist with absorption.
- If there's any residue, expose to sunlight or ultraviolet light. (If using ultraviolet light, protect areas around the stain with cardboard.) Check every 2 hours.

On cotton/fabric

- Quickly pour a large quantity of white vinegar through the stain.
- If stubborn, heat white vinegar in the microwave until it's steaming. Pour through the stain until removed.
- In all cases, wash according to the fabric. Dry on the clothesline or clothes airer.

BAT POO

On car

- Wipe with 2 drops of glycerine on a cloth. Leave for 90 minutes.
- Wipe with damp pantyhose.

On cotton/fabric

- Remove excess under the tap using cold water.
- Wipe with 2 drops of glycerine on a cloth. Leave for 90 minutes.
- Blot with or soak in white vinegar.
- Wash according to the fabric. Dry on the clothesline or clothes airer.

BATH

For age stains

- Ensure the surface is dry.
- Place a denture tablet over the stain and secure it with masking tape.

⚠ WARNING

Don't use denture tablets on plastic or polycarbonate baths.

- Spray water over the denture tablet. Leave overnight.
- Remove the denture tablet and scrub over the stain with bicarb and white vinegar on a scrubbing brush.
- For widespread staining, fill the bath to the rim with hot water and add 12 denture tablets. Leave overnight. Empty the bath and scrub.
- In both cases, when clean, seal the surface by wiping with 2 drops of glycerine on a cloth.
- For plastic or polycarbonate baths, mix equal parts glycerine and talcum powder and wipe on the stain with pantyhose. Leave for 24 hours, then wipe with a damp cloth.

For bore water, lime scale and rust marks

- Dampen with water and sprinkle with talcum powder to create a paste.
- Put on rubber gloves and apply *CLR* or *Ranex* over the talcum powder paste. Don't get *CLR* or *Ranex* on your skin because it can cause irritation.
- Leave for 10 minutes.
- When the mark is removed, neutralise the chemicals by wiping with white vinegar on a cloth.

For essential oils on fibreglass

- Mix 1 teaspoon of dishwashing liquid, 1 teaspoon of glycerine and 1 teaspoon of talcum powder.
- Rub in the mixture with pantyhose. Leave for 90 minutes.
- Wipe with a damp cloth. Repeat if necessary.

TIPS

Regularly clean the mesh part of your bath's tap nozzle. Remove the nozzle and soak it in a container with CLR *or* Ranex. *Wear gloves when using* CLR *or* Ranex.

If there are marks on the bath from metallic objects, such as steel wool, rub with a damp pencil eraser.

BATHERS

(see 'Swimming Costume')

BATTERY ACID

(Alkaline)

NOTE: Wear rubber gloves to protect your hands.

On concrete

- Scrub with white vinegar using a broom.
- For a rust stain, apply *CLR* or *Ranex*. Don't get *CLR* or *Ranex* on your skin because it can cause irritation. Scrub with a broom.
- Rinse with a hose.

On cotton/fabric

- Pour white vinegar through the stain.
- Wash according to the fabric. Dry in sunshine.

BÉARNAISE SAUCE

On carpet/upholstery

- Remove excess by blotting with paper towel.
- Scribble with a cake of bathroom soap run under cold water.
- Massage with a couple of drops of dishwashing liquid on your fingertips until the liquid feels like jelly.
- Wipe with a damp cloth until dishwashing liquid is removed.
- Absorb moisture by covering the area with paper towel. Place a book on top of the paper towel to assist with absorption.

On cotton/fabric

- Remove excess under the tap using cold water.
- Scribble with a cake of bathroom soap.
- Massage with a couple of drops of dishwashing liquid on your fingertips until the liquid feels like jelly.
- Rinse using cold water.
- Wash according to the fabric. Dry on the clothesline or clothes airer.

BÉCHAMEL SAUCE

On carpet/upholstery

- Remove excess by blotting with paper towel.
- Scribble with a cake of bathroom soap run under cold water.
- Massage with a couple of drops of dishwashing liquid on your fingertips until the liquid feels like jelly.
- Wipe with a damp cloth until the dishwashing liquid is removed.

- Absorb moisture by covering the area with paper towel. Place a book on top of the paper towel to assist with absorption.

On cotton/fabric (not wool)

- Remove excess under the tap using cold water.
- Scribble with a cake of bathroom soap.
- Massage with a couple of drops of dishwashing liquid on your fingertips until the liquid feels like jelly.
- Rinse under blood-heat (body temperature) water.
- Wash according to the fabric. Dry on the clothesline or clothes airer.

On wool

- Scribble with a cake of bathroom soap and run under cold water.
- Massage with 1 teaspoon of cheap shampoo on your fingertips.
- Rinse in blood-heat (body temperature) water.
- Rinse in 1 teaspoon of cheap hair conditioner and blood-heat water.
- Gently wring and dry flat on a towel in the shade.

BED BUGS

On mattress

- Apply tea tree oil to your fingertips and wipe around the edge of the mattress, bed frame, skirting boards and nearby furnishings.
- Mix 3 teaspoons of tea tree oil, 1 teaspoon of dishwashing liquid and 1 litre of water in a spray pack and spray over all the areas referred to in the first step.

- Use surface insecticide spray over the edges and ends of the bed, but not over the top of the mattress and not just before going to bed.
- Alternatively, apply 1–2 drops of oil of pennyroyal to the edge seam of the mattress.

⚠ WARNING

Oil of pennyroyal can be harmful to pregnant women and pregnant pets. Change the sheets daily until bed bugs are eradicated.

BEDDING

(see 'Mattress')

BEER

On carpet/upholstery (not leather)

- Remove excess by blotting with paper towel.
- Mix 1 teaspoon of dishwashing liquid with 2 cups of cold water to generate a sudsy mix. If the stain is old, tightly wring a cloth in white vinegar and blot over the mark first.
- Scrub with only the suds on a toothbrush. Work in all directions – north, south, east and west.
- In all cases, absorb moisture by covering the area with paper towel. Place a book on top of the paper towel to assist with absorption.

On cotton/fabric

- Remove excess under the tap using cold water.
- Make a paste of *Vanish NapiSan Oxi Action* and cold water the consistency of spreadable butter.

- Apply to the stain and leave for 15 minutes.
- Wash according to the fabric. Dry on the clothesline or clothes airer.

On leather

- Wipe with 2 drops of glycerine on a cotton ball.
- Wipe with white spirits on a cotton ball. Wipe in even, parallel strokes over the entire panel of leather.
- Sprinkle with talcum powder.
- When dry, brush off.
- Wipe with leather conditioner. Make your own – see **Household formulas**.

BEES

To deter

- Mix 4 teaspoons of dried mint or 8 teaspoons of freshly chopped mint with 1 litre of boiling water in a spray pack. Let it sit for 15 minutes.
- Lightly spray over the affected area.

BEESWAX

On carpet/upholstery

- Put ice cubes in a zip-lock bag and place on top of the wax.
- When the wax is chilled, remove excess by combing with a plastic comb. Vacuum as you comb.
- When you've removed as much wax as possible, wipe with 2 drops of tea tree oil on a cotton ball or cloth to remove residue.

- Absorb moisture by covering the area with paper towel. Place a book on top of the paper towel to assist with absorption.

On cotton/fabric

- If possible, place in the freezer for 15 minutes. If not, place ice cubes on top of the wax.
- When the wax is chilled, remove as much as possible by rubbing the fabric with the wax on it against itself or scraping the wax with a plastic comb.
- Rub 2 drops of tea tree oil over the wax residue.
- Wash according to the fabric. Dry on the clothesline or clothes airer.

On timber

- Rub with 2 drops of tea tree oil on a cloth.
- For French polish, dampen some silk under water and polish over the wax.

BEETROOT

On carpet/upholstery

- Remove excess by lifting with a plastic comb or by blotting with paper towel.
- Place white vinegar on a cloth and wring tightly so it's damp but not wet. Blot over the mark.
- Place the vinegar cloth in one hand and a dry cloth in the other and wipe hand over hand, as though stroking a cat, until the stain is removed.
- Absorb moisture by covering the area with paper towel. Place a book on top of the paper towel to assist with absorption.

On cotton/fabric (not wool)

- Remove excess under the tap using cold water.
- For a small stain, pour through with white vinegar.
- For a large stain, fill a 9-litre bucket with cold water and 1 cup of white vinegar. Soak for 20 minutes.
- Wash according to the fabric. Dry on the clothesline or clothes airer.

On laminate

- For a fresh stain, wipe with white vinegar on a cloth.
- For an old stain, wipe with 2 drops of glycerine on a cotton bud or cotton ball. Leave for 5 minutes. Wipe with white vinegar on a cloth.
- Wipe with a damp cloth.

On wool

- Blot with white vinegar until the beetroot colour is removed.
- Massage with 1 teaspoon of cheap shampoo on your fingertips.
- Rinse in blood-heat (body temperature) water.
- Rinse in 1 teaspoon of cheap hair conditioner and blood-heat water.
- Gently wring and dry flat on a towel in the shade.

BENCHTOPS

For scorch marks on laminate/Formica

- For heavy staining, wipe with 2 drops of glycerine on a cloth. Leave for 5 minutes.
- Wipe with bicarb and white vinegar on a cloth.

- Avoid abrasive cleaners because they can scratch the surface.

For scratches in granite/marble

- To work out if the benchtops are sealed, place your eye level with the surface and shine a torch along the top of the benchtop. If the light shines in an uninterrupted beam, the benchtops are coated in polyurethane. If the beam has lights and dots, it's not sealed.
- To work out if the benchtops are sealed with shellac, hold a pin in a pair of pliers and heat the end of the pin. Place the heated end on an inconspicuous area of the benchtop. If it smells like burnt hair, it's shellac.
- If sealed with polyurethane, remove scratches by wiping with a small amount of *Brasso* on a cloth, using speed rather than pressure. This partially melts the polyurethane. It will look worse before it looks better.
- If the polyurethane is damaged, you will need to reseal the entire surface, which is a big job. You can buy proprietary wipe-on polyurethane products but they are not suitable for heavy damage. Seek professional help.
- If sealed with shellac, remove scratches with shellac on a cloth.
- If unsealed, make a paste of equal parts glycerine and whiting and apply with a cloth to polish out scratches.

For stains or scratches on quartz-based benchtops

- Remove glues or resins with a single-sided razor blade held at a low angle.
- Fill chips with a malleable epoxy resin – make sure the colour matches.

To clean

- Mix 1 teaspoon of lavender oil and 1 litre of water in a spray pack – then spray and wipe.
- For tiles, sprinkle with bicarb and splash with white vinegar.
- Scrub with a nylon brush.
- Wipe with a damp cloth.
- For unsealed timber, rub with a damp tea bag or cold tea on pantyhose.
- For sealed timber, wipe with a little dishwashing liquid and water on a cloth, or sprinkle with bicarb, splash with white vinegar and wipe with a damp cloth.

To polish

- Use two pairs of pantyhose – one damp and one dry. Rub the damp pair over the surface and follow right away with the dry pair.
- Polish unsealed timber with a fine coating of beeswax or carnauba wax – you only need 1 teaspoon for every 4 metres of benchtop.

BERRY

When removing berry stains, don't use soap or heat because it will set the stain.

On carpet/upholstery

- Remove excess by lifting with a plastic comb or by blotting with paper towel.
- For berry stains that change colour (blueberry, blackberry), wipe with 2 drops of glycerine on a cloth.

Leave for 5 minutes. Then place white vinegar on a cloth and wring tightly so it's damp but not wet. Blot over the mark. Place the vinegar cloth in one hand and a dry cloth in the other and wipe hand over hand, as though stroking a cat, until the stain is removed.

- For mulberry, wipe with a green mulberry – pick one from a mulberry tree.
- For other berries (strawberry, raspberry, etc.), place white vinegar on a cloth and wring tightly so it's damp but not wet. Blot over the mark.
- Absorb moisture by covering the area with paper towel. Place a book on top of the paper towel to assist with absorption.

On concrete/sandstone

- Wipe with white spirits on a cotton ball.
- Rinse with a damp cloth.

On cotton/fabric (not silk/wool)

- Remove excess under the tap using cold water.
- For berry stains that change colour (blueberry, blackberry), wipe with 2 drops of glycerine on a cloth. Then tightly wring a cloth in white vinegar and blot over the mark.
- For mulberry, wipe with a green mulberry – pick one from a mulberry tree.
- For other berries (strawberry, raspberry, etc.), tightly wring a cloth in white vinegar and blot over the mark.
- In all cases, wash according to the fabric. Dry in sunshine.

On silk/wool

- Blot with white vinegar on a cloth until the berry colour is removed.
- Massage with 1 teaspoon of cheap shampoo on your fingertips.
- Rinse in blood-heat (body temperature) water.
- Rinse in 1 teaspoon of cheap hair conditioner and blood-heat water.
- Gently wring and dry flat on a towel in the shade. Ensure silk is dried away from the wind so the fibres don't tangle and leave a dusty look.

TIP

Make your own silk. Keep silkworms in a box and feed them fresh mulberry leaves. When a cocoon has formed, simmer it in boiling water for 20 minutes until the resinous material loosens. Allow to cool and then unreel it. Use it as silk thread.

BETADINE

On carpet/upholstery

- Remove excess by blotting with paper towel.
- Massage with 2 drops of lavender oil on a cloth. Place white vinegar on a cloth and wring tightly so it's damp but not wet. Blot over the mark.
- Alternatively, remove excess then scrub with 2 drops of glycerine on a toothbrush in all directions – north, south, east and west. For an old stain, leave overnight. Rub with a little dishwashing liquid on a cloth. Wipe with a damp

cloth until the dishwashing liquid is removed. Tightly wring a cloth in white vinegar, fold the cloth flat and polish out the glycerine without pushing it into the back of the carpet or upholstery.

- In both cases, absorb moisture by covering the area with paper towel. Place a book on top of the paper towel to assist with absorption.

On cotton/fabric

- Massage with 2 drops of lavender oil on a cloth.
- Wash according to the fabric. Dry on the clothesline or clothes airer.

On stone

- Sprinkle with talcum powder like icing sugar on a cake.
- Spray with white vinegar. Leave for 15 minutes.
- Scrub with 2 drops of lavender oil – use a brush on rough surfaces and a cloth on smooth surfaces.

BIRD POO

The solution depends on what the bird eats – protein, seed or fruit.

On cotton/fabric

- Remove excess under the tap using cold water.
- To remove protein (generally brown or black poo), scribble over the stain with a cake of bathroom soap run under cold water.
- Rinse using cold water. Wash according to the fabric. Dry on the clothesline or clothes airer.

- To remove seed (generally white poo), scribble over the stain with a cake of bathroom soap run under blood-heat (body temperature) water.
- Rinse using blood-heat water. Wash according to the fabric. Dry on the clothesline or clothes airer.
- To remove fruit (generally purple or orange poo), wipe with 2 drops of glycerine on a cloth and leave for 90 minutes. Then blot with white vinegar.
- In all cases, rinse using cold water. Wash according to the fabric. Dry on the clothesline or clothes airer.

TIP

To stop birds hovering over your clothesline and potentially soiling your washing, tie coloured ribbons to the line and allow them to flutter. You could also hang some old CDs on the line. Birds don't like sharp movements.

On sandstone/timber

- Remove excess with a stiff brush.
- For protein (generally brown or black poo), rub over the head of a stiff broom with a cake of bathroom soap run under cold water.
- Sweep over the stains until removed.
- Rinse using cold water.
- For seed (generally white poo), remove excess then rub over the head of a stiff broom with a cake of bathroom soap run under blood-heat (body temperature) water.
- Sweep over the stains until removed.
- Rinse using blood-heat water.

- For fruit (generally purple or orange poo), remove excess then wipe with 2 drops of glycerine on a toothbrush. Leave for 90 minutes. Then wipe with white vinegar on a toothbrush.
- Rinse using blood-heat water.

On wrought iron

- Rub over the head of a stiff broom with a cake of bathroom soap and run under cold water.
- Sweep over the stains until removed.
- Rinse with a hose or wipe with a damp cloth.

BIRO

(see 'Pen')

BITUMEN

(see 'Tar')

BLACK BEAN SAUCE

On carpet/upholstery

- Remove excess by blotting with paper towel.
- Place white vinegar on a cloth and wring tightly so it's damp but not wet. Blot over the mark.
- Place the vinegar cloth in one hand and a dry cloth in the other and wipe hand over hand, as though stroking a cat, until the stain is removed.
- Absorb moisture by covering the area with paper towel. Place a book on top of the paper towel to assist with absorption.

On cotton/fabric

- Quickly pour a large quantity of white vinegar through the stain.
- If stubborn, heat white vinegar in the microwave until it's steaming. Pour through the stain until removed.
- In all cases, wash according to the fabric. Dry on the clothesline or clothes airer.

BLANKET

To clean

- For wool, mohair and silk, wash with 1 teaspoon of cheap shampoo in 9 litres of blood-heat (body temperature) water.
- Rinse with 1 teaspoon of cheap hair conditioner in 9 litres of blood-heat water.
- For polar fleece, acrylic and cotton, wash in the washing machine with laundry detergent.
- Dry on the clothesline pegged in a U shape. Place a sheet over the top to protect the fibres from the sun.

BLEACH

On carpet

- Replace the colour with folk art paint (available from art suppliers or craft stores) that matches the colour of the carpet. You may need to mix the colour from a couple of tubes.
- Test the paint on an inconspicuous corner of the carpet to make sure it's an exact match. Allow each test section of paint to dry because it could change colour.

- When you have the right colour, use a toothbrush to brush the paint into the bleached spot on the carpet. Feather the edges so you don't get an obvious line.
- Move a hair dryer backwards and forwards across the paint to set it.

On cotton/fabric/silk (not wool)

- Prevent further bleaching by wiping with white vinegar on a cloth.
- If there's a pale section, you'll need to re-dye it. Use silk dye for silk.
- Wash according to the fabric. Dry on the clothesline or clothes airer. Ensure silk is dried away from the wind so the fibres don't tangle and leave a dusty look.

On timber

- To replace the tannins in the bleached area, wipe with a damp tea bag or rub with pantyhose run under cold black tea.
- Polish with a fine coating of beeswax or carnauba wax – you only need 1 teaspoon for every 4 metres of timber.

On wool

- Prevent further bleaching by wiping with white vinegar on a cloth.
- For a brown mark, mix 2 cups of 3 per cent hydrogen peroxide in a 9-litre bucket of blood-heat (body temperature) water.
- Immerse the item and put a plate on top of it to keep it fully submerged in the solution. Leave for 6 hours.
- Remove and place in a 9-litre bucket of blood-heat water with 1 cup of white vinegar.

- If there's a pale section, you'll need to re-dye it using specialist wool dye.
- Rinse in 1 teaspoon of cheap shampoo and blood-heat water.
- Gently wring and dry flat on a towel in the shade.

BLENDER

To clean

- Heat ½ cup of white vinegar in the microwave until it's steaming, but not boiling.
- Place inside the blender, and add 2 teaspoons of bicarb.
- Switch the blender on for 1 minute. Don't forget to put the lid on.
- Rinse with water.

BLIND

To clean cotton/fabric

- Place 1 cup of unprocessed wheat bran in a large bowl. Add drops of white vinegar one at a time, stirring as you go, until the mixture resembles breadcrumbs. It shouldn't be wet.
- Place the mixture into the toe of pantyhose and tie up tightly. The tied section will be the size of a tennis ball.
- Wipe over the blinds as though using an eraser.
- When finished, store pantyhose in a zip-lock bag in the freezer to use again.
- For insect droppings, use the technique described above.
- For remaining insect droppings, fill a 9-litre bucket with cold water and enough dishwashing liquid to generate a sudsy mix.

- Apply only the suds to the stains with a damp cloth.
- Wipe with a damp cloth.

TIP

Have a peg handy in case the front doorbell rings while you're cleaning the blinds. That way you know where to resume cleaning.

BLOOD

This is a protein stain so use only cold water.

On carpet/upholstery

- If you've already used a product to remove the blood, neutralise by blotting with white vinegar on a cloth. Scrub with 2 drops of glycerine on a toothbrush and leave for 90 minutes. Then follow the instructions below.
- Remove as much as possible by blotting with paper towel.
- Scribble stain with a cake of bathroom soap run under cold water.
- Scrub with a toothbrush in every direction – north, south, east and west.
- Wipe with a cold damp cloth.
- Absorb moisture by covering the area with paper towel. Place a book on top of the paper towel to assist with absorption.

On cotton/fabric (not silk/wool)

- Quickly pour a large quantity of cold water through the stain.

- Scribble with a cake of bathroom soap. Rub the fabric against itself using your hands.
- If there's a shadow mark, soak in ½ lid *Vanish NapiSan Oxi Action* and 7 litres of cold water for 30 minutes. Don't use on silk or wool.
- If the stain has set, wipe with 2 drops of glycerine on a cotton ball before washing according to the fabric. Dry on the clothesline or clothes airer.
- In all cases, wash according to the fabric. Dry on the clothesline or clothes airer.

On mattress

- For a fresh stain, scribble with a cake of bathroom soap run under cold water.
- Wipe with a damp cloth.
- Leave to dry. Repeat, if needed.
- For an old stain, mix equal parts cornflour, glycerine and water to the consistency of thickened cream.
- Leave on the stain until it dries.
- Brush off with a stiff brush.
- You may need to repeat these steps a few times as old stains can be particularly difficult to remove.

On silk/wool

- Scribble with a cake of bathroom soap run under cold water.
- Wash in 1 teaspoon of cheap shampoo and blood-heat (body temperature) water.
- Gently wring and dry flat on a towel in the shade. Ensure silk is dried away from the wind so the fibres don't tangle and leave a dusty look.

On stone/timber

- For new stains, rinse with cold water.
- For old stains, mix plaster of Paris and water to the consistency of peanut butter.
- Spread 5 mm to 1 cm thick over the stain.
- Allow to dry completely. If it feels cold on the back of your hand, it's not dry.
- Sweep away with a broom. Repeat, if needed.

BLUEBERRY

(see 'Berry')

BLUSH MAKE-UP

(see 'Make-up')

BLU-TACK

On carpet/upholstery

- Place a lump of *Blu-Tack* in the freezer and leave for 10 minutes or until frozen.
- Punch the frozen *Blu-Tack* over the stained *Blu-Tack*. It will come away.
- If the frozen *Blu-Tack* becomes too warm, put it back in the freezer.
- For residue, sprinkle with talcum powder and roll over it with tightly rolled pantyhose until removed.

On walls

- Place a lump of *Blu-Tack* in the freezer and leave for 10 minutes or until frozen.
- Punch the frozen *Blu-Tack* over the stained *Blu-Tack*. It will come away.

BODY ODOUR/PERSPIRATION

In natural fibres (not silk/wool)

- Make a paste of *Vanish NapiSan Oxi Action* and water to the consistency of spreadable butter. Don't use on wool or silk.
- Place over the stains. Leave for 5 minutes.
- Wash according to the fabric. Dry on the clothesline or clothes airer.

In silk/wool

- Scribble with a cake of bathroom soap run under cold water.
- Wash in 1 teaspoon of cheap shampoo and blood-heat (body temperature) water.
- Gently wring and dry flat on a towel in the shade. Ensure silk is dried away from the wind so the fibres don't tangle and leave a dusty look.

TIP

If there are stiff marks in the clothing from deodorant, find a different brand of deodorant that better suits your body chemistry.

After showering, wipe a mild solution of 3 per cent hydrogen peroxide or witch-hazel over your armpits to help reduce odour.

In synthetic fibres

- Wipe with methylated spirits on a cloth.
- Make a paste of *Vanish NapiSan Oxi Action* and water to the consistency of spreadable butter.

- Place over the stain. Leave for 5 minutes.
- Wash according to the fabric. Dry on the clothesline or clothes airer.

BOLOGNESE SAUCE

The stain is from protein, fat and tomato paste.

On carpet/upholstery

- Remove excess by lifting with a plastic comb or by blotting with paper towel.
- Scribble with a cake of bathroom soap run under cold water.
- Massage with a couple of drops of dishwashing liquid on your fingertips until the liquid feels like jelly.
- Wipe with a damp cloth until the dishwashing liquid is removed.
- To remove the tomato colour, place white vinegar on a cloth and wring tightly before blotting over the mark. Then expose to sunlight or ultraviolet light. (If using ultraviolet light, protect areas around the stain with cardboard.) Check every 2 hours. Leave up to 24 hours.
- In all cases, absorb moisture by covering the area with paper towel. Place a book on top of the paper towel to assist with absorption.

On cotton/fabric

- Remove excess under the tap using cold water.
- Scribble with a cake of bathroom soap run under cold water.
- Massage with a couple of drops of dishwashing liquid on your fingertips until the liquid feels like jelly.

- For a tomato colour, remove excess then blot with or soak in white vinegar and hang in sunshine before washing.
- Wash according to the fabric. Dry in sunshine.

BOOT POLISH

(see 'Shoe Polish')

BRASS

To work out if something is made of brass, hold a magnet to it. If it doesn't stick, it's brass.

To clean

- First, work out if it's coated in lacquer. To do this, take a pin or needle, hold it in a pair of pliers and heat on the stove. Touch the pin or needle to an inconspicuous part of the brass. If there's a burning smell, it's coated in lacquer.
- If lacquered, wipe with a damp cloth.
- If not lacquered, wipe with bicarb and white vinegar on pantyhose. Rinse with a damp cloth.

TIP

If the brass item fits inside the leg of a pair of pantyhose, speed up your cleaning. Place it inside the leg and hold the pantyhose like a skipping rope. Fill one saucer with bicarb and another with white vinegar and move the brass item between the two saucers. To inhibit tarnishing, wipe with a little sweet almond oil on a cloth.

BREAST MILK

This is high in protein and sugars.

On carpet/upholstery

- Remove excess by blotting with paper towel.
- Scribble with a cake of bathroom soap run under cold water.
- Wipe with a damp cloth.
- Absorb moisture by covering the area with paper towel. Place a book on top of the paper towel to assist with absorption.

On cotton/fabric

- Remove excess under the tap using cold water.
- Scribble with a cake of bathroom soap. Rub the fabric against itself using your hands.
- Rinse using cold water.
- Wash in cold water. Dry on the clothesline or clothes airer.

TIP

Never soak items stained with breast milk in bleach detergent – it will cook the stain. Always wash in cold water.

BROCCOLI

(Cooked)

On carpet/upholstery

- Remove excess by lifting with a plastic comb or by blotting with paper towel.

- Scribble with a cake of bathroom soap run under blood-heat (body temperature) water.
- Scrub with a toothbrush in all directions – north, south, east and west.
- Wipe with a damp cloth.
- Absorb moisture by covering the area with paper towel. Place a book on top of the paper towel to assist with absorption.

On cotton/fabric

- Remove excess under the tap using cold water.
- Scribble with a cake of bathroom soap. Rub the fabric against itself using your hands.
- Wash according to the fabric. Dry on the clothesline or clothes airer.

BURN MARK

Burn marks can be light, medium or dark.

On carpet

- If the carpet is made of nylon, you will need to patch it – see '*How to patch carpet*' (pages 67–8).
- If the carpet is made of natural fibres, first test if it is colourfast. Wring a white cloth in white vinegar and place it on an inconspicuous part of the carpet. If any colour transfers to the cloth, it's not colourfast.
- For light burns on colourfast carpet made from natural fibres, cut a cloth to the size of the burnt area. Wring the cloth in 3 per cent hydrogen peroxide and place it over the mark for 2 minutes. Remove and wipe stain with a damp cloth.

- For light burns on non-colourfast carpet made from natural fibres, shave across the burnt fibres with a disposable razor.
- For medium burns on colourfast carpet made from natural fibres, cut a cloth to the size of the burnt area. Wring the cloth in 3 per cent hydrogen peroxide and place it over the mark for 2 minutes. Remove and wipe stain with white vinegar on a cloth.
- For medium burns on non-colourfast carpet made from natural fibres, shave across the burnt fibres with a disposable razor.
- For dark burns on colourfast or non-colourfast carpet made from natural fibres, comb through the carpet with a metal lice comb. Remove as much singe as possible and vacuum, then slide the comb horizontally so it sits under the burn. Shave across the burnt fibres with a disposable razor.
- If a burn on a carpet made from natural fibres is significant, you will have to patch the carpet – see '*How to patch carpet*'.

HOW TO PATCH CARPET

- Cut around the damaged part of the carpet with a Stanley knife to create a neat shape.
- Find a piece of carpet (left over or from inside a cupboard) a little larger than the stained area. Make sure the pattern is in the same direction.
- Make a paper template of the stained area.
- Transfer to the piece of patch carpet and cut the patch carpet around the template with a sharp knife.
- Attach carpet tape (available from carpet manufacturers, dealers and some supermarkets) under the edges of the damaged carpet with the adhesive side facing upwards.

- Ensure half of the tape is under the old carpet and the other half is exposed in the hole.
- Press the patch of carpet into the hole, sticking it to the exposed half of the tape.
- Brush the carpet in both directions until the fibres line up on the edges.
- Stand on the area for 5 minutes to make sure it sticks well.
- Place a heavy book or books on top of the patch for 24 hours.

On cotton/fabric (not polyester)

- Mix 1 teaspoon of 3 per cent hydrogen peroxide in 2 cups of water.
- Wring a cloth in the solution and place over the mark.
- Iron over it on a cool setting.

On glass

- Mix equal parts cigarette ash, bicarb and white vinegar.
- Wipe on the mixture with pantyhose. Leave for 1 hour.
- When dry, polish with damp pantyhose.

On laminate

- Mix equal parts cigarette ash and toothpaste. Alternatively, mix equal parts *Gumption* and white spirits.
- Polish with the mixture using pantyhose.
- If the burn has penetrated into the laminate, lightly sand with 000 sandpaper until the mark is removed. Then use a laminate repair kit, available from hardware stores. It comes in a variety of colours.

On polyester

- Dampen the surface with white vinegar on a cloth.
- Wring a cloth of a similar weave in white vinegar and place over the mark.
- Run a warm (not hot) iron over the top.
- If the mark doesn't come out, it's permanently damaged.

On sealed timber

- If the burn hasn't penetrated the polyurethane, wring a cloth in 3 per cent hydrogen peroxide and place it over the stained area only.
- Leave for 20 minutes.
- Remove the cloth.
- If the burn has penetrated the surface, use the technique described above and then rub with a little *Brasso* on a cloth. For a burn the size of a 5 cent piece, use 1 drop of *Brasso* on a cloth and rub lightly and quickly in the direction of the grain. It will look worse before it looks better.

BUTTER

On carpet/upholstery

- Remove excess by blotting with paper towel.
- Massage with a couple of drops of dishwashing liquid on your fingertips until the liquid feels like jelly.
- Wipe with a damp cloth until the dishwashing liquid is removed.
- Absorb moisture by covering the area with paper towel. Place a book on top of the paper towel to assist with absorption.

On cotton/fabric (not wool)

- Remove excess under the tap using cold water.
- Massage with a couple of drops of dishwashing liquid on your fingertips until the liquid feels like jelly.
- Wash according to the fabric. Dry on the clothesline or clothes airer.

On wool

- Massage with 1 teaspoon of cheap shampoo on your fingertips.
- Rinse in blood-heat (body temperature) water.
- Rinse in 1 teaspoon of cheap hair conditioner and blood-heat water.
- Gently wring and dry flat on a towel in the shade.

C

CANDLE SOOT

On carpet/upholstery

- Vacuum. Candle soot is very greasy.
- Cut a cake of bathroom soap in half lengthways and round the edges. Dampen it under water and use like a rolling pin across the soot. The soot will stick to the soap. Remove the soot from the soap using water as you go.
- Absorb moisture by covering the area with paper towel. Place a book on top of the paper towel to assist with absorption.

On timber

- Vacuum any loose particles.
- Wipe with 2 drops of dishwashing liquid on pantyhose.
- Rinse with a damp cloth.

CANDLE WAX

(see 'Wax')

CANDY

(see 'Lollies')

CAR

For a coffee spill

- For a fresh spill, remove excess by blotting with paper towel. Scribble with a cake of bathroom soap run under cold water. Wipe with a damp cloth.
- For an old spill, wipe with 2 drops of glycerine on a cloth. Sprinkle with talcum powder. Allow to dry, then vacuum.

For mystery stains

- Mix 2 tablespoons of bicarb, 2 tablespoons of white vinegar, 2 tablespoons of methylated spirits, 2 teaspoons of glycerine, 2 teaspoons of eucalyptus oil and 1 cup of water in a spray pack.
- Spray over mystery stains.
- Blot with a damp cloth.

For odour

- Sprinkle bicarb over the upholstery.
- Leave for 20 minutes.
- Vacuum.
- Add 2 drops of lavender oil to a damp tea bag and place it over an air vent.

TIP

To minimise water use when cleaning the exterior of your car, mix 3 cups of strong black tea, 1 teaspoon of tea tree oil and 1 teaspoon of dishwashing liquid in a 9-litre bucket of blood-heat (body temperature) water. Stuff the head of a clean, soft kitchen broom into the leg of pantyhose and secure. Use the broom to sweep the liquid from the back to the front of the car in even, parallel strokes – the opposite direction to that in which dirt hits the car. Pour the remainder of the solution from the bucket over the car. Rinse with a bucket of clean water.

For sweat marks on fabric seats

- Place 1 cup of unprocessed wheat bran in a large bowl. Add drops of white vinegar one at a time, stirring as you go, until the mixture resembles breadcrumbs. It shouldn't be wet.

- Place in the toe of pantyhose and tie off. Rub over the fabric as though using an eraser.
- Alternatively, apply the mixture directly and scrub with a brush.
- Vacuum.

CARAMEL

On carpet/upholstery

- Remove excess by lifting with a plastic comb or by blotting with paper towel.
- Mix equal parts white vinegar and blood-heat (body temperature) water.
- Scrub with a toothbrush or pantyhose in all directions (north, south, east and west) until removed. Work from the outside to the inside of the stain.
- Absorb moisture by covering the area with paper towel. Place a book on top of the paper towel to assist with absorption.
- When almost dry, repeat.
- If a shadow returns in a couple of weeks, repeat again.

On cotton/fabric

- Remove excess under the tap using cold water.
- Rinse with blood-heat (body temperature) water.
- Wash according to the fabric. Dry on the clothesline or clothes airer.

CARPET

To refresh

- Mix equal parts unprocessed wheat bran and bicarb and sprinkle over the carpet. Bran is an abrasive and bicarb is a deodoriser.
- Sweep the mixture into the carpet fibres with a clean broom.
- Leave for 5 minutes before vacuuming.

SHANNON'S DIY CARPET STEAM-CLEAN

- Hire a carpet cleaner – available at supermarkets.
- Use half the amount of cleaning product that comes with the machine (saving the other half for later) and add 2 tablespoons of bicarb, 2 tablespoons of white vinegar, 2 tablespoons of methylated spirits, 2 teaspoons of glycerine and 2 teaspoons of eucalyptus oil. This is a great general cleaner so store it in a spray pack and use when needed.

CARPET BEETLE

Carpet beetle eats carpet and its jute backing, leaving a black, sooty mark near the skirting board or doorframe.

For black marks

- Sprinkle with uniodised salt and brush backwards and forwards over it.
- Vacuum.

TIP

Deter carpet beetle with whole cloves, each stabbed into a bay leaf. Place at 1.5-metre intervals along the walls.

CARROT

On carpet/upholstery

- Remove excess by lifting with a plastic comb or by blotting with paper towel.
- Place white vinegar on a cloth and wring tightly so it's damp but not wet. Blot over the mark.
- For stubborn stains, expose to sunlight or ultraviolet light. (If using ultraviolet light, protect areas around the stain with cardboard.) Check every 2 hours.
- In all cases, absorb moisture by covering the area with paper towel. Place a book on top of the paper towel to assist with absorption.

On cotton/fabric

- Remove excess under the tap using cold water.
- Blot with or soak in white vinegar. Hang in the sunshine.
- When the stain has faded, wash according to the fabric. Dry on the clothesline or clothes airer.

CAST IRON

For rust

- Sprinkle with uniodised salt.
- Cut a potato in half and rub over the salt until the rust is removed.
- Rinse under water and dry.
- Heat on a stovetop until completely dry.
- Add cooking oil; reheat until the oil begins to fume.
- Allow to cool and wipe with paper towel.
- Cover with a little cooking oil using paper towel. This seasons the iron.

To clean

- When cold, wipe with cheap cooking oil using paper towel.
- Heat until the oil fumes.
- Allow to cool. Wipe dry with paper towel.
- Cover with a little cooking oil using paper towel. This seasons the iron.
- If still dirty, scrub with a nylon brush and hot water. Dry and re-season.

CAT HAIR

On blankets/jumpers/upholstery

- Put on a pair of rubber gloves and wash your gloved hands with a cake of bathroom soap and water. Shake your hands dry.
- Wipe over the cat hair. It will stick to the gloves.

TIP

If you stroke your cat while the gloves are on, it will remove extra fur and reduce cleaning.

CAT URINE

You need to remove every bit of urine or the smell will linger.

On carpet/upholstery

- For fresh stains, remove excess by blotting with paper towel.
- Place white vinegar on a cloth and wring tightly so it's damp but not wet. Blot over the mark.

- For old stains, first find where the urine is. In a darkened room, turn on an ultraviolet light and the urine stains will show up yellow.
- Mark around the yellow stains with a piece of white chalk so you can identify the offending areas.
- Wipe inside the chalk marks with a cloth tightly wrung in white vinegar.
- In all cases, absorb moisture by covering the area with paper towel. Place a book on top of the paper towel to assist with absorption.

On stone

- Wipe with white vinegar on a cloth.
- If stubborn, mix plaster of Paris and water to the consistency of peanut butter. To each cup of mixture, add 2 teaspoons of white vinegar.
- Spread 5 mm to 1 cm thick over the stain.
- Allow to dry completely. If it feels cold on the back of your hand, it's not dry.
- When dry, brush away.

On timber

- For fresh stains, remove excess by blotting with paper towel.
- Place white vinegar on a cloth and wring tightly so it's damp but not wet. Blot over the mark.
- For old stains, find where the urine is. In a darkened room, turn on an ultraviolet light and the urine stains will show up yellow.
- Mark around the yellow stains with a piece of white chalk so you can identify the offending areas.

- Wipe inside the chalk marks with a cloth tightly wrung in white vinegar.
- If the urine has soaked through the floorboard grooves, make a paste of plaster of Paris and water to the consistency of peanut butter. For every cup of paste, add 2 teaspoons of white vinegar.
- Spread 5 mm to 1 cm thick over the floorboards.
- Allow to dry completely. If it feels cold on the back of your hand, it's not dry.
- When dry, brush off with a broom.

TIP

To deter cats, use anything containing camphor, such as mothballs, naphthalene flakes or Vicks VapoRub. *Mix 1 mothball and 1 litre of water in a spray pack. Shake well. Mist around the areas where you have trouble with cats. Wipe* Vicks VapoRub *around doorframes. A light scattering of naphthalene flakes under the house will keep cats away.*

NOTE: *Do not use mothballs or naphthalene flakes if you have children under 3 years of age.*

Camphor can bleach carpet.

CAVIAR

Some caviar is coloured with lumpfish roe, which is more challenging to remove.

On carpet/upholstery

- Remove excess by lifting with a plastic comb or by blotting with paper towel.
- Place white vinegar on a cloth and wring tightly so it's damp but not wet. Blot over the mark.
- If stubborn, rot some full cream milk in the sun until it forms solids.
- Place the solids over the stain until the ink is absorbed.
- Remove the solids by lifting with a plastic comb.
- Wipe with a damp cloth.
- Massage with a couple of drops of dishwashing liquid on your fingertips until the liquid feels like jelly.
- Wipe with a damp cloth until the dishwashing liquid is removed.
- In all cases, absorb moisture by covering the area with paper towel. Place a book on top of the paper towel to assist with absorption.

On cotton/fabric

- Remove excess under the tap using cold water. Blot with or soak in white vinegar.
- If stubborn, rot some full cream milk in the sun until it forms solids. Place the solids on the stain until the ink is absorbed. Remove using cold water.
- In all cases, wash according to the fabric. Dry on the clothesline or clothes airer.

CHALK

On carpet/upholstery

- Wipe with a slice of wholemeal brown bread (not wholegrain).

- If this doesn't work, mix ½ teaspoon of dishwashing liquid with 1 cup of water and wipe on with a cloth.
- Place white vinegar on a cloth and wring tightly so it's damp but not wet. Blot over the mark.
- Absorb moisture by covering the area with paper towel. Place a book on top of the paper towel to assist with absorption.
- Alternatively, wipe with white spirits on a cloth.
- Sprinkle with talcum powder.
- When dry, vacuum.

On cotton/fabric

- Remove excess under the tap using cold water.
- Scribble with a cake of bathroom soap. Rub the fabric against itself using your hands.
- Wash according to the fabric. Dry on the clothesline or clothes airer.

CHANDELIER

To clean

- Turn it off at the switch.
- Put a sheet or towel on the floor underneath the chandelier big enough to catch any drips.
- On a ladder, remove the light bulbs and put a small plastic bag over each fitting so you don't get moisture in the electrics.
- Dust the tops of the chandelier with a soft brush.
- Spray a generous amount of chandelier spray cleaner (available at lighting shops) over the chandelier until it starts to drip. The dirt and dust will run off.
- When the chandelier is completely dry, return the light bulbs.

CHARCOAL

On carpet/upholstery

- Remove excess by vacuuming.
- Scrub with 2 drops of dishwashing liquid on a toothbrush.
- Wipe with a damp cloth until the dishwashing liquid is removed.
- Absorb moisture by covering the area with paper towel. Place a book on top of the paper towel to assist with absorption.

On cotton/fabric

- Remove excess by shaking.
- Scrub with 2 drops of dishwashing liquid on a toothbrush.
- Wash according to the fabric. Dry on the clothesline or clothes airer.

CHEESE SAUCE

On carpet/upholstery

- Chill first by covering with ice cubes in a zip-lock bag.
- Remove excess by lifting with a plastic comb or by blotting with paper towel.
- Scribble with a cake of bathroom soap run under cold water.
- Absorb moisture by covering the area with paper towel. Place a book on top of the paper towel to assist with absorption.

On cotton/fabric

- Place in the freezer until the cheese sauce goes hard.
- Remove excess by lifting with a plastic comb or using cold water.
- Scribble with a cake of bathroom soap. Rub the fabric against itself using your hands. Alternatively, soak in ½ lid of *Vanish NapiSan Oxi Action* and 9 litres of cold water for 30 minutes. Don't use on wool, silk or leather.
- Wash according to the fabric. Dry on the clothesline or clothes airer.

CHERRY

On carpet/upholstery

- Remove excess by lifting with a plastic comb or by blotting with paper towel.
- Place white vinegar on a cloth and wring tightly so it's damp but not wet. Blot over the mark.
- If stubborn, mix ½ teaspoon of dishwashing liquid and 1 teaspoon of white vinegar in 1 cup of cold water. Wipe the mixture on using a cloth. Wipe off with a damp cloth.
- In all cases, absorb moisture by covering the area with paper towel. Place a book on top of the paper towel to assist with absorption.

On cotton/fabric

- Remove excess under the tap using cold water.
- Blot with or soak in white vinegar.
- If stubborn, mix ½ teaspoon of dishwashing liquid and 1 teaspoon of white vinegar in 4 litres of cold water. Soak for 30 minutes.
- In all cases, wash according to the fabric. Dry on the clothesline or clothes airer.

CHEWING GUM

On carpet/upholstery (not leather)

- Put ice cubes in a zip-lock bag and place over the gum.
- When the chewing gum has hardened, remove as much as possible with a dull blade without cutting the carpet or upholstery.
- Rub in circles with a little tea tree oil on tightly rolled pantyhose.
- Sprinkle with talcum powder and rub with pantyhose until removed.
- Vacuum.

On cotton/fabric

- Place in the freezer, or place ice cubes in a zip-lock bag over the gum.
- When the chewing gum has hardened, remove as much as possible with a dull knife.
- Rub in circles with tea tree oil on a tissue. Little gum balls will form that can be plucked from the cotton or fabric.
- Repeat until the gum is removed.
- Wash according to the fabric. Dry on the clothesline or clothes airer.

On leather

- Put ice cubes in a zip-lock bag on the gum.
- When the gum has hardened, remove as much as possible with scissors or a blade. Be careful not to cut the surface of the leather.
- Wipe with 2 drops of tea tree oil on a cotton bud. Leave for 1 hour.

- Rub off with pantyhose.
- Wipe with leather conditioner. Make your own – see **Household formulas**.

CHICKEN NOODLE SOUP

On carpet/upholstery

- Remove excess by lifting with a plastic comb or by blotting with paper towel.
- Mix ½ teaspoon of dishwashing liquid in cold water to generate a sudsy mix.
- Apply only the suds with a toothbrush, working north, south, east and west.
- Wipe with white vinegar on a cloth.
- Remove yellow marks with 2 drops of lavender oil on a cloth.
- Absorb moisture by covering the area with paper towel. Place a book on top of the paper towel to assist with absorption.

On cotton/fabric

- Remove excess under the tap using cold water.
- Massage with a little dishwashing liquid on your fingertips until the liquid feels like jelly.
- Rinse in blood-heat (body temperature) water.
- Remove any remaining yellow marks with lavender oil.
- Wash according to the fabric. Dry on the clothesline or clothes airer.

CHILLI SAUCE

(see also 'Sweet Chilli Sauce')

On carpet/upholstery

- Remove excess by lifting with a plastic comb or by blotting with paper towel.
- Place white vinegar on a cloth and wring tightly so it's damp but not wet. Blot over the mark.
- Massage with a couple of drops of dishwashing liquid on your fingertips until the liquid feels like jelly.
- Wipe with a cold damp cloth until the dishwashing liquid is removed.
- Absorb moisture by covering the area with paper towel. Place a book on top of the paper towel to assist with absorption.
- When dry, vacuum and scrub with a brush.

On cotton/fabric

- Remove excess under the tap using cold water.
- Blot with or soak in white vinegar or lemon juice.
- Wash according to the fabric. Dry in sunshine.

CHIMNEY

To work out when it's time to clean your chimney, scrape a fingernail on the inside when cold. If soot flakes off, rather than smears off, it's time for a clean. Other clues are excess smoke from the fire and soot falling down the chimney into the fireplace.

CHINA ORNAMENT

China ornaments should be cleaned every 6 months to prevent crazing.

To clean

- Add a tiny amount of sweet almond oil to a paintbrush and wipe over dusty areas. The dust will stick to the oil.
- For stubborn dust, use a hair dryer on a cool setting.
- If china is crazed or discoloured, add 2 denture tablets to a sink filled with blood-heat (body temperature) water. Soak the items overnight. Dry in sunshine.

TIP

Don't put good china in water hotter than you could leave your hand in.

CHIPS

(see 'Potato Chips')

CHOCOLATE

On carpet/upholstery

- Remove excess by lifting with a plastic spatula or credit card.
- Scribble with a cake of bathroom soap run under cold water.
- If there's residue, massage with a couple of drops of dishwashing liquid on your fingertips until the liquid feels like jelly. If the jelly mixture dries out, add a little cold water to your fingertips and continue massaging.

- In all cases, absorb moisture by covering the area with paper towel. Place a book on top of the paper towel to assist with absorption.

On cotton/fabric (not polyester satin/wool)

- Remove excess by lifting with a plastic comb using cold water.
- Scribble with a cake of bathroom soap. Rub the fabric against itself using your hands.
- If there's residue, massage with a couple of drops of dishwashing liquid until the liquid feels like jelly.
- In all cases, rinse using cold water.
- Wash in the washing machine on a warm or hot cycle. Dry in sunshine.

On cooktop

- Lay a wet cloth over the chocolate.
- Hold up one edge of the cloth and apply heat from a hair dryer so the chocolate melts into the cloth.

On polyester satin

- Place a dry cotton ball at the back of the stain.
- Working from the outside to the inside and rubbing in circles, wipe the front of the stain with white spirits on a cotton ball.
- Wash according to the fabric. Dry on the clothesline or clothes airer.

On stone

- Scrub with 2 drops of dishwashing liquid and cold water on a toothbrush.

- If stubborn, mix plaster of Paris and water to the consistency of peanut butter.
- To each cup of mixture, add 1 teaspoon of dishwashing liquid.
- Spread 5 mm to 1 cm thick over the stain.
- Allow to dry completely. If it feels cold on the back of your hand, it's not dry.
- When dry, brush off.

On wool

- Massage with a couple of drops of dishwashing liquid on your fingertips until the liquid feels like jelly.
- Rinse in cold water.
- Wash in 1 teaspoon of cheap shampoo and blood-heat (body temperature) water.
- Rinse in blood-heat water.
- Gently wring and dry flat on a towel in the shade.

CHUTNEY

On carpet/upholstery

- Remove excess by lifting with a plastic comb or by blotting with paper towel.
- Mix equal parts white vinegar and blood-heat (body temperature) water.
- Apply sparingly with a toothbrush or pantyhose, scrubbing in all directions (north, south, east and west) until removed.
- Absorb moisture by covering the area with paper towel. Place a book on top of the paper towel to assist with absorption.
- When almost dry, repeat.
- If a shadow returns in a couple of weeks, repeat again.

On cotton/fabric

- Remove excess by lifting with a plastic comb using cold water.
- Blot with or soak in white vinegar.
- Wash according to the fabric. Dry on the clothesline or clothes airer.

CIGARETTE ASH

On carpet/upholstery

- Remove excess by vacuuming.
- Scribble with a cake of bathroom soap run under cold water.
- Wipe with a damp cloth.
- Vacuum.
- Sprinkle with bicarb. Leave for 15 minutes.
- Vacuum.
- Absorb moisture by covering the area with paper towel. Place a book on top of the paper towel to assist with absorption.

On cotton/fabric

- Remove excess by shaking.
- Scribble with a cake of bathroom soap run under cold water. Rub the fabric against itself using your hands.
- Sprinkle with bicarb. Leave for 15 minutes.
- Wash according to the fabric. Dry on the clothesline or clothes airer.

CIGARETTE STAINING

On carpet/upholstery

- Mix equal parts bicarb and unprocessed wheat bran.
- Sprinkle the mixture over the stain and sweep backwards and forwards with a brush.
- Leave for 5 hours.
- Vacuum thoroughly.
- For residue, mix 2 tablespoons of bicarb, 2 tablespoons of white vinegar, 2 tablespoons of methylated spirits, 2 teaspoons of glycerine, 2 teaspoons of eucalyptus oil, 2 teaspoons of dishwashing liquid and 1 litre of water in a spray pack. Lightly spray over the area. Wipe with a damp cloth.
- Absorb moisture by covering the area with paper towel. Place a book on top of the paper towel to assist with absorption.

On curtains/washable fabric

- In a bath, mix 2 cups of white vinegar, 1 cup of bicarb and 2 teaspoons of dishwashing liquid in blood-heat (body temperature) water.
- Immerse the items and stomp over them with clean feet.
- Soak for 30 minutes.
- Rinse in blood-heat water.
- Gently wring. Dry in sunshine.

On walls

- Mix 2 tablespoons of cigarette ash, 2 tablespoons of bicarb and 2 tablespoons of white vinegar in a bowl. Leave for 5 minutes.

- Put on rubber gloves and wipe the mixture over the walls using rolled up pantyhose. Leave for 5 minutes.
- Remove with damp pantyhose.

CINNAMON OIL

On carpet/upholstery

- Remove excess by blotting with paper towel.
- Massage with a couple of drops of dishwashing liquid on your fingertips until the liquid feels like jelly.
- Wipe with a damp cloth until the dishwashing liquid is removed.
- Absorb moisture by covering the area with paper towel. Place a book on top of the paper towel to assist with absorption.

On cotton/fabric

- Remove excess under the tap using cold water.
- Massage with a couple of drops of dishwashing liquid on your fingertips until the liquid feels like jelly.
- Wash according to the fabric. Dry on the clothesline or clothes airer.

On laminate/polycarbonate

- Make a paste of glycerine and talcum powder.
- Apply the mixture using pantyhose. Leave for 90 minutes.
- Polish off with damp pantyhose. Repeat, if needed.

On timber

- Mix plaster of Paris and water to the consistency of peanut butter.

- To each cup of mixture, add 1 teaspoon of dishwashing liquid.
- Spread 5 mm to 1 cm thick over the stain.
- Allow to dry completely. If it feels cold on the back of your hand, it's not dry.
- When dry, brush away.
- Alternatively, dab a little car polish over the area.

⚠ WARNING

Using car polish will remove a fine layer of the timber or coating from the surface.

CITRONELLA SPRAY

On carpet/upholstery

- Remove excess by blotting with paper towel.
- Massage with a couple of drops of dishwashing liquid on your fingertips until the liquid feels like jelly.
- Wipe with a damp cloth until the dishwashing liquid is removed.
- Absorb moisture by covering the area with paper towel. Place a book on top of the paper towel to assist with absorption.

CLAY

On carpet/upholstery

- Remove excess by rubbing with a brush and vacuuming.
- Wipe with a cold damp cloth in all directions – north, south, east and west.
- Rub with paper towel, hand over hand, until dry.

- Vacuum.
- For red clay, sprinkle with uniodised salt and sweep backwards and forwards with a brush until removed.
- Vacuum.

On cotton/fabric

- Mix ½ cup of white vinegar and ¼ cup of uniodised salt.
- Soak fabric in mixture and leave for 30 minutes.
- Remove by rubbing the fabric against itself using your hands.
- Rinse using cold water.
- Wash according to the fabric. Dry on the clothesline or clothes airer.

COCA-COLA

(see 'Soft Drink')

COCKROACH DROPPINGS

On curtains

- Wipe with damp pantyhose.
- Sprinkle uniodised salt on pantyhose and scrub.
- Wipe with 2 drops of glycerine on a cloth. Leave for 90 minutes.
- Rub with pantyhose that have been dipped in soapy water.
- Rinse. Add 1 cup of uniodised salt to the rinse water to deter cockroaches.

COCKROACHES

To deter

- Mix 1 cup of uniodised salt, 1 teaspoon of lavender oil and 1 litre of water in a spray pack.
- Spray the solution around doors, windows, drains, air vents and other areas where cockroaches lurk. Respray when you see cockroaches – more often during summer.

COCKTAIL SAUCE

On carpet/upholstery

- Remove excess by blotting with paper towel.
- Massage with a couple of drops of dishwashing liquid on your fingertips until the liquid feels like jelly.
- Wipe with a damp cloth until the dishwashing liquid is removed.
- Absorb moisture by covering the area with paper towel. Place a book on top of the paper towel to assist with absorption.

On cotton/fabric

- Remove excess under the tap using cold water.
- Massage with a couple of drops of dishwashing liquid on your fingertips until the liquid feels like jelly.
- Wash according to the fabric. Dry on the clothesline or clothes airer.

COCOA

(see 'Chocolate')

COCONUT OIL

(see 'Cooking Oil')

COFFEE

On carpet/upholstery

- For fresh spills, remove excess by blotting with paper towel. Place white vinegar on a cloth and wring tightly so it's damp but not wet. Blot over the mark.
- If the coffee contains milk, massage with a couple of drops of dishwashing liquid on your fingertips until the liquid feels like jelly. Wipe with a damp cloth until the dishwashing liquid is removed.
- For old spills, scrub with 2 drops of glycerine on a toothbrush. Work from the outside to the inside of the stain. Leave for 90 minutes. Tightly wring a cloth in white vinegar, fold the cloth flat and polish out the glycerine without pushing it into the back of the carpet or upholstery.
- In all cases, absorb excess moisture by covering the area with paper towel. Place a book on top of the paper towel to assist with absorption.

On cotton/fabric

- If fresh, blot with or soak in white vinegar.
- If old, wipe with 2 drops of glycerine and leave for 90 minutes. Then blot with or soak in white vinegar.
- In both cases, wash according to the fabric. Dry on the clothesline or clothes airer.

On laminate

- Mix equal parts *Gumption* and glycerine.
- Apply the mixture with rolled up pantyhose.
- Wipe with a damp cloth.

COLOGNE

(see 'Aftershave Cologne')

COLOUR RUN

(see 'Dye')

COLOURED PENCIL

On carpet/upholstery

- Place 2 drops of tea tree oil on a slice of brown bread and wipe over the marks.
- Wipe with methylated spirits on a cotton bud until the colour bleeds.
- Cover with talcum powder.
- When it dries, vacuum. Repeat, if needed.

On walls

- Place 2 drops of tea tree oil on a slice of brown bread and wipe over the marks.
- Wipe with methylated spirits on a cloth.

COMPUTER

Be careful when cleaning computer screens. They are delicate.

To clean

- Turn the computer off.
- Wipe the screen with one damp and one dry pair of pantyhose. Rub with the damp pair and then rub with the dry pair.

- To clean between keyboard keys, use a cotton bud dipped in white vinegar. Or place the keyboard inside the leg of pantyhose, turn it over and vacuum through the pantyhose using your vacuum cleaner's brush attachment.

TIP

A square of leather makes an ideal mousepad.

CONCEALER MAKE-UP

(see 'Make-up')

CONCRETE

(see 'Polished Concrete')

COOKING OIL

On carpet/upholstery (not leather)

- Remove excess by blotting with paper towel.
- Massage with a couple of drops of dishwashing liquid on your fingertips until the liquid feels like jelly.
- Wipe with a damp cloth until the dishwashing liquid is removed.
- Absorb moisture by covering the area with paper towel. Place a book on top of the paper towel to assist with absorption.

On cotton/fabric

- Remove excess under the tap using cold water.
- Massage with a couple of drops of dishwashing liquid on your fingertips until the liquid feels like jelly.

- Wash according to the fabric. Dry on the clothesline or clothes airer.

On glazed tiles/pavers

- Mix plaster of Paris and water to the consistency of peanut butter.
- To each cup of mixture, add 1 teaspoon of dishwashing liquid.
- Spread 5 mm to 1 cm thick over the stain.
- Allow to dry completely. If it feels cold on the back of your hand, it's not dry.
- When dry, remove with a scrubbing brush. Repeat, if needed.

On granite/marble

- Remove excess by blotting with paper towel.
- Massage with a couple of drops of dishwashing liquid until the liquid feels like jelly.
- Wipe with a damp cloth.
- For any remaining stains, mix plaster of Paris and water to the consistency of peanut butter.
- To each cup of mixture, add 1 teaspoon of dishwashing liquid.
- Spread 5 mm to 1 cm thick over the stain.
- Allow to dry completely. If it feels cold on the back of your hand, it's not dry.
- When dry, remove with a plastic or wooden spatula so you don't scratch the surface.

On leather

- Place a drop of water on the leather. If it beads, it's hard-tanned leather. If it penetrates, it's soft-tanned leather.

- For hard-tanned leather (shiny, waxy finish), wipe with 2 drops of white spirits on a cloth. Work in even, parallel strokes across the entire panel of leather. Sprinkle with talcum powder. When dry, brush off.
- For soft-tanned leather (low sheen finish/kid/kangaroo hide), oil with leather conditioner and leave for 2 weeks – it takes that long to dry. The stains will lighten as the leather dries.

TIP

If you get grease on a book, cover the spot above and underneath with blotting paper and run a warm iron on top. If the stain remains, wipe two pieces of blotting paper with a little dishwashing liquid, place them above and underneath the stain and press firmly with a very cool iron on top. It's the pressure, not the heat, that shifts the remaining oil.

COPPER

For tarnish

- Sprinkle with equal parts bicarb and white vinegar.
- Allow the paste to dry.
- Buff off with a clean, dry cloth or pantyhose.
- Wipe with a little sweet almond oil on a cloth. This prevents further tarnishing.

For verdigris on stone

- Place a denture tablet over the stain and secure it with masking tape.
- Spray water over the denture tablet. Leave overnight.

- Remove the denture tablet and scrub over the stain with bicarb and white vinegar on a scrubbing brush.
- Rinse with a hose.

CORDIAL

(Fruit)

On carpet/upholstery

- Remove excess by blotting with paper towel.
- Place white vinegar on a cloth and wring tightly so it's damp but not wet. Blot over the mark.
- For an old stain, wipe with 2 drops of glycerine on a cloth. Leave for 90 minutes. Then blot with white vinegar on a cloth.
- For remaining coloured stains, expose to sunlight or ultraviolet light. (If using ultraviolet light, protect areas around the stain with cardboard.) Check every 2 hours.
- In all cases, absorb moisture by covering the area with paper towel. Place a book on top of the paper towel to assist with absorption.

On cotton/fabric

- Remove excess under the tap using cold water.
- Blot with or soak in white vinegar. Hang in the sunshine until the stain fades.
- Wash according to the fabric. Dry on the clothesline or clothes airer.

CORN

On carpet/upholstery

- Remove excess by lifting with a plastic comb or by blotting with paper towel.
- Massage with a couple of drops of dishwashing liquid on your fingertips until the liquid feels like jelly. It will go grey in colour.
- Wipe with a cold damp cloth until the dishwashing liquid is removed.
- Absorb moisture by covering the area with paper towel. Place a book on top of the paper towel to assist with absorption.

On cotton/fabric

- Remove excess under the tap using cold water.
- Massage with a couple of drops of dishwashing liquid on your fingertips until the liquid feels like jelly. It will go grey.
- Wash according to the fabric. Dry on the clothesline or clothes airer.

CORN CHIP COLOURING

On carpet/upholstery

- Remove excess corn chips by lifting with a plastic comb or vacuuming.
- Sprinkle with unprocessed wheat bran and scrub backwards and forwards with a brush. Don't use moisture.
- Vacuum.

On cotton/fabric

- Scrub with unprocessed wheat bran.
- If it gets wet, wipe with 2 drops of lavender oil. Leave for 5 minutes.
- Wash according to the fabric. Dry on the clothesline or clothes airer.

CORRECTION FLUID

On carpet/upholstery

- Wipe only the correction fluid mark with *Liquid Paper Remover* on a cotton bud.
- Wipe with paper towel.
- Alternatively, wipe only the correction fluid mark with white spirits or eucalyptus oil on a cotton bud. Because white spirits and eucalyptus oil can strip colour, test the surface first by dipping a toothpick in the solvent and testing on an inconspicuous area. If colour comes away, don't use the solvent.

On cotton/fabric

- Wipe only the correction fluid mark with *Liquid Paper Remover* on a cotton bud.
- Alternatively, wipe only the correction fluid mark with white spirits or eucalyptus oil on a cotton bud. Because white spirits and eucalyptus oil can strip colour, test the surface first by dipping a toothpick in the solvent and testing on an inconspicuous area. If colour comes away, don't use the solvent.
- In both cases, wash according to the fabric. Dry on the clothesline or clothes airer.

On sealed timber

- Put on rubber gloves. Wring a cloth in boiling water.
- When the cloth is almost dry, lay it over the mark for 30 seconds.
- Remove and scrape with a credit card held at an angle. The mark will come away.

COSMETICS

(see 'Make-up')

COUCH

To clean fabric

- The cleaning method will depend on what the couch is made of. Consult the care label first. It's usually located on the base of the couch. If there's no care label, consult 'Mystery Stains'.
- Stains with a ring or circle around the edge contain protein and are removed by scribbling with a cake of bathroom soap run under cold water.
- For a greasy stain, massage with a couple of drops of dishwashing liquid on your fingertips until the liquid feels like jelly. Wipe with a damp cloth.
- For grime marks, mix unprocessed wheat bran and drops of white vinegar until the mixture resembles breadcrumbs. Rub over the marks with a stiff, clean brush.
- For removable covers, wash with ½ cup of white vinegar and ½ cup of cheap shampoo in the washing machine.
- Vacuum the couch once a week using the small attachment, making sure to clean under and behind cushions.

To clean leather

- Wipe with leather conditioner. Make your own – see **Household formulas**.

TIP

If you see a leather couch thrown out during council clean-ups, remove the leather at the back of the couch with a Stanley knife. It's generally in pristine condition and can be reused.

COUGH SYRUP

Cough syrup is high in sugar.

On carpet/upholstery

- Remove excess by blotting with paper towel.
- Mix equal parts white vinegar and blood-heat (body temperature) water.
- Scrub the mixture with a toothbrush or pantyhose in all directions – north, south, east and west.
- Absorb moisture by covering the area with paper towel. Place a book on top of the paper towel to assist with absorption.
- When almost dry, repeat.
- If a shadow returns in a couple of weeks, repeat again.

On cotton/fabric

- Remove excess under the tap using cold water.
- Blot with or soak in white vinegar.
- Wash according to the fabric. Dry on the clothesline or clothes airer.

CRANBERRY SAUCE

On carpet/upholstery

- Remove excess by lifting with a plastic comb or by blotting with paper towel.
- Mix equal parts white vinegar and blood-heat (body temperature) water.
- Scrub the mixture with a toothbrush or pantyhose in all directions – north, south, east and west.
- Absorb moisture by covering the area with paper towel. Place a book on top of the paper towel to assist with absorption.
- When almost dry, repeat.
- If a shadow returns in a couple of weeks, repeat again.

On cotton/fabric

- Remove excess under the tap using cold water.
- Blot with or soak in white vinegar.
- Wash according to the fabric. Dry on the clothesline or clothes airer.

CRAYON

On carpet/upholstery

- Remove excess by lifting with a plastic comb or by blotting with paper towel.
- Wipe with tea tree oil on pantyhose – roll over the crayon mark in a circle. The crayon wax will stick to the pantyhose.
- Absorb moisture by covering the area with paper towel. Place a book on top of the paper towel to assist with absorption.

On cotton/fabric

- Remove excess under the tap using cold water.
- Mix 2 drops of tea tree oil with 1 teaspoon of dishwashing liquid.
- Massage the mixture over the crayon marks with your fingertips.
- Rinse under blood-heat (body temperature) water.
- Wash according to the fabric. Dry on the clothesline or clothes airer.

On walls

- Rub the mark with 2 drops of tea tree oil on a slice of brown bread.
- Alternatively, rub with a pencil eraser run under soapy water. The wax in the crayon will roll off in balls.
- In both cases, wipe with a damp cloth.

CREAM

On carpet/upholstery

- Remove excess by lifting with a plastic comb or by blotting with paper towel.
- To remove proteins, mix ½ teaspoon of dishwashing liquid in 1 cup of cold water to generate a sudsy mix. Apply only the suds using a toothbrush.
- To remove fats, mix ½ teaspoon of dishwashing liquid in 1 cup of hot water. Apply only the suds using a toothbrush.
- Absorb moisture by covering the area with paper towel. Place a book on top of the paper towel to assist with absorption.
- Alternatively, wipe with white spirits on a cotton ball.

- Sprinkle with talcum powder to absorb the white spirits.
- When dry, vacuum.

On cotton/fabric

- Remove excess under the tap using cold water.
- Massage with a little dishwashing liquid on your fingertips until the liquid feels like jelly.
- Soak in 1/2 lid of *Vanish NapiSan Oxi Action* and 9 litres of water for 30 minutes. Don't use on wool, silk or leather.
- Wash according to the fabric. Dry on the clothesline or clothes airer.

CREAM CHEESE

On carpet/upholstery

- Remove excess by lifting with a plastic comb or by blotting with paper towel.
- Scribble with a cake of bathroom soap run under cold water.
- Massage with a couple of drops of dishwashing liquid on your fingertips until the liquid feels like jelly.
- Wipe with a damp cloth until the dishwashing liquid is removed.
- Absorb moisture by covering the area with paper towel. Place a book on top of the paper towel to assist with absorption.

On cotton/fabric

- Remove excess by running under the tap using cold water. Scribble with a cake of bathroom soap. Massage with a couple of drops of dishwashing liquid on your fingertips until the liquid feels like jelly.

- Alternatively, soak in ½ lid of *Vanish NapiSan Oxi Action* and 9 litres of water for 30 minutes. Don't use on wool, silk or leather.
- In both cases, wash according to the fabric. Dry on the clothesline or clothes airer.

CRÊPE PAPER

On carpet/upholstery

- Remove excess by blotting with paper towel.
- Mix 2 drops of lavender oil and 2 drops of glycerine to form a paste.
- Apply the mixture with a cloth. Leave for 2 minutes.
- Remove with a damp cloth.
- Absorb moisture by covering the area with paper towel. Place a book on top of the paper towel to assist with absorption.

On cotton/fabric

- Mix 2 drops of lavender oil and 2 drops of glycerine to form a paste.
- Place over the item for 90 minutes.
- Wash according to the fabric. Dry on the clothesline or clothes airer.

CRICKET BALL STAIN

On cotton/fabric

- Wipe with white spirits on a cotton ball.
- Wash according to the fabric. Dry on the clothesline or clothes airer.

CROCKERY

Crockery can be made of china, porcelain, pottery, glass or polycarbonate resin.

For crazing/discoloration

- Add 2 denture tablets to a sink of blood-heat (body temperature) water and soak items overnight.
- Dry in sunshine.

TIPS

To prevent china plates from chipping and cracking in cupboards, put paper towel between the plates. Never put gold-rimmed china in the microwave or dishwasher. Place a glass of water inside china cabinets to prevent crazing.

To clean

- Hand wash in dishwashing liquid and hot water.
- For extra sparkle, add 1 tablespoon of white vinegar to the rinse water.
- Never soak pottery because it can lift the glaze.

CROISSANT

The stain is from butter or margarine.

On carpet/upholstery

- Remove excess by blotting with paper towel.
- Massage with a couple of drops of dishwashing liquid on your fingertips until the liquid feels like jelly.

- Wipe with a damp cloth until the dishwashing liquid is removed.
- Absorb moisture by covering the area with paper towel. Place a book on top of the paper towel to assist with absorption.
- Consult 'Honey', 'Jam', etc. if needed.

On cotton/fabric

- Remove excess under the tap using cold water.
- Massage with a couple of drops of dishwashing liquid on your fingertips until the liquid feels like jelly.
- Wash according to the fabric. Dry on the clothesline or clothes airer.
- Consult 'Honey', 'Jam', etc. if needed.

CURRY

(see also 'Tandoori', 'Vindaloo')

On carpet/upholstery

- Remove excess by lifting with a plastic comb or by blotting with paper towel.
- Mix 1 teaspoon of lavender oil and 1 litre of water in a spray pack. Lightly spray over the area and scrub with pantyhose or a cloth.
- Alternatively, massage with 2 drops of lavender oil on your fingertips until the stain starts to move.
- To remove greasy marks, massage with a couple of drops of dishwashing liquid on your fingertips until the liquid feels like jelly.
- In all cases, place white vinegar on a cloth and wring tightly so it's damp but not wet. Blot over the mark.

- Absorb moisture by covering the area with paper towel. Place a book on top of the paper towel to assist with absorption.
- If there's a dye stain, expose to sunlight or ultraviolet light. (If using ultraviolet light, protect areas around the stain with cardboard.) Check every 2 hours.

On chopping board

- Wipe with 2 drops of lavender oil on a cloth.
- Scrub with dishwashing liquid and water.

On cotton/fabric

- Remove excess under the tap using cold water.
- Place a dry cotton ball behind the stain. Blot the front of the stain with lavender oil on a cotton ball.
- Alternatively, rub with talcum powder.
- In both cases, wash according to the fabric. Dry on the clothesline or clothes airer.

On plastic container

- Mix 1 teaspoon of lavender oil in a 9-litre bucket of water.
- Place items inside the bucket and leave overnight.
- Remove and dry in sunshine.

CUSTARD

On carpet/upholstery

- Remove excess by lifting with a plastic comb or by blotting with paper towel.
- Scribble with a cake of bathroom soap run under cold water.
- Wipe with a damp cloth.

- Massage with a couple of drops of dishwashing liquid on your fingertips until the liquid feels like jelly.
- Wipe with a damp cloth until the dishwashing liquid is removed.
- Absorb moisture by covering the area with paper towel. Place a book on top of the paper towel to assist with absorption.

On cotton/fabric

- Remove excess under the tap using cold water.
- Scribble with a cake of bathroom soap. Rub the fabric against itself using your hands. For residue, massage with a couple of drops of dishwashing liquid on your fingertips until the liquid feels like jelly.
- Alternatively, make a paste of *Vanish NapiSan Oxi Action* and water to the consistency of spreadable butter and place over the stain. Leave for 20 minutes. Don't use on wool, silk or leather.
- In both cases, wash according to the fabric. Dry on the clothesline or clothes airer.

CUTLERY

To clean

- Wash stainless steel cutlery in dishwashing liquid and hot water.
- For rust spots, sprinkle with bicarb and white vinegar on pantyhose. Then wash in dishwashing liquid and hot water.
- Wash gold cutlery with bicarb and white vinegar.
- Wash brass cutlery with bicarb and white vinegar and then wipe with a little sweet almond oil on a cloth. Brass tarnishes quickly.

D

DAMP

In wardrobe

- Use a cloth to wipe interior walls with ¼ teaspoon of oil of cloves mixed in a 250-ml bottle of baby oil. Relabel bottle.
- Tie 6 sticks of white blackboard chalk together with string or ribbon and leave inside the wardrobe to absorb moisture. When the chalk sticks are wet, place them in the sun until they dry out. You can use them over and over again.
- For serious continuous damp, seek professional advice.

DATE

On carpet/upholstery

- Remove excess by lifting with a plastic comb or by blotting with paper towel.
- Mix equal parts white vinegar and blood-heat (body temperature) water.
- Scrub the mixture with a toothbrush or pantyhose in all directions – north, south, east and west.
- Absorb moisture by covering the area with paper towel. Place a book on top of the paper towel to assist with absorption.
- When almost dry, repeat.
- If a shadow returns in a couple of weeks, repeat again.

On cotton/fabric

- Remove excess under the tap using cold water.
- Blot with or soak in white vinegar.
- Wash according to the fabric. Dry on the clothesline or clothes airer.

DECKING

(Bamboo/eco/timber)

For iron marks

- Proprietary products are available from hardware stores that remove iron and fix tannin leaching.

For moss

- Mix 2 tablespoons of copper sulphate solution in a 9-litre bucket of hot or cold water.
- Sweep the mixture over the decking with a broom.
- Allow to dry. It will blow away in a couple of days.

For mould

- Mix 2 drops of oil of cloves in a 9-litre bucket of water.
- Sweep the mixture over the decking with a broom. Leave for 24 hours.
- Rinse with a hose.

For weather exposure

- Mix 1 teaspoon of dishwashing liquid and 1 cup of black tea in a 9-litre bucket of blood-heat (body temperature) water.
- Sweep the mixture over the decking with a broom.
- Rinse with a hose, then re-oil the timber.

To clean

- For sealed timber, mix 3 teaspoons of dishwashing liquid in a 9-litre bucket of blood-heat (body temperature) water. Don't use dishwashing liquid on unsealed timber because it dries out the timber and creates splinters.
- Sweep the mixture over the decking with a broom.

- For unsealed timber, rinse with a mixture of strong black tea (4–5 tea bags in 4 cups of boiling water) and 1 drop of oil of cloves in a 9-litre bucket. Wipe the hot mixture over the timber. This will help prevent a silvery colour.

DEODORANT

On cotton/fabric (not silk/wool)

- If it contains synthetic fibres, wipe with a little methylated spirits first.
- Make a paste of *Vanish NapiSan Oxi Action* and water to the consistency of spreadable butter. Don't use on wool, silk.
- Apply to the stain. Leave for 20 minutes.
- Wash according to the fabric. Dry on the clothesline or clothes airer.

On leather

- Wipe with white spirits on a cloth using even parallel strokes across the entire panel.
- Sprinkle with talcum powder.
- When dry, brush away.
- Wipe with leather conditioner. Make your own – see **Household formulas**.

On silk/wool

- Scribble with a cake of bathroom soap run under cold water.
- Rinse with 1 teaspoon of cheap shampoo and blood-heat (body temperature) water.
- Gently wring and dry flat on a towel in the shade. Ensure silk is dried away from the wind so the fibres don't tangle and leave a dusty look.

DESSERT STAIN

Desserts can contain sugar, fat and food colouring.

On carpet/upholstery (not leather)

- Remove excess by lifting with a plastic comb or by blotting with paper towel.
- To remove sugars, tightly wring a cloth in white vinegar. Place the vinegar cloth in one hand and a dry cloth in the other and wipe hand over hand, as though stroking a cat.
- To remove fat, massage with a couple of drops of dishwashing liquid on your fingertips until the liquid feels like jelly.
- Wipe with a damp cloth until the dishwashing liquid is removed.
- To remove food colouring, expose to sunlight or ultraviolet light. (If using ultraviolet light, protect areas around the stain with cardboard.) Check every 2 hours.
- Absorb moisture by covering the area with paper towel. Place a book on top of the paper towel to assist with absorption.

On cotton/fabric

- Remove excess under the tap using cold water.
- To remove sugars, blot with or soak in white vinegar.
- To remove fat, massage with a couple of drops of dishwashing liquid on your fingertips until the liquid feels like jelly.
- Rinse under blood-heat (body temperature) water.
- To remove food colouring, blot with white vinegar and hang in sunshine until the stain fades before washing.
- In all cases, wash according to the fabric. Dry on the clothesline or clothes airer.

On leather

- Remove excess by blotting with paper towel.
- Wipe with white spirits on a cloth in even, parallel strokes across the entire panel.
- Sprinkle with talcum powder.
- When dry, brush off.

DIESEL OIL

On concrete/pavers

- Wipe with white spirits or turpentine on a cloth. Leave for 1 hour.
- Scrub with dishwashing liquid and hot water on a brush or broom.
- Rinse with a hose.

On cotton/fabric

- For synthetic fibres, wipe with methylated spirits on a cloth first, then follow instructions below.
- For natural fibres, massage with a couple of drops of dishwashing liquid on your fingertips until the liquid feels like jelly.
- Rinse under blood-heat (body temperature) water.
- Wash according to the fabric. Dry on the clothesline or clothes airer.
- If there's odour, mix 2 cups of full cream milk in a 9-litre bucket of water.
- Soak overnight. Then follow the instructions above.

DIRT

On antique/delicate fabric

- Scribble with a cake of bathroom soap run under blood-heat (body temperature) water.
- Rinse under blood-heat water.
- Lay flat on a towel in sunshine to dry.
- For stubborn stains, blast with a cool hair dryer and brush with a soft brush until removed.

On carpet/upholstery (not leather)

- Remove excess by vacuuming.
- Mix equal parts white vinegar, bicarb and water in a spray pack. Alternatively, mix ½ teaspoon of dishwashing liquid and 1 litre of water in a spray pack.
- Lightly spray over the surface. Leave for 5 minutes.
- Rub with a cloth.
- Absorb moisture by covering the area with paper towel. Place a book on top of the paper towel to assist with absorption.
- When dry, vacuum.

On cotton/fabric (not wool)

- Remove excess under the tap using cold water.
- Mix *Vanish NapiSan Oxi Action* and blood-heat (body temperature) to hot water to the consistency of spreadable butter. Don't use on wool, silk or leather.
- Apply to the stain and leave for 20 minutes.
- Wash according to the fabric. Dry on the clothesline or clothes airer.

On leather

- Wipe with saddle soap on a damp cloth.
- Polish with a clean cloth.
- Wipe with leather conditioner. Make your own – see **Household formulas**.
- For kid leather, mix unprocessed wheat bran and drops of white vinegar until the mixture resembles breadcrumbs.
- Either place the mixture in the toe of pantyhose and wipe over the kid leather, or apply directly. The latter is a bit messier.

On secateur blades

- Rub with lemon juice on a cloth.
- Rub with a cork coated in coarse uniodised salt.
- Wipe with a clean cloth.

On suede

- Mix 1 cup of unprocessed wheat bran with drops of white spirits until the mixture resembles breadcrumbs.
- Place the mixture in a pillowcase and add the suede item.
- Sit on the pillowcase for an hour a day over the course of a week.
- Remove the item (outside the house) and shake until it's free of bran.
- If there are grubby marks, wipe with a little white spirits on a cotton ball, then sprinkle with talcum powder. When dry, use a brush over the suede.

On wool

- Sprinkle with uniodised salt.
- Rub with a clean handkerchief or piece of linen along the grain – don't rub in circles.

- Give the wool a good shake and brush with a bristle brush.
- Wash in 1 teaspoon of cheap shampoo and blood-heat (body temperature) water.
- Rinse in blood-heat water.
- Gently wring and dry flat on a towel in the shade.

DOG HAIR

On carpet/fabric/upholstery

- Put on disposable rubber gloves.
- Wash your gloved hands with bathroom soap and water. Shake your hands dry.
- Wipe over the dog hair. It will stick to the gloves.

DOG POO

This is high in proteins and fats.

On carpet/upholstery

- Remove excess by lifting with a plastic comb or by blotting with paper towel.
- Scribble with a cake of bathroom soap run under cold water. If stubborn, scrub with a toothbrush or pantyhose.
- Leave to dry.
- Vacuum.
- Alternatively, remove excess then fill a bucket with cold water and enough dishwashing liquid to generate a sudsy mix.
- Apply only the suds with a toothbrush, using as little water as possible.

- Fill a bucket with blood-heat (body temperature) water and dishwashing liquid and apply only the suds with a toothbrush.
- Absorb moisture by covering the area with paper towel. Place a book on top of the paper towel to assist with absorption.

DOG URINE

On carpet/upholstery

- For new stains, absorb excess by blotting with paper towel.
- Wipe with white vinegar on a cloth or toothbrush. Repeat, if needed.
- For old stains, first find where the urine is. In a darkened room, turn on an ultraviolet light and the urine stains will show up yellow.
- Mark around the yellow stains with a piece of white chalk so you can see where to clean.
- Wipe inside the chalk marks with a cloth tightly wrung in white vinegar.
- For new and old stains, absorb moisture by covering the area with paper towel. Place a book on top of the paper towel to assist with absorption.

On stone/timber

- Wipe with white vinegar on a cloth.
- If stubborn, mix plaster of Paris and water to the consistency of peanut butter.
- To each cup of mixture, add 2 teaspoons of white vinegar.
- Spread 5 mm to 1 cm thick over the stain.

- Allow to dry completely. If it feels cold on the back of your hand, it's not dry.
- When dry, brush away.

TIP

To deter dogs, wipe the area with a little lavender oil on a cloth. Or mix 1 teaspoon of lavender oil and 1 litre of water in a spray pack and lightly mist over the area.

DONER KEBAB

(see 'Kebab')

DOONA

(Feather/wool)

To clean

- Fill a bath with blood-heat (body temperature) water and 1 tablespoon of cheap shampoo.
- Lay the doona in the bath and stomp over it with clean feet to remove dirt and grime.
- Empty the bath, fill it again with clean, blood-heat water and stomp on the doona again.
- Drain water from the bath and tread on the doona to squeeze out as much moisture as possible.
- Place the doona in a large garbage bag, rather than a basket, so you don't leave a drip trail.
- Hang it on the clothesline using lots of pegs, so you don't place stress on one spot. Peg it by the two outside edges on separate lines to form a U shape. This allows air to circulate. If you don't have a clothesline, borrow a friend's or string a line in sunshine. It must be dried outside.

- When it's almost completely dry, whack it with your hand or a tennis racquet. This fluffs up the fibres or loosens the feathers.

DRAIN

To clean

- Flatten a metal coat-hanger and wrap one end with pantyhose. Knot them tightly.
- Use the coat-hanger like a bottle brush and scrub inside the drain.
- Put ½ cup of bicarb down the drain and leave for 20 minutes, followed by ½ cup of white vinegar and leave for 20 minutes.
- Pour a full kettle of boiling water down the drain. It will stink at first, but the smell will dissipate.

DRESSING

(see 'Salad Dressing')

DRIED FRUIT

On carpet/upholstery

- Remove excess by lifting with a plastic comb or by blotting with paper towel.
- Mix equal parts white vinegar and blood-heat (body temperature) water.
- Scrub the mixture with a toothbrush or pantyhose in all directions – north, south, east and west.
- Absorb moisture by covering the area with paper towel. Place a book on top of the paper towel to assist with absorption.

- When almost dry, repeat.
- If a shadow returns in a couple of weeks, repeat again.

On cotton/fabric

- Remove excess by lifting with a plastic comb using cold water.
- Blot with or soak in white vinegar.
- Wash according to the fabric. Dry on the clothesline or clothes airer.

DYE

(Fabric; see also 'Hair Dye' or 'Vegetable Dye')

On carpet/upholstery (not leather)

- For coloured carpet, mix 1 part *SOS Colour Run* to 5 parts water. For white or pale cream carpet, use *Colour Run Remover: Whites*.
- Apply the mixture with a cloth. Place the cloth in one hand and a dry cloth in the other and wipe hand over hand, as though stroking a cat, until the stain is removed.
- Wipe with blood-heat (body temperature) water on a cloth.
- Absorb moisture by covering the area with paper towel. Place a book on top of the paper towel to assist with absorption.

On cotton/fabric (not delicate)

- Soak overnight in a 9-litre bucket of the hottest water the fabric can manage (check the label) and either *SOS Colour Run* or *Colour Run Remover: Whites* (as appropriate). Use twice as much as suggested on the packet.

- Wash according to the fabric. Dry on the clothesline or clothes airer.

On delicate fabric

- Rot some full cream milk in the sun until it forms solids.
- Place the solids over the stain.
- When the dye is absorbed into the solids, rinse using cold water.
- Wash according to the fabric. Dry on the clothesline or clothes airer.

TIPS

Most clothing labels give temperature instructions. As a general rule, cotton can be heated to boiling point, nylon to 40°C and silk and wool to 30°C.

To make clothes colourfast, mix 4 cups of uniodised salt in a 9-litre bucket of water, place clothes in the bucket and leave for 5 minutes. Wash according to the fabric. Salt removes excess surface dye and acts as a setting agent.

On leather

- Mix 1 part either *SOS Colour Run* or *Colour Run Remover: Whites* (as appropriate) to 20 parts water.
- Apply the mixture with a cloth. Place the cloth in one hand and a dry cloth in the other and wipe hand over hand, as though stroking a cat, until the stain is removed.
- Sprinkle with talcum powder.
- When dry, brush away.
- Wipe with leather conditioner. Make your own – see **Household formulas**.

On timber

- If coated in polyurethane, wipe with a little *Brasso* on a cloth. Rub in the direction of the grain and polish with a soft cloth. It will look worse before it looks better.
- If coated in shellac, wipe with a small amount of *SOS Colour Run* on a cotton ball and rub in the direction of the grain until the colour is removed. Wipe with furniture polish. Make your own – see **Household formulas**.

E

EARDROPS

(Non-prescription)

Some eardrops contain bleach. Remove stains immediately.

On carpet/upholstery

- Remove excess by blotting with paper towel.
- Place 1 cup of unprocessed wheat bran in a large bowl. Add drops of white vinegar one at a time, stirring as you go, until the mixture resembles breadcrumbs. It shouldn't be wet. If the eardrops contain wax, add 2 drops of tea tree oil to the mix.
- Scrub backwards and forwards with a brush.
- Vacuum.

On cotton/fabric

- Wipe with white vinegar on a cloth and wash immediately according to the fabric.
- If the eardrops contain wax, wipe with 2 drops of tea tree oil before wiping with white vinegar.
- Dry on the clothesline or clothes airer.

EGG

In frying pan/saucepan

- Place half an eggshell, a strip of foil and 1 cup of white vinegar in the saucepan.
- Leave for half an hour.
- Rinse using cold water. The egg stain will wipe off.

On brick

- For raw egg, scrub with a cake of bathroom soap and cold water on a stiff brush. Don't use dishwashing liquid or spray products.
- For cooked egg, scrub with 2 drops of glycerine on a stiff brush. Leave for 90 minutes. Scrub with a cake of bathroom soap and cold water on a stiff brush.
- In both cases, rinse with cold water.

TIP

Remove egg from bricks either early in the morning or late in the evening when the brick is cold because heat makes the proteins in egg become hard and more difficult to remove.

On carpet/upholstery

- For raw egg, wrap two combs in two separate tissues so the teeth come through the tissue. Slide the combs towards each other and lift the egg.
- Scribble with a cake of bathroom soap run under cold water.
- Wipe with a damp cloth.
- Absorb moisture by covering the area with paper towel. Place a book on top of the paper towel to assist with absorption.
- For an old stain, break it up by lifting with a plastic comb while wiping with a warm, steaming cloth. Then use the above technique.
- For cooked egg, remove excess by lifting with a plastic comb.

- Scribble with a cake of bathroom soap run under cold water.
- Wipe with a damp cloth.
- Absorb moisture by covering the area with paper towel. Place a book on top of the paper towel to assist with absorption.

EGG YOLK

(Raw)

This is higher in protein than egg white.

On carpet/upholstery

- Remove excess by blotting with paper towel.
- Massage with a couple of drops of dishwashing liquid on your fingertips until the liquid feels like jelly.
- Wipe with a damp cloth.
- Absorb moisture by covering the area with paper towel. Place a book on top of the paper towel to assist with absorption.

On cotton/fabric

- Remove excess by using cold water.
- Scribble with a cake of bathroom soap run under cold water. If needed, rub in with your fingertips.
- Soak in cold water for 30 minutes.
- Wash on a blood-heat (body temperature) setting. If there's residue, repeat.

EGGPLANT

On carpet/upholstery

- Remove excess by lifting with a plastic comb or by blotting with paper towel.
- For raw eggplant, mix 1 part *SOS Colour Run* with 5 parts water. For white or pale cream carpet, use *Colour Run Remover: Whites.*
- Apply the mixture with a cloth. Place the cloth in one hand and a dry cloth in the other and wipe hand over hand, as though stroking a cat, until the stain is removed.
- Absorb moisture by covering the area with paper towel. Place a book on top of the paper towel to assist with absorption.
- For cooked eggplant, massage with a couple of drops of dishwashing liquid on your fingertips until the liquid feels like jelly.
- Wipe with a damp cloth until the dishwashing liquid is removed.
- Absorb moisture by covering the area with paper towel. Place a book on top of the paper towel to assist with absorption.

On cotton/fabric

- Remove excess by lifting with a plastic comb or under blood-heat (body temperature) water.
- Massage with a couple of drops of dishwashing liquid on your fingertips until the liquid feels like jelly.
- Rinse under blood-heat water.
- Wash according to the fabric. Dry on the clothesline or clothes airer.

ENERGY DRINK

On carpet/upholstery

- Remove excess by blotting with paper towel.
- Mix equal parts white vinegar and blood-heat (body temperature) water.
- Scrub the mixture with a toothbrush or pantyhose in all directions – north, south, east and west.
- To remove colouring, expose to sunlight or ultraviolet light. (If using ultraviolet light, protect areas around the stain with cardboard.) Check every 2 hours.
- Absorb moisture by covering the area with paper towel. Place a book on top of the paper towel to assist with absorption.
- When almost dry, repeat.
- If a shadow returns in a couple of weeks, repeat again.
- For old stains, wipe with 2 drops of glycerine on a cotton ball and leave for a few minutes.
- Sprinkle with bicarb and scrub with a nylon brush.
- Place white vinegar on a cloth and wring tightly so it's damp but not wet. Blot over the mark.
- Absorb moisture by covering the area with paper towel. Place a book on top of the paper towel to assist with absorption.

On cotton/fabric

- Remove excess under the tap using cold water.
- Blot with or soak in white vinegar.
- Hang in sunshine until colour is removed.
- Wash according to the fabric. Dry on the clothesline or clothes airer.

On stone

- Blot with white vinegar.
- If stubborn, mix plaster of Paris and water to the consistency of peanut butter.
- To each cup of mixture, add 2 teaspoons of white vinegar.
- Spread 5 mm to 1 cm thick over the stain.
- Allow to dry completely. If it feels cold on the back of your hand, it's not dry.
- When dry, brush away.

ENGINE GREASE

On carpet/upholstery

- Wrap tissues around a plastic comb and place it under the stain. Remove excess by combing off the stain. If you can't get under the stain, remove excess by lifting with a plastic comb or by blotting with paper towel. Don't spread it.
- Massage with 2 drops of baby oil on your fingertips until the stain moves.
- Massage with a couple of drops of dishwashing liquid on your fingertips until the liquid feels like jelly.
- Wipe with a damp cloth. Repeat, if needed.
- Absorb moisture by covering the area with paper towel. Place a book on top of the paper towel to assist with absorption.

On cotton/fabric (not silk/wool)

- Remove excess by blotting with paper towel.
- Wipe with baby oil on a cotton ball in circles.
- Massage with a couple of drops of dishwashing liquid on your fingertips until the liquid feels like jelly.

- Soak in ½ lid of *Vanish NapiSan Oxi Action* and 9 litres of hot water for 20 minutes. Don't use on silk or wool.
- Wash according to the fabric. Dry on the clothesline or clothes airer.

On timber

- Wipe with baby oil on a cotton ball until the stain appears muddy.
- Put on rubber gloves and massage with a couple of drops of dishwashing liquid on your gloved fingertips until the liquid changes texture and becomes like jelly.
- Wipe with blood-heat (body temperature) water on a cloth.
- If engine grease remains, massage with dishwashing liquid again.

On silk/wool

- Wipe with baby oil on a cotton ball.
- Massage with a couple of drops of dishwashing liquid on your fingertips until the liquid feels like jelly.
- Rinse under blood-heat (body temperature) water.
- Wash in 1 teaspoon of cheap shampoo and blood-heat water.
- Rinse with 1 teaspoon of cheap hair conditioner and blood-heat water.
- Gently wring and dry flat on a towel in the shade. Ensure silk is dried away from the wind so the fibres don't tangle and leave a dusty look.

ESSENTIAL OIL

On carpet/upholstery

- Remove excess by blotting with paper towel.
- Massage with a couple of drops of dishwashing liquid on your fingertips until the liquid feels like jelly.
- Wipe with a damp cloth until the dishwashing liquid is removed.
- Absorb moisture by covering the area with paper towel. Place a book on top of the paper towel to assist with absorption.

On cotton/fabric

- Remove excess under the tap using cold water.
- Massage with a couple of drops of dishwashing liquid on your fingertips until the liquid feels like jelly.
- Rinse using cold water.
- Wash according to the fabric. Dry on the clothesline or clothes airer.

On fibreglass

- Mix 1 teaspoon of dishwashing liquid, 1 teaspoon of glycerine and 1 teaspoon of talcum powder to form a paste.
- Scrub with the mixture using pantyhose or a cloth.
- Leave for 90 minutes.
- Polish with a soft cloth. Repeat, if needed.

On timber

- If on unsealed timber, mix plaster of Paris and water to the consistency of peanut butter.

- To each cup of mixture, add 1 teaspoon of dishwashing liquid.
- Spread 5 mm to 1 cm thick over the stain.
- Allow to dry completely. If it feels cold on the back of your hand, it's not dry.
- When dry, brush away.
- If on sealed timber, wipe with a damp cloth. It won't have penetrated into the timber.

Guide to essential oils and scents

Item	Properties	Where to use	How to use
Bay leaves	Kill pantry moths	Pantries, kitchen cupboards and wardrobes	Place a dried leaf on each shelf
Bicarb	Absorbs gaseous smells, deodoriser	Anywhere there is a nasty smell	Place 2 tablespoons on a saucer near the offending odour
Cedar chips	Clean scent that prevents insects	Particularly good for moths in cupboards and wardrobes. Great for sick rooms because they make breathing easier	Place in sachets or saucers
Cinnamon, vanilla and herbal oils	Encourage appetite	Kitchen, dining room	Use in sachets or simply wipe directly onto surfaces

Item	Properties	Where to use	How to use
Fruit oils	Warm, welcoming fragrance, although apart from lemon they do encourage insects	Kitchen, dining room	1 teaspoon of fruit oil per 1-litre spray pack of water. Lightly mist as an air freshener
Lavender oil	Relieves headache, helps relaxation and smells clean. Antibacterial. Great insecticide for mozzies and flies	Bedroom, living area, bathroom, kitchen, cupboards, on your skin	1 teaspoon of lavender oil per 1-litre spray pack of water
Lily, freesia, lily of the valley and other strong floral oils	Good at temporarily masking very nasty odours and wonderful on clothes	Anywhere there is a nasty pong or wardrobes and drawers to scent your clothes	¼ teaspoon of floral oil per 1-litre spray pack of water. Lightly mist as an air freshener
Oil of cloves	Antibacterial and anti-mould. Has a festive scent	Anywhere you find mould	¼ teaspoon of oil of cloves per 1-litre spray pack of water. Lightly mist over mould and leave to dry. Mould spores will die and drop off in a couple of days

Item	Properties	Where to use	How to use
Rose oil	Creates a cosy, romantic feel	Bedroom, living area, on your skin	1 teaspoon of rose oil per 1-litre spray pack of water
Tea tree oil	Clean, fresh smell and is a great disinfectant, antibacterial and antifungal	Just about anywhere	1 teaspoon of tea tree oil per 1-litre spray pack of water

EYE SHADOW

(see 'Make-up')

F

FABRIC DRESSING

(see 'New Clothing')

FAECES

(Human)

On carpet/upholstery

- Remove excess by lifting with a plastic comb or by blotting with paper towel.
- Scribble with a cake of bathroom soap run under cold water.
- Wipe with a damp cloth.
- Massage with a couple of drops of dishwashing liquid on your fingertips until the liquid feels like jelly.
- Wipe with a damp cloth until the dishwashing liquid is removed.
- Absorb moisture by covering the area with paper towel. Place a book on top of the paper towel to assist with absorption.

On cotton/fabric

- Remove excess under the tap using cold water.
- Scribble with a cake of bathroom soap run under cold water.
- Massage with a couple of drops of dishwashing liquid on your fingertips until the liquid feels like jelly.
- Rinse using cold water.
- Alternatively, mix ½ lid of *Vanish NapiSan Oxi Action* in a 9-litre bucket of cold water and soak for 20 minutes. Don't use on wool, silk or leather.
- In both cases, wash according to the fabric. Dry in sunshine.

FAKE TAN

On carpet/upholstery

- Sprinkle with talcum power and rub with paper towel.
- Massage with equal parts lavender oil and dishwashing liquid on your fingertips until the liquid feels like jelly.
- Wipe with a cold damp cloth.
- Absorb moisture by covering the area with paper towel. Place a book on top of the paper towel to assist with absorption. Repeat, if needed.

On cotton/fabric

- Sprinkle with talcum power and rub with paper towel.
- Massage with equal parts lavender oil and dishwashing liquid on your fingertips until the liquid feels like jelly.
- Rinse using cold water.
- Wash according to the fabric. Dry on the clothesline or clothes airer.

FANTA

(see 'Soft Drink')

FAT

(see 'Cooking Oil')

FAUX FUR

To clean

- For a dry clean, place 1 cup of unprocessed wheat bran in a large bowl. Add drops of white vinegar one at a time, stirring as you go, until the mixture resembles breadcrumbs. It shouldn't be wet.

- Place in the toe of pantyhose, tie off tightly and rub over the faux fur. Brush with a hairbrush to fluff it up.
- For a wet clean, add 1 teaspoon of cheap shampoo to a 9-litre bucket of blood-heat (body temperature) water.
- Soak for 20 minutes.
- Rinse on the spin cycle of the washing machine.
- Dry flat in the shade. Never put faux fur in a dryer.
- Brush with a hairbrush to fluff it up.

FELT TIP PEN

(see 'Pen')

FIG

On carpet/upholstery

- Remove excess by lifting with a plastic comb or by blotting with paper towel.
- Blot with white vinegar on a cloth.
- If stubborn, wipe with 2 drops of glycerine on a cloth, then wipe with white vinegar on a cloth.
- In all cases, absorb moisture by covering the area with paper towel. Place a book on top of the paper towel to assist with absorption.

On cotton/fabric

- Remove excess by lifting with a plastic comb.
- Apply 2 drops of glycerine to the stain.
- Leave for 90 minutes.
- Wash according to the fabric. Dry in sunshine.

FISH

(see 'Seafood')

FISH SAUCE

This is high in protein and oil.

On carpet/upholstery

- Remove excess by blotting with paper towel.
- To remove protein, scrub with a cake of bathroom soap and cold water on a toothbrush.
- To remove oil, massage with a couple of drops of dishwashing liquid on your fingertips until the liquid feels like jelly.
- In all cases, wipe with a damp cloth.
- Absorb moisture by covering the area with paper towel. Place a book on top of the paper towel to assist with absorption.

On cotton/fabric

- Remove excess under the tap using cold water.
- Massage with a couple of drops of dishwashing liquid on your fingertips until the liquid feels like jelly.
- Rinse using cold water.
- Wash according to the fabric. Dry on the clothesline or clothes airer.

FLEAS

To deter

- Mix 4 teaspoons of dried mint or 8 teaspoons of freshly chopped mint with 1 litre of boiling water in a spray pack. Let the mixture sit for 15 minutes.
- Lightly spray over the affected area.
- For carpet and upholstery, vacuum.

FLOORS

To clean carpet

- Mix 2 tablespoons of bicarb, 2 tablespoons of white vinegar, 2 tablespoons of methylated spirits, 2 teaspoons of glycerine, 2 teaspoons of eucalyptus oil and 1 litre of water in a spray pack.
- Lightly spray the mixture over the carpet.
- Leave for 20 minutes, then vacuum.
- Alternatively, sprinkle a little bicarb on the carpet, then vacuum.
- Stains should be spot cleaned. Consult the appropriate stain and solution.

To clean concrete (polished)

- Sprinkle with a little bicarb. Spray with white vinegar in a spray pack.
- While fizzing, scrub with a broom.
- Wipe with an old T-shirt wrapped around a broom. Allow to dry.
- Apply carnauba wax with a polishing machine (available from hire companies or vacuum cleaner shops). Don't use beeswax because it's too soft.

To clean cork/timber

- For instructions on how to work out the timber sealant, see page 416.
- For cork and timber sealed in polyurethane, clean with 1 cup of white vinegar in a 9-litre bucket of blood-heat (body temperature) water. Add 2 drops of lavender oil for a fresh scent.
- For cork and timber floors sealed in tung oil, varnish or wax, clean with 1 cup of cold black tea in a 9-litre bucket

of blood-heat water. Tea raises the tannin levels in cork and timber, helping retain their colour and quality.

- For unsealed timber, mix strong black tea (4–5 tea bags in 4 cups of boiling water) with 1 drop of oil of cloves in a 9-litre bucket of hot water. Wipe with a broom or cloth.

TIPS

To repair a dent in timber, place a wet, hot tea bag over the indentation and leave until the timber has expanded. If the floorboards are squeaking from rubbing together, sprinkle talcum powder over the timber and jump up and down or stomp on them to make sure the talcum powder gets into the cracks in the boards. It's a great task for the kids. Reapply as needed.

To clean limestone/marble

- This flooring is porous and alkaline-based so don't use white vinegar. Instead, clean with pH neutral soap.
- Grate 1 teaspoon of bathroom soap into a 9-litre bucket of blood-heat (body temperature) water and stir well.
- Wipe the mixture over the surface with a cloth or old T-shirt wrapped around a broom.
- Allow to dry.
- To seal, coat with a thin layer of good-quality liquid marble flooring wax or wipe with skim milk.

To clean tiles

- Sprinkle with a little bicarb. Spray with a little white vinegar.
- While fizzing, sweep with a broom.
- To finish, wipe with a damp cloth.
- To clean grout, scrub with a plastic (not metal) scourer.

TIP

Remove tile marks with a pencil eraser.

FLUORESCENT PEN

On carpet/upholstery (not leather)

- Slightly dampen the stain with water and sprinkle with uniodised salt.
- Put ice cubes in a zip-lock bag and place on top until the ice melts.
- Remove and blot the stain with a damp cloth.
- Scribble with a cake of bathroom soap and wipe with a damp cloth.
- Absorb moisture by covering the area with paper towel. Place a book on top of the paper towel to assist with absorption.

On cotton/fabric

- Add 1 kg of uniodised salt to a 9-litre bucket of water.
- Dip the garment in the salt solution.
- Remove and put inside a plastic bag.
- Place the bag in the freezer and leave overnight.
- Remove from the plastic bag.
- Wash according to the fabric. Dry on the clothesline or clothes airer.

On leather

- Rub with white spirits on a cotton bud. Wipe in even, parallel strokes over the entire panel of leather.
- Sprinkle with talcum powder.

- When dry, brush the talcum powder off with your hand. Repeat if necessary.
- Wipe with leather conditioner. Make your own – see **Household formulas**.

FLY SPRAY

On cotton/fabric

- Mix dishwashing liquid and blood-heat (body temperature) water to generate suds.
- Scrub with only the suds on a toothbrush.
- Rinse in blood-heat water.
- Wash according to the fabric. Dry on the clothesline or clothes airer.

On wallpaper

- Gently rub with 2 drops of tea tree oil on a slice of brown bread.

On walls

- If it's an oil-based spray, scrub with 2 drops of dishwashing liquid on pantyhose.
- Wipe with a damp cloth.
- For orange stains, expose to ultraviolet light until the colour fades.

FLYSCREEN

To clean

- Protect wooden doors by hanging an old sheet over them. This will prevent the timber from being splattered as you clean.

- Close the window or door.
- Dampen the screen with water on a cloth. Clean from the outside to the inside.
- Wipe with black tea on a cloth. Clean the safety grilles as well.
- Cover a soft broom head with pantyhose and sweep over the screen.

FOOD COLOURING

On carpet/upholstery

- Remove excess by blotting with paper towel.
- Place white vinegar on a cloth and wring tightly so it's damp but not wet. Blot over the mark.
- To remove dye, expose to sunlight or ultraviolet light. (If using ultraviolet light, protect areas around the stain with cardboard.) Check every 2 hours.
- Absorb moisture by covering the area with paper towel. Place a book on top of the paper towel to assist with absorption.

On cotton/fabric

- Remove excess under the tap using blood-heat (body temperature) water.
- Blot with or soak in white vinegar.
- Wash according to the fabric. Dry in sunshine.

FRENCH FRIES

(see 'Potato Chips')

FRUIT FLY

To eradicate

- Use a small glass jar with a lid (a metal lid works best but plastic lids are fine). Make sure the glass is clean.
- Punch holes in the lid every 2 mm using scissors.
- Half-fill the jar with 1 tablespoon of *Vegemite* and ½ cup of vinegar (any variety).
- The fruit fly will be attracted to the mixture and fly into the jar.

FRUIT JUICE

NOTE: Apple, grape, lime, orange and pineapple juice need to be treated differently – see the relevant entry.

On carpet/upholstery

- Remove excess by blotting with paper towel.
- Place white vinegar on a cloth and wring tightly so it's damp but not wet. Blot over the mark.
- Absorb moisture by covering the area with paper towel. Place a book on top of the paper towel to assist with absorption.

On cotton/fabric

- Remove excess under the tap using cold water.
- Blot with or soak in white vinegar. Alternatively, soak with ½ lid of *Vanish NapiSan Oxi Action* in a 9-litre bucket of water for 30 minutes. Don't use on wool, silk or leather.
- Wash according to the fabric. Dry on the clothesline or clothes airer.

On stone

- Remove excess by blotting with paper towel.
- Scrub with dishwashing liquid on a toothbrush.
- Wipe with a damp cloth.
- If stubborn, mix plaster of Paris and water to the consistency of peanut butter.
- To each cup of mixture, add 1 teaspoon of dishwashing liquid.
- Spread 5 mm to 1 cm thick over the stain.
- Allow to dry completely. If it feels cold on the back of your hand, it's not dry.
- When dry, brush away.

FUR

To clean

- Place the item in a large pillowcase and add 1 kg of unprocessed wheat bran.
- Secure the top of the pillowcase and shake vigorously for about 3 minutes.
- Open the pillowcase and lightly shake the item as you remove it, so the bran remains in the pillowcase.

FURNITURE BEETLE

To eradicate

- Mix 4 teaspoons of dried mint or 8 teaspoons of freshly chopped mint with 1 litre of boiling water in a spray pack. Let it sit for 15 minutes.
- Spray over the area and leave for 24 hours.

G

GARLIC

On carpet/upholstery

- Remove excess by lifting with a plastic comb or by blotting with paper towel.
- Wipe with 2 drops of glycerine on a cloth.
- Leave for 90 minutes.
- Wipe with a damp cloth.
- Absorb moisture by covering the area with paper towel. Place a book on top of the paper towel to assist with absorption.

On cotton/fabric

- Remove excess under the tap using cold water.
- Wipe with 2 drops of glycerine.
- Leave for 90 minutes.
- Wash according to the fabric. Dry on the clothesline or clothes airer.

GARLIC ODOUR

On china/glass/plastic

- Mix 1 tablespoon of uniodised salt and 1 teaspoon of finely chopped parsley.
- Wipe the mixture over the item using a dry cloth.
- Rinse in water.

TIP

Remove the smell of garlic from your hands by rubbing with bicarb or parsley stems.

GASOLINE

(see 'Diesel Oil' or 'Petrol')

GATORADE

(see 'Energy Drink')

GELATINE

On carpet/upholstery

- If dry, vacuum. If wet, chill with ice cubes in a zip-lock bag.
- Remove excess by lifting with a plastic comb or by blotting with paper towel.
- Scribble with a cake of bathroom soap run under cold water.
- Scrub with a toothbrush or pantyhose in all directions – north, south, east and west.
- Absorb moisture by covering the area with paper towel. Place a book on top of the paper towel to assist with absorption.

On cotton/fabric

- If dry, shake off. If wet, chill with ice cubes.
- Scribble with a cake of bathroom soap under cold water. Rub the fabric against itself using your hands.
- Wash according to the fabric. Dry on the clothesline or clothes airer.

GINGER ALE

(see 'Soft Drink')

GLASS

For glass cancer

- Glass cancer is the haze on glass that looks like soap scum or water marks. It's caused by chemical residue and the damage is permanent. Don't use harsh abrasives on glass (including commercial glass cleaners).
- To clean glass and alleviate cancer, wipe with white vinegar on a cloth. Then wipe firmly with 1 teaspoon of sweet almond oil on a cloth.

For glues/grime/resins

- On glass, run a razor blade at a low angle over the glass.

For lime scale

- Wipe with white vinegar on rolled up pantyhose.

For scorch marks

- Sprinkle with bicarb to the same thickness as icing sugar on a cake.
- Spray the bicarb with white vinegar.
- While it's fizzing, scrub with a nylon brush.
- Rinse with a damp cloth. Repeat, if needed.

For scratches

- To remove light scratches, wipe with sweet almond oil on a cloth.
- To remove heavy scratches, wipe with a paste of glycerine and whiting. Alternatively, use jewellers rouge. Apply with a rotary tool or electric buff.

To clean windows

- Mix equal parts methylated spirits and water in a spray pack or use undiluted white vinegar in a spray pack.
- Spray the solution over the glass.
- Wipe with paper towel or a squeegee. Wipe with vertical stripes on the outside of the window and horizontal stripes on the inside. That way you can tell which side a smudge is on. Use vertical stripes on the outside because it's the direction the rain falls.

TIPS

Don't use newspaper to clean windows. It used to be good when the ink contained lamp black, but today's newspapers use rubber-based ink, which smears. Use paper towel instead.

If you break glass on the floor, ensure you've collected all the shards by lying a lit torch on the floor so the beam runs across it. Any remaining shards will sparkle in the light. Wear shoes when clearing glass. Pick up small shards by pressing over the area with a slice of brown bread.

GLITTER

On carpet/upholstery

- Vacuum as much glitter as possible.
- Cut a cake of bathroom soap in half lengthways and round the edges. Dampen it in water and use like a rolling pin across the glitter. The glitter will stick to the soap. Clear the glitter from the soap under water as you go.

- Alternatively, vacuum excess, then put on rubber gloves and wash your gloved hands with a cake of bathroom soap and water. Shake your hands dry. When dry, wipe over the glitter. It will stick to the rubber.
- In both cases, absorb moisture by covering the area with paper towel. Place a book on top of the paper towel to assist with absorption.
- For glitter acrylic paint, wring a cloth in methylated spirits, place over the stain, cover area with plastic wrap and leave for 4 hours. Remove and wipe stain with a damp cloth.

On cotton/fabric

- Place the item on a clean towel and lightly spray over the glitter with hairspray.
- Leave until the hairspray goes hard.
- Cut a cake of bathroom soap in half lengthways and round the edges to create a soap sausage. Dampen it in water and use like a rolling pin across the glitter. The glitter will stick to the soap. Clear the glitter from the soap under water as you go.
- Wash according to the fabric. Dry on the clothesline or clothes airer.
- For glitter acrylic paint, soak in methylated spirits for 4 hours. Then wash according to the fabric. Dry on the clothesline or clothes airer.

GLUCOSE SYRUP

On carpet/upholstery

- Remove excess by blotting with paper towel.
- Scribble with a cake of bathroom soap run under blood-heat (body temperature) water.

- Scrub with a toothbrush or pantyhose in all directions – north, south, east and west.
- Blot with equal parts white vinegar and water on a cloth.
- Absorb moisture by covering the area with paper towel. Place a book on top of the paper towel to assist with absorption.
- When almost dry, repeat.
- If a shadow returns in a couple of weeks, repeat again.

On cotton/fabric

- Remove excess under the tap using cold water.
- Scribble with a cake of bathroom soap run under blood-heat (body temperature) water. Rub the fabric against itself using your hands.
- Rinse in equal parts white vinegar and water.
- Wash according to the fabric. Dry on the clothesline or clothes airer.

On stone

- Wipe with a cake of bathroom soap and blood-heat (body temperature) water on a cloth.
- Mix plaster of Paris and water to the consistency of peanut butter.
- To each cup of mixture, add 1 teaspoon of dishwashing liquid.
- Spread 5 mm to 1 cm thick over the stain.
- Allow to dry completely. If it feels cold on the back of your hand, it's not dry.
- When dry, brush away.

GLUE

Different glues have different solvents.

- **Superglue** – remove with superglue remover or acetone.
- **Craft and PVA glues** (which go on white and dry clear) – use steam.
- **Two-part epoxy glues** (e.g. *Araldite*) – remove with acetone.
- **Gums and paper glues** – wipe with a damp cloth.
- **Children's craft glue** – use blood-heat (body temperature) water and a cake of bathroom soap and scribble over the stain.
- **Contact adhesives** – remove with tea tree oil.

On carpet

- Wrap a fine-toothed metal comb in a tissue so the teeth come through the tissue. Don't use a plastic comb.
- Place the comb at an angle to the carpet and wedge it underneath the glue.
- Dip a cotton ball in the appropriate solvent and rub over the top of the stain with the comb underneath. Use extra cotton balls, if needed. Replace the tissue if it gets wet.
- For an epoxy glue stain, warm with a hair dryer after wedging the comb underneath.
- Wring a cloth in boiling water and place it over the glue until the cloth cools.
- Pinch and pull the cloth to remove as much of the adhesive as possible.
- Repeat a few times before using the solvent.
- To remove the smell of acetone, wipe with equal parts methylated spirits and water on a cloth.

On glass/windscreen

- Work the appropriate solvent into the glue and leave for 24 hours.
- Carefully remove with a plastic knife.
- If it doesn't come away, aim a heat gun at the glue. Only use the heat gun in short bursts or you could crack the glass.

On quartz/stone benchtops

- Remove glues or resins with a single-sided razor blade held at a low angle.
- Wipe with appropriate solvent (see previous page) on a cloth.
- If stubborn, wring a cloth in solvent and place it over the glue for 5 minutes.
- Remove the cloth then remove the glue with a razor blade held at a low angle.

On timber

- Dampen pantyhose with water and heat in the microwave for 10 seconds – no longer or the pantyhose will melt.
- Rub over the glue in the direction of the grain using speed, not pressure.
- Dry thoroughly with a cloth.

On tulle

- Boil the kettle to generate steam.
- Hold the affected area over the steam for 1 minute.
- Rub over the glue with pantyhose. The glue will be pulled off.

On walls

- Place a drop of tea tree oil on the glue patch and cover with plastic wrap.
- Leave for 20 minutes.
- Remove the plastic wrap and slide a plastic knife under the glue.
- If it doesn't come away, replace the plastic wrap and leave for another 20 minutes before trying again.

GOLDEN SYRUP

(see 'Maple Syrup')

GRAFFITI

On hard and soft surfaces

- For *Texta*, oil-based paint or spray paint, wipe with white spirits on pantyhose or a cloth.
- For water-based children's paint, wipe a damp cloth with a cake of bathroom soap and rub over the stained area. Wipe with a damp cloth.
- For vinyl-based paint, mix plaster of Paris and water to the consistency of peanut butter. To every cup of mixture, add 1 teaspoon of methylated spirits. Spread 5 mm to 1 cm thick over the stain. Allow to dry completely then brush away.
- For ink-based paint, rot full cream milk in the sun and place the solids over the stain. The ink will be absorbed into the solids. Remove and wipe stain clean with a damp cloth.

GRAPE JUICE

On carpet/upholstery

- Remove excess by blotting with paper towel.
- For an old stain, wipe with 2 drops of glycerine on a cloth. Leave for 90 minutes. Then follow the instructions below.
- For a fresh stain, sprinkle with bicarb. Leave for 5 minutes, then vacuum.
- Place white vinegar on a cloth and wring tightly so it's damp but not wet. Blot over the mark.
- Absorb moisture by covering the area with paper towel. Place a book on top of the paper towel to assist with absorption.

On cotton/fabric

- Rinse under the tap using cold water.
- For an old stain, wipe with glycerine and leave for 90 minutes.
- For a fresh stain, blot with or soak in white vinegar.
- In both cases, wash according to the fabric. Dry in sunshine.

GRAPHITE POWDER

On carpet/upholstery

- Vacuum as much as possible.
- Cut a cake of bathroom soap in half lengthways and round the edges. Dampen it in water and use like a rolling pin across the powder. The powder will stick to the soap. Clear the powder from the soap under water as you go.

- Absorb moisture by covering the area with paper towel. Place a book on top of the paper towel to assist with absorption.

On cotton/fabric

- Place the item on a clean towel and lightly spray with hairspray.
- Leave until the hairspray goes hard. It will come off in the wash.
- Alternatively, cut a cake of bathroom soap in half lengthways and round the edges. Dampen it in water and use like a rolling pin across the powder. The powder will stick to the soap. Clear the powder from the soap with water as you go.
- In both cases, wash according to the fabric. Dry on the clothesline or clothes airer.

GRASS

On carpet/upholstery

- Remove excess by vacuuming.
- Wipe with white spirits on a cloth.
- Sprinkle with talcum powder.
- When dry, vacuum.
- Place white vinegar on a cloth and wring tightly so it's damp but not wet. Blot over the mark.
- Absorb moisture by covering the area with paper towel. Place a book on top of the paper towel to assist with absorption.

On cotton/fabric

- Remove excess under the tap using cold water.
- Blot with or soak in white spirits.
- Wash according to the fabric. Dry on the clothesline or clothes airer.

On stone

- Wipe with white spirits on a cloth.
- Mix plaster of Paris and water to the consistency of peanut butter.
- To each cup of mixture, add 1 teaspoon of white spirits.
- Spread 5 mm to 1 cm thick over the stain.
- Allow to dry completely. If it feels cold on the back of your hand, it's not dry.
- When dry, brush away.

GRAVY

On carpet/upholstery

- Remove excess by lifting with a plastic comb or by blotting with paper towel.
- Scribble with a cake of bathroom soap run under cold water.
- Scrub with a toothbrush in all directions.
- Wipe with a damp cloth.
- Massage with a couple of drops of dishwashing liquid on your fingertips until the liquid feels like jelly.
- Wipe with a damp cloth until the dishwashing liquid is removed.
- Absorb moisture by covering the area with paper towel. Place a book on top of the paper towel to assist with absorption.

On cotton/fabric

- Remove excess under the tap using cold water.
- Scribble with a cake of bathroom soap run under cold water.
- Massage with a couple of drops of dishwashing liquid on your fingertips until the liquid feels like jelly.
- Rinse with blood-heat (body temperature) water.
- Wash according to the fabric. Dry on the clothesline or clothes airer.

On marble

- Remove excess by lifting with a plastic comb or by blotting with paper towel.
- If the stain has penetrated, mix plaster of Paris and water to the consistency of peanut butter.
- To each cup of mixture, mix in 1 tablespoon of dishwashing liquid.
- Spread 5 mm to 1 cm thick over the stain.
- Allow to dry completely. If it feels cold on the back of your hand, it's not dry.
- When dry, wipe off with a cold damp cloth.

GREASE

(see 'Engine Grease' or 'Cooking Oil')

GREEN TEA

On carpet/upholstery

- Remove excess by blotting with paper towel.
- For a fresh stain, place white vinegar on a cloth and wring tightly so it's damp but not wet. Blot over the mark.
- For an old stain, wipe with glycerine and leave for 90 minutes, then follow instructions for a fresh stain.

- In both cases, absorb moisture by covering the area with paper towel. Place a book on top of the paper towel to assist with absorption.

On cotton/fabric

- Remove excess under the tap using cold water.
- For a fresh stain, blot with or soak in white vinegar.
- For an old stain, wipe with glycerine and leave for 90 minutes, then follow instructions for a fresh stain.
- In both cases, wash according to the fabric. Dry on the clothesline or clothes airer.

GROUT

For mould

- Mix ¼ teaspoon of oil of cloves and 1 litre of water in a spray pack.
- Lightly spray the solution and leave for 24 hours.
- Wipe with a damp cloth.
- If mould sits on the surface, wipe with white vinegar on a cloth after treating with the oil of cloves solution.

To clean

- Scrub with bicarb and white vinegar on a toothbrush or plastic scourer.

TIP

Remove old grout with a grout rake. Run the rake backwards and forwards along the grout until the grout becomes powdery. Clean the area thoroughly and apply new grout. Wipe off excess grout before it dries.

GUACAMOLE

On carpet/upholstery

- Remove excess by lifting with a plastic comb or by blotting with paper towel.
- Massage with a couple of drops of dishwashing liquid on your fingertips until the liquid feels like jelly.
- Wipe with a damp cloth until the dishwashing liquid is removed.
- Absorb moisture by covering the area with paper towel. Place a book on top of the paper towel to assist with absorption.

On cotton/fabric

- Remove excess under the tap using cold water.
- Massage with a couple of drops of dishwashing liquid on your fingertips until the liquid feels like jelly.
- Rinse under blood-heat (body temperature) water.
- Wash according to the fabric. Dry on the clothesline or clothes airer.

On granite/marble

- Remove excess by lifting with a plastic comb or by blotting with paper towel.
- Mix plaster of Paris and water to the consistency of peanut butter.
- To each cup of mixture, add 1 teaspoon of dishwashing liquid.
- Spread 5 mm to 1 cm thick over the stain.
- Allow to dry completely. If it feels cold on the back of your hand, it's not dry.
- When dry, remove with a scrubbing brush. Repeat, if needed.

H

HAIR DYE

On carpet/upholstery

- Apply a small quantity of the same brand and colour of hair dye.
- Rub with your fingertips in circles until the stain moves.
- Add 2 drops of anti-dandruff shampoo and continue to rub.
- Wipe with a damp cloth. Repeat with anti-dandruff shampoo until removed.
- For hair chalk, blot with white vinegar on a tightly wrung cloth.
- In all cases, absorb moisture by covering the area with paper towel. Place a book on top of the paper towel to assist with absorption.

On cotton/fabric

- Apply a small quantity of the same brand and colour of hair dye.
- Rub with your fingertips in circles until the stain moves.
- Add 2 drops of anti-dandruff shampoo and continue to rub.
- Rinse using cold water.
- Wash according to the fabric. Dry on the clothesline or clothes airer.
- For hair chalk, blot with or soak in white vinegar.

On timber

- Use the same brand and colour of hair dye.
- Place the hair dye on a cloth and rub over the mark in circles until the stain loosens.

- Follow immediately with anti-dandruff shampoo on a cloth until the stain lifts.
- Wring a cloth in blood-heat (body temperature) water and wipe over the surface.

HAIR GEL

On carpet/upholstery

- Remove excess by lifting with a plastic comb or by blotting with paper towel.
- Massage with a couple of drops of dishwashing liquid on your fingertips until the liquid feels like jelly.
- Wipe with a warm, damp cloth.
- If the gel contains wax, mix ½ teaspoon of tea tree oil with ½ teaspoon of dishwashing liquid and rub over the hair gel with your fingertips.
- Wipe with a warm, damp cloth until the dishwashing liquid is removed.
- In all cases, absorb moisture by covering the area with paper towel. Place a book on top of the paper towel to assist with absorption.

On cotton/fabric

- Remove excess under the tap using blood-heat (body temperature) water.
- Massage with a couple of drops of dishwashing liquid on your fingertips until the liquid feels like jelly.
- Rinse under blood-heat water.
- Wash according to the fabric. Dry on the clothesline or clothes airer.

HAIRSPRAY

On carpet/upholstery

- Spray with hairspray – it contains its own solvent.
- Wipe with a damp cloth.
- Absorb moisture by covering the area with paper towel. Place a book on top of the paper towel to assist with absorption.

On cotton/fabric (not wool)

- Spray with hairspray – it contains its own solvent.
- Rinse using cold water.
- Wash according to the fabric. Dry on the clothesline or clothes airer.

On timber

- Spray with hairspray – it contains its own solvent. Wipe with pantyhose or a cloth.
- Alternatively, spray rolled up pantyhose with hairspray and wipe over the timber.
- Alternatively, wipe with 2 drops of cheap shampoo on a cloth.
- In all cases, rinse with a damp cloth.

On wool

- Spray with hairspray – it contains its own solvent.
- Wash in 1 teaspoon of cheap shampoo and blood-heat (body temperature) water.
- Rinse in 1 teaspoon of cheap hair conditioner and blood-heat water.
- Gently wring and dry flat on a towel in the shade.

TIP

To protect your clothes against spills, after washing them and while they're still wet, lightly spray with hairspray. If you spill food, it will wipe off with paper towel.

HAMBURGER

This contains protein, fat and sauces.

On carpet/upholstery

- Remove excess by lifting with a plastic comb or by blotting with paper towel.
- Scribble with a cake of bathroom soap run under cold water.
- Wipe with a damp cloth.
- Massage with a couple of drops of dishwashing liquid on your fingertips until the liquid feels like jelly.
- Wipe with a damp cloth until the dishwashing liquid is removed.
- If needed, consult 'Mustard' and 'Tomato Sauce' entries.
- Absorb moisture by covering the area with paper towel. Place a book on top of the paper towel to assist with absorption.

On cotton/fabric (not wool)

- Remove excess under the tap using cold water.
- Scribble with a cake of bathroom soap.
- Rinse using cold water.
- Massage with a couple of drops of dishwashing liquid on your fingertips until the liquid feels like jelly.
- Rinse under blood-heat (body temperature) water.

- If needed, consult 'Mustard' and 'Tomato Sauce' entries.
- Wash according to the fabric. Dry on the clothesline or clothes airer.

On granite/marble

- Remove excess by lifting with a plastic comb or by blotting with paper towel.
- If the stain has penetrated, mix plaster of Paris and water to the consistency of peanut butter.
- To each cup of mixture, mix in 1 teaspoon of dishwashing liquid.
- Spread 5 mm to 1 cm thick over the stain.
- Allow to dry completely. If it feels cold on the back of your hand, it's not dry.
- When dry, brush away.

On wool

- Massage with a little cheap shampoo on your fingertips.
- Rinse in blood-heat (body temperature) water.
- Rinse in 1 teaspoon of cheap hair conditioner and blood-heat water.
- Gently wring and dry flat on a towel in the shade.

HANDBAG

To clean exterior

- For leather, use saddle soap.
- For suede, place 1 cup of unprocessed wheat bran in a large bowl. Add drops of white vinegar one at a time, stirring as you go, until the mixture resembles breadcrumbs. It shouldn't be wet. Scrub over the suede with a brush.

- For fabric, scribble with a cake of bathroom soap and rub with a just-damp pair of pantyhose in a tight ball. Remove excess soap by rubbing with clean damp pantyhose. Dry in the shade so it doesn't warp (many fabric bags have cardboard linings).
- For vinyl, make a paste of glycerine and talcum powder. Rub the mixture over the vinyl with rolled up pantyhose and leave for 5 minutes. Wipe off.
- For rattan, mix 2 tablespoons of uniodised salt in 1 cup of water. Allow to dissolve. Wipe the salt solution across the surface with rolled up pantyhose. Leave in the shade to dry. When dry, brush off the salt.

To clean interior

- Some bag linings can be removed. Others are attached but can be pulled outside the bag. If the lining doesn't come out, vacuum using the brush attachment.
- If the lining is cotton, clean with dishwashing liquid and water on a scrubbing brush. Rinse with a damp cloth.
- If there are lipstick, make-up or ballpoint pen marks, wipe with white spirits on a cotton ball.
- To dry, put the exterior of the bag in the shade and the lining in the sun. If you can't do this, dry the whole bag in the shade. The lining must be completely dry before you place it back inside the bag.

TIPS

Remove grease stains from handbags with cornstarch. When storing suitcases, keep a tea bag or cake of bathroom soap inside to keep bugs and damp at bay. To prevent dye and ink transferring to clothing, spray the exterior of the handbag with hairspray.

HAT

Felt

For lint

- Apply sticky tape and pull off. The lint will come away.

For sweat marks

- For heavy staining on light-coloured hats, mix Fuller's earth and water to the consistency of soft butter.
- Paint the mixture over the sweat marks with a paintbrush.
- Leave to dry completely. Brush off.
- For heavy staining on dark-coloured hats, mix potter's plaster and water to the consistency of soft butter.
- Place the mixture over the sweat stain with a paintbrush.
- Leave to dry completely.
- Brush off.

To clean

- Mix dishwashing liquid and blood-heat (body temperature) water to generate a sudsy mix.
- Scrub with only the suds on a toothbrush.
- Wipe with a damp cloth.
- Dry in the shade.

Straw

For sweat marks

- Mix 2 tablespoons of cornflour with drops of water until lumpy.
- Apply to the sweat marks and leave to dry.
- When dry, brush off.

To clean

- Mix 2 tablespoons of uniodised salt in 1 cup of water. Allow to dissolve.
- Wipe hat with the salt solution using rolled up pantyhose.
- Allow to dry in the shade.
- When dry, brush off the salt.

HEAT MARK

(White)

For instructions on how to work out the timber sealant, see page 416.

On timber sealed with polyurethane

- Rub with a small amount of *Brasso* on a cloth in the direction of the grain. It will look worse before it looks better.

On timber sealed with varnish, shellac or wax

- Warm beeswax in the microwave in 10-second bursts.
- Peel a piece of lemon using a peeler. Don't get any lemon juice on the peel.
- Apply the warm beeswax to the yellow side of the lemon peel.
- Rub peel over the mark in the direction of the grain using speed, not pressure.

HEATER OIL

On carpet/upholstery

- Remove excess by blotting with paper towel.
- Massage with dishwashing liquid (2 drops per 15-cm circle) on your fingertips until the liquid feels like jelly.

- Wipe with a damp cloth until the dishwashing liquid is removed.
- Absorb moisture by covering the area with paper towel. Place a book on top of the paper towel to assist with absorption.

On cotton/fabric

- Remove under the tap using blood-heat (body temperature) water.
- Massage with a couple of drops of dishwashing liquid on your fingertips until the liquid feels like jelly.
- Rinse under blood-heat water.
- Wash according to the fabric. Dry on the clothesline or clothes airer.

HERBAL TEA

(see 'Green Tea' or 'Tea')

HIGHCHAIR

To clean

- Wipe with 2 drops of tea tree oil and blood-heat (body temperature) water on a cloth.
- For hardened food, wring a cloth or sponge in hot water and place over the food for 10 minutes. This will soften the food. Then wipe with 2 drops of tea tree oil and blood-heat water on a cloth.

TIP

If your child makes a huge mess when eating, place a flattened garbage bag underneath the highchair to catch rejected food. If your child throws food, suspend a doona cover to create a tent over the highchair.

HIGHLIGHTER PEN

(see 'Fluorescent Pen')

HOISIN SAUCE

On carpet/upholstery

- Remove excess by lifting with a plastic comb or by blotting with paper towel.
- Place white vinegar on a cloth and wring tightly so it's damp but not wet. Blot over the mark.
- Place the vinegar cloth in one hand and a dry cloth in the other and wipe hand over hand, as though stroking a cat, until the stain is removed.
- Absorb moisture by covering the area with paper towel. Place a book on top of the paper towel to assist with absorption.

On cotton/fabric (not wool)

- Remove excess under the tap using cold water.
- Blot with or soak in white vinegar.
- Rinse using cold water.
- Wash according to the fabric. Dry on the clothesline or clothes airer.

On wool

- Blot with or soak in white vinegar.
- Massage with a little cheap shampoo on your fingertips.
- Rinse in 1 teaspoon of cheap hair conditioner and blood-heat (body temperature) water.
- Gently wring and dry flat on a towel in the shade.

HOLLANDAISE SAUCE

On carpet/upholstery

- Remove excess by lifting with a plastic comb or by blotting with paper towel.
- Massage with a couple of drops of dishwashing liquid on your fingertips until the liquid feels like jelly.
- Wipe with a damp cloth until the dishwashing liquid is removed.
- Absorb moisture by covering the area with paper towel. Place a book on top of the paper towel to assist with absorption.

On cotton/fabric (not wool)

- Remove excess under the tap using cold water.
- Massage with a couple of drops of dishwashing liquid on your fingertips until the liquid feels like jelly.
- Rinse using cold water.
- Wash according to the fabric. Dry on the clothesline or clothes airer.

On wool

- Massage with a little cheap shampoo on your fingertips.
- Rinse in blood-heat (body temperature) water.
- Rinse in 1 teaspoon of cheap hair conditioner and blood-heat water.
- Gently wring and dry flat on a towel in the shade.

HONEY

On carpet/upholstery

- Remove excess by lifting with a plastic comb or by blotting with paper towel.
- Scribble with a cake of bathroom soap run under blood-heat (body temperature) water.
- Scrub with a toothbrush or pantyhose in all directions – north, south, east and west.
- Blot with equal parts white vinegar and water on a cloth.
- Absorb moisture by covering the area with paper towel. Place a book on top of the paper towel to assist with absorption.
- When almost dry, repeat.
- If a shadow returns in a couple of weeks, repeat again.

On cotton/fabric (not wool)

- Remove excess under the tap using cold water.
- Scribble with a cake of bathroom soap run under blood-heat (body temperature) water. Rub the fabric against itself using your hands.
- Rinse in equal parts white vinegar and water.
- Wash according to the fabric. Dry on the clothesline or clothes airer.

On stone

- Wipe with a cake of bathroom soap and blood-heat (body temperature) water on a cloth.
- Mix plaster of Paris and water to the consistency of peanut butter.
- To each cup of mixture, add 1 teaspoon of dishwashing liquid.

- Spread 5 mm to 1 cm thick over the stain.
- Allow to dry completely. If it feels cold on the back of your hand, it's not dry.
- When dry, brush away.

On wool

- Scribble with a cake of bathroom soap run under blood-heat (body temperature) water.
- Massage with a little cheap shampoo on your fingertips.
- Rinse in equal parts white vinegar and blood-heat water.
- Rinse in 1 teaspoon of cheap hair conditioner and blood-heat water.
- Gently wring and dry flat on a towel in the shade.

HOT CHOCOLATE

On carpet/upholstery

- Remove excess by blotting with paper towel.
- Scribble with a cake of bathroom soap run under cold water.
- Wipe with a damp cloth.
- Place white vinegar on a cloth and wring tightly so it's damp but not wet. Blot over the mark.
- Absorb moisture by covering the area with paper towel. Place a book on top of the paper towel to assist with absorption.

On cotton/fabric (not wool)

- Remove excess under the tap using cold water.
- Scrub with a cake of bathroom soap and cold water. Rub the fabric against itself using your hands.

- Blot with or soak in white vinegar.
- Wash according to the fabric. Dry on the clothesline or clothes airer.

On wool

- Massage with a little cheap shampoo on your fingertips.
- Rinse in blood-heat (body temperature) water.
- Rinse in 1 teaspoon of cheap hair conditioner and blood-heat water.
- Gently wring and dry flat on a towel in the shade.

HOTPLATE

(Cast iron)

For rust

- Cut a lemon in half and sprinkle one of the cut ends with uniodised salt.
- Scrub over the rust with the cut end until the rust disappears.
- Wipe with cooking oil on paper towel to season and prevent further rust.

TIP

If you use the hotplate regularly, it won't go rusty.

To clean

- Sprinkle with a little bicarb, splash with white vinegar and scrub with a nylon brush.
- When still warm, pour a little cooking oil on top and wipe with paper towel.

- For stubborn stains, after cleaning with bicarb and white vinegar, sprinkle equal parts sugar and white vinegar over a heated hotplate until the vinegar evaporates. It will look like toffee.
- Remove the toffeed sugar with a scraper.
- When cool, wipe with paper towel.
- Coat with cooking oil to season and prevent rust.

HUMMUS

This is a protein and oil stain.

On carpet/upholstery

- Remove excess by lifting with a plastic comb or by blotting with paper towel.
- Scribble with a cake of bathroom soap run under cold water.
- Massage with a couple of drops of dishwashing liquid on your fingertips until the liquid feels like jelly.
- Wipe with a damp cloth until the dishwashing liquid is removed.
- Absorb moisture by covering the area with paper towel. Place a book on top of the paper towel to assist with absorption.

On cotton/fabric (not wool)

- Remove excess under the tap using cold water.
- Scribble with a cake of bathroom soap.
- Massage with a couple of drops of dishwashing liquid on your fingertips until the liquid feels like jelly.
- Wash according to the fabric. Dry on the clothesline or clothes airer.

On wool

- Massage with a little cheap shampoo on your fingertips.
- Rinse in blood-heat (body temperature) water.
- Rinse in 1 teaspoon of cheap hair conditioner and blood-heat water.
- Gently wring and dry flat on a towel in the shade.

ICE BLOCK

(Flavoured)

On carpet/upholstery

- Remove excess by blotting with paper towel.
- Place white vinegar on a cloth and wring tightly so it's damp but not wet. Blot over the mark.
- Absorb moisture by covering the area with paper towel. Place a book on top of the paper towel to assist with absorption.
- For a coloured stain, expose to sunlight or ultraviolet light. (If using ultraviolet light, protect areas around the stain with cardboard.) Check every 2 hours.

On cotton/fabric (not wool)

- Remove excess under the tap using cold water.
- Blot with or soak in white vinegar until the stain is removed.
- Wash according to the fabric. Dry in sunshine.

On wool

- Massage with a little cheap shampoo on your fingertips.
- Rinse in blood-heat (body temperature) water.
- Rinse in 1 teaspoon of cheap hair conditioner and blood-heat water.
- Gently wring and dry flat on a towel in the shade.

ICE CREAM

This is a protein, fat and sugar stain. Remove proteins first.

On carpet/upholstery

- Remove excess by blotting with paper towel.
- Scribble with a cake of bathroom soap run under cold water.
- Scrub with a toothbrush in all directions – north, south, east and west.
- Massage with a couple of drops of dishwashing liquid on your fingertips until the liquid feels like jelly.
- Wipe with a damp cloth.
- Place white vinegar on a cloth and wring tightly so it's damp but not wet. Blot over the mark.
- Place the vinegar cloth in one hand and a dry cloth in the other and wipe hand over hand, as though stroking a cat, until the stain is removed.
- Absorb moisture by covering the area with paper towel. Place a book on top of the paper towel to assist with absorption.

On cotton/fabric (not wool)

- Remove excess under the tap using cold water.
- Scribble with a cake of bathroom soap run under cold water.
- Massage with a couple of drops of dishwashing liquid on your fingertips until the liquid feels like jelly.
- Rinse in blood-heat (body temperature) water.
- Blot with or soak in white vinegar until the stain is removed.
- Wash according to the fabric. Dry on the clothesline or clothes airer.

On wool

- Massage with a little cheap shampoo on your fingertips.
- Rinse in blood-heat (body temperature) water.
- Blot with or soak in white vinegar.
- Rinse in 1 teaspoon of cheap hair conditioner and blood-heat water.
- Gently wring and dry flat on a towel in the shade.

ICING

On carpet/upholstery

- Remove excess by lifting with a plastic comb or by blotting with paper towel.
- Tightly wring a cloth in white vinegar and blot over the mark.
- Massage with a couple of drops of dishwashing liquid on your fingertips until the liquid feels like jelly.
- Wipe with a damp cloth until the dishwashing liquid is removed.
- Absorb moisture by covering the area with paper towel. Place a book on top of the paper towel to assist with absorption.

On cotton/fabric

- Remove excess under the tap using cold water.
- Blot with or soak in white vinegar.
- Massage with a couple of drops of dishwashing liquid on your fingertips until the liquid feels like jelly.
- Rinse in blood-heat (body temperature) water.
- Wash according to the fabric. Dry on the clothesline or clothes airer.

INK

(see 'Pen')

INSECT

(Squashed)

On carpet/upholstery

- Remove excess by lifting with a plastic comb or by blotting with paper towel.
- Wipe with 2 drops of glycerine on a toothbrush.
- Scribble with a cake of bathroom soap run under cold water.
- Scrub with a toothbrush in all directions – north, south, east and west.
- Wipe with a cold, damp cloth.
- Absorb moisture by covering the area with paper towel. Place a book on top of the paper towel to assist with absorption.
- For insect faeces (which look like an orange splash), scribble with a cake of bathroom soap run under cold water.
- Wipe with a cold, damp cloth.
- In all cases, absorb moisture by covering the area with paper towel. Place a book on top of the paper towel to assist with absorption.

On cotton/fabric

- Remove excess under the tap using cold water.
- Wipe with 2 drops of glycerine on a cloth.
- Scribble with a cake of bathroom soap run under cold water. Rub the fabric against itself using your hands.
- Wash according to the fabric. Dry on the clothesline or clothes airer.

IODINE

On carpet/upholstery

- Remove excess by blotting with paper towel.
- If stained black, wipe with glycerine and leave overnight. Then follow instructions below.
- If fresh, blot with methylated spirits on a cotton bud or cotton ball.
- Wipe with a damp cloth.
- Absorb moisture by covering the area with paper towel. Place a book on top of the paper towel to assist with absorption.

On cotton/fabric

- Remove excess under the tap using cold water.
- Blot with or soak in methylated spirits.
- Wash according to the fabric. Dry on the clothesline or clothes airer.

On stone

- Blot with methylated spirits on a cotton bud or cloth.
- If stubborn, mix plaster of Paris and water to the consistency of peanut butter.
- To each cup of mixture, add 1 teaspoon of methylated spirits.
- Spread 5 mm to 1 cm thick over the stain.
- Allow to dry completely. If it feels cold on the back of your hand, it's not dry.
- When dry, brush away.

IRON

(Clothes)

For black marks

- Place an old towel over the ironing board and pull pantyhose over the end of the board until taut.
- Sprinkle bicarb on the pantyhose and spray the surface of a cold iron with white vinegar.
- Run the iron over the pantyhose. Repeat, if necessary.

For blocked holes

- Put on rubber gloves and add 2 drops of *CLR* or *Ranex* to the water slot of a cold iron. Don't get *CLR* or *Ranex* on your skin because it can cause irritation.
- Turn the iron on.
- Hold the iron horizontally over a sink and press the steam button.
- Repeat with clean water.

For white flecks

- Pour a weak tea solution – 1 tea bag in 1 cup of blood-heat (body temperature) water left to steep for 30 seconds – or equal parts white vinegar and water into a cold iron.
- Turn on the iron.
- Over a sink, press the steam button until the liquid works through the iron.
- Repeat with clean water and continue to press the steam function until the iron sprays clean water.
- To prevent this problem from recurring, remove water from the iron after using it.

TIPS

If you're in a hurry or can't be bothered to iron, try the bachelor's ironing technique. Hang the garment in the bathroom while you're showering. When you put it on, the heat from your body will interact with the slightly damp garment and creases will disappear.

Another technique is to fill a spray pack with 1 litre of water and 1 teaspoon of lavender oil and spray it over your clothes before wearing them.

IRONING SCORCH MARK

On cotton/fabric (not polyester)

- Wring a clean cloth in 3 per cent hydrogen peroxide and place it over the mark.
- Iron over it on a cool setting.

On polyester

- Dampen the surface with white vinegar.
- Wring a cloth with a similar weave in white vinegar and place over the mark.
- Run a warm (not hot) iron over the top.
- If the mark doesn't come out, the polyester is permanently damaged.

TIP

If clothes become shiny from ironing, wring a clean white cloth in white vinegar and place over the shiny area. Run a cool iron on top. This also gives clothes a quick spruce-up if they've been in the cupboard for too long.

IVORY

For yellowing

- Ivory yellows with age and you can't make it white again.

To clean

- Mix sweet almond oil and talcum powder to the consistency of runny cream.
- Wipe on the mixture with a cotton bud.
- Polish off immediately with a damp cotton bud.

J

JAM

On carpet/upholstery

- Remove excess by lifting with a plastic comb or by blotting with paper towel.
- Place white vinegar on a cloth and wring tightly so it's damp but not wet. Blot over the mark.
- Place the vinegar cloth in one hand and a dry cloth in the other and wipe hand over hand, as though stroking a cat, until the stain is removed.
- For a light brown stain, scrub with 2 drops of glycerine on a toothbrush.
- Leave for 90 minutes.
- Tightly wring a cloth in white vinegar, fold the cloth flat and polish out the glycerine without pushing it into the back of the carpet or upholstery.
- In all cases, absorb moisture by covering the area with paper towel. Place a book on top of the paper towel to assist with absorption.

On cotton/fabric (not wool)

- Remove excess under the tap using cold water.
- Blot with or soak in white vinegar. For a light brown stain, wipe with 2 drops of glycerine and leave for 90 minutes.
- Wash according to the fabric. Dry on the clothesline or clothes airer.

On wool

- Remove excess under the tap using cold water.
- Blot with or soak in white vinegar.

- Massage with cheap shampoo on your fingertips.
- Rinse in blood-heat (body temperature) water.
- Rinse in 1 teaspoon of cheap hair conditioner and blood-heat water.
- Gently wring and dry flat on a towel in the shade.

JELLY BEANS

(see 'Lollies')

JELLY DESSERT

On carpet/upholstery

- Remove excess by lifting with a plastic comb or by blotting with paper towel.
- Place white vinegar on a cloth and wring tightly so it's damp but not wet. Blot over the mark.
- Absorb moisture by covering the area with paper towel. Place a book on top of the paper towel to assist with absorption.

On cotton/fabric

- Remove excess by lifting with a plastic comb or using cold water.
- Blot with or soak in white vinegar.
- If soaking, remove from vinegar. Leave for 20 minutes.
- Wash according to the fabric. Dry on the clothesline or clothes airer.

JEWELLERY

To clean

- To clean beads, enamel, glass, silver and titanium, mix ½ teaspoon of dishwashing liquid in a 9-litre bucket of blood-heat (body temperature) water. Don't use dishwashing liquid on pearls, jade or opal. Gently scrub with the mixture using a toothbrush. Dry each piece with a clean cloth.
- To clean platinum, gold and diamonds, fill a bowl with 1 cup of blood-heat (body temperature) water and 1 teaspoon of white vinegar. Apply the solution with a sable paintbrush.
- Clean pearls in a mild salt solution – 1 teaspoon of uniodised salt for 600 ml of water.
- For opal and jade, grate 1 teaspoon of bathroom soap into 1 litre of water. Shake well. Apply the mixture with a cotton bud and dry quickly.
- Clean precious stones with a little water only.
- Clean ivory with sweet almond oil on a cotton bud.
- Wipe earring hooks with methylated spirits on a cotton ball.

TIP

Don't wash items in a sink in case the plug comes loose. You don't want your precious jewellery going down the drain.

JUICER

To clean exterior

- Wipe with bicarb and white vinegar on a cloth. If stubborn, scrub with a nylon brush or pantyhose.

- Wipe with a damp cloth.
- In some cases, staining will have penetrated into the plastic. It's still safe to use.

To clean interior

- Heat ½ cup of white vinegar in the microwave until it's steaming, but not boiling.
- Place inside the juicer and add 2 teaspoons of bicarb.
- Switch on for 1 minute.
- Rinse with water.
- For brown marks, mix ½ teaspoon of glycerine and 1 cup of blood-heat (body temperature) water. Pour into the juicer. Turn the machine on for 1 minute. Rinse thoroughly with water.
- For orange stains, place 1 teaspoon of lavender oil and 1 litre of water in the juicer. Leave overnight before rinsing.

JUMPER

For pilling

- Mix 2 tablespoons of Fuller's earth in a 15-litre bucket of blood-heat (body temperature) water.
- Immerse the item and leave for 5–10 minutes. Don't leave it for longer or it will bleach.
- Rinse in blood-heat water.
- Gently wring and dry flat on a towel in the shade.
- As it dries, put a line of pins on the towel in the shape you want and stretch into shape. Brush away the pilling with a soft brush. Remove remaining pills with a plastic razor.
- For synthetic jumpers, stretch over the end of an ironing board and shave with a plastic razor.

For shrinkage/stretching

- For dark-coloured jumpers, mix 2 tablespoons of Fuller's earth in a 15-litre bucket of blood-heat (body temperature) water.
- For light-coloured jumpers, mix 4 tablespoons of Fuller's earth in a 15-litre bucket of blood-heat (body temperature) water.
- Alternatively, for dark- or light-coloured jumpers, add 2 tablespoons of Epsom salts to a 15-litre bucket of blood-heat (body temperature) water.
- In all cases, immerse the item and gently agitate with your hands until it's thoroughly wet.
- Leave for 10–15 minutes. Don't leave it for longer or it will bleach.
- Rinse in blood-heat water.
- Gently wring and dry flat on a towel in the shade.
- Gently stretch it back into shape as it's drying. Put a line of pins on the towel in the shape you want. To make the stretch even, hold a wide-toothed comb on each inside edge of the jumper and stretch outwards using the combs.

To clean

- Soak in 1 teaspoon of cheap shampoo and blood-heat (body temperature) water for 20 minutes.
- Rinse in blood-heat water.
- Rinse in 1 teaspoon of cheap hair conditioner and blood-heat water.
- Gently wring and dry flat on a towel in the shade.

JUTE

To clean carpet/upholstery

- Mix ½ teaspoon of glycerine with ½ teaspoon of dishwashing liquid.
- Apply the mixture using a toothbrush. Work from the outside to the inside of the stain.
- Leave for 90 minutes.
- Wipe with a damp cloth.
- Absorb moisture by covering the area with paper towel. Place a book on top of the paper towel to assist with absorption.

K

KEBAB

On carpet/upholstery

- Remove excess by lifting with a plastic comb or by blotting with paper towel.
- Scribble with a cake of bathroom soap run under cold water.
- Wipe with a damp cloth.
- Massage with a couple of drops of dishwashing liquid on your fingertips until the liquid feels like jelly.
- Wipe with a damp cloth until dishwashing liquid is removed.
- Tightly wring a cloth in white vinegar and blot over the mark.
- Absorb moisture by covering the area with paper towel. Place a book on top of the paper towel to assist with absorption.

On cotton/fabric (not wool)

- Remove excess by running under the tap using cold water.
- Scribble with a cake of bathroom soap run under cold water. Rub the fabric against itself using your hands.
- Blot with or soak in white vinegar until the stain is removed.
- Rinse using cold water.
- Wash according to the fabric. Dry in sunshine.

On wool

- Remove excess under the tap using cold water.
- Blot with or soak in white vinegar.
- Massage with a couple of drops of cheap shampoo on your fingertips.

- Rinse in blood-heat (body temperature) water.
- Rinse in 1 teaspoon of cheap hair conditioner and blood-heat water.
- Gently wring and dry flat on a towel in the shade.

KETCHUP

(see 'Tomato Sauce')

KETTLE

For lime scale/tartar

- Empty the kettle. Add 2 tablespoons of uncooked rice, 2 tablespoons of bicarb and 2 tablespoons of white vinegar.
- Cover the openings with your hands and shake for 1 minute.
- Rinse thoroughly with water.
- Alternatively, add 1 teaspoon of citric acid powder, fill with water and bring to the boil. Allow the water to cool.
- Remove and rinse thoroughly.
- Alternatively, fill the kettle with 1 cup of white vinegar or ½ cup of lemon juice.
- Leave for 1 hour.
- Add water and boil.
- Discard the water, refill the kettle with clean water and boil again.

For scaling

- Put on rubber gloves and add 1 teaspoon of *CLR* or *Ranex* to a kettle filled with water. Don't get *CLR* or *Ranex* on your skin because it can cause irritation.
- Leave for 1 hour.

- Remove and rinse with water. Make sure you rinse thoroughly.

KIWI FRUIT

On carpet/upholstery

- Remove excess by lifting with a plastic comb or by blotting with paper towel.
- For old stains, wipe with 2 drops of glycerine on a cloth. Leave for 90 minutes. Then follow instructions below.
- For fresh stains, place white vinegar on a cloth and wring tightly so it's damp but not wet. Blot over the mark.
- Place the vinegar cloth in one hand and a dry cloth in the other and wipe hand over hand, as though stroking a cat, until the stain is removed.
- In all cases, absorb moisture by covering the area with paper towel. Place a book on top of the paper towel to assist with absorption.

On cotton/fabric

- Remove excess under the tap using cold water.
- For old stains, wipe with 2 drops of glycerine. Leave for 90 minutes. Then follow instructions below.
- For fresh stains, blot with or soak in white vinegar until the stain is removed.
- Wash according to the fabric. Dry in sunshine.

KNIFE

For rust

- Rub with bicarb on a damp cloth. Alternatively, wipe with lemon juice on a cloth.
- Rinse under water.

To clean

- Hand wash in dishwashing liquid and hot water. Don't wash in the dishwasher because it blunts them.
- Dry thoroughly.

TIP

While chopping onions and garlic, regularly dip the knife in a glass of water. Onions and garlic blunt knives, so always rinse after chopping.

L

LAKSA

On carpet/upholstery

- Remove excess by lifting with a plastic comb or by blotting with paper towel.
- Massage with a couple of drops of dishwashing liquid on your fingertips until the liquid feels like jelly.
- Wipe with a damp cloth until the dishwashing liquid is removed.
- For a yellow-coloured stain, wipe with 2 drops of lavender oil on a cloth.
- For a sauce stain, tightly wring a cloth in white vinegar and blot over the mark.
- For pink staining, expose to sunlight or ultraviolet light. (If using ultraviolet light, protect areas around the stain with cardboard.) Check every 2 hours.
- In all cases, absorb moisture by covering the area with paper towel. Place a book on top of the paper towel to assist with absorption.

On cotton/fabric

- Remove excess under the tap using cold water.
- Massage with a couple of drops of dishwashing liquid on your fingertips until the liquid feels like jelly.
- Rinse using cold water.
- For a yellow-coloured stain, wipe with 2 drops of lavender oil on a cloth.
- For a sauce stain, blot with or soak in white vinegar.
- For pink staining, blot with white vinegar and hang in sunshine until the stain fades before washing.
- In all cases, wash according to the fabric. Dry on the clothesline or clothes airer.

LAMP

To clean base

- If ceramic, wipe with white vinegar on a cloth.
- If hand-painted, place 1 cup of unprocessed wheat bran in a large bowl. Add drops of white vinegar one at a time, stirring as you go, until the mixture resembles breadcrumbs. It shouldn't be wet. Place in the toe of pantyhose, tie off and wipe over base.
- If glass, wipe with white vinegar on a cloth.
- If marble, apply liquid wax polish such as *CeraFluida* with pantyhose.
- If metal, wipe with bicarb and white vinegar on a cloth.
- If plastic, wipe with equal parts glycerine and talcum powder on a cloth.
- If timber, wipe with cold black tea on a cloth.

To clean shade

- For fabric lamp shades, place 1 cup of unprocessed wheat bran in a large bowl. Add drops of white vinegar one at a time, stirring as you go, until the mixture resembles breadcrumbs. It shouldn't be wet.
- Place in the toe of pantyhose, tie off and wipe over the lamp shade.
- For glass lamp shades, tightly wring a cloth in warm water and wipe over the glass. If stubborn, blot with white vinegar on a cloth.
- For fly speck, mix equal parts tea tree oil and water.
- Apply the mixture on a cotton bud. Spin the cotton bud over each speck.

TIPS

To deter bugs, mix 1 teaspoon of lavender oil with 1 litre of water in a spray pack and lightly mist over the shades. Wipe lamp bulbs with lavender oil to deter moths.

To prevent a halogen light from corroding, wipe the connection on the bulb with a cloth once a week. While cleaning, wipe over light bulb with a cloth to remove dust.

LEAF STAIN

On tiles

- Scrub with 2 drops of glycerine using a broom.
- Leave for 90 minutes.
- Add 1 teaspoon of dishwashing liquid to a 9-litre bucket of water.
- Sweep suds backwards and forwards over the stain with a broom.
- If the leaves are eucalyptus, add 1 tablespoon of eucalyptus oil to the solution.
- Rinse with clean water.

LEMONADE

(see 'Soft Drink')

LIGHTER FLUID

On carpet/upholstery

- Remove excess by blotting with paper towel.
- Massage with a couple of drops of dishwashing liquid on your fingertips until the liquid feels like jelly.

- Wipe with a damp cloth until dishwashing liquid is removed.
- Absorb moisture by covering the area with paper towel. Place a book on top of the paper towel to assist with absorption.

On cotton/fabric

- Remove excess by blotting with paper towel.
- Massage with a couple of drops of dishwashing liquid on your fingertips until the liquid feels like jelly.
- Rinse using cold water.
- Wash according to the fabric. Dry on the clothesline or clothes airer.

LILY POLLEN

On benchtops

- Wipe with 2 drops of lavender oil on a cloth until removed.
- For larger areas, lightly spray with 1 teaspoon of lavender oil in a 1-litre spray pack of water. Wipe with pantyhose.

On carpet/upholstery

- Remove excess by lifting with a plastic comb. Don't spread the stain.
- Blot with 2 drops of lavender oil on a cloth, working from the outside to the inside of the stain until removed.
- Wipe with a damp cloth.
- Absorb moisture by covering the area with paper towel. Place a book on top of the paper towel to assist with absorption.

On cotton/fabric

- Remove excess by lifting with a plastic comb. Don't spread the stain.
- Blot with 2 drops of lavender oil on a cotton ball, while holding a clean cotton ball at the back of the stain.
- Repeat until removed.
- Wash according to the fabric. Dry on the clothesline or clothes airer.

LIME JUICE

On carpet/upholstery

- Remove excess by blotting with paper towel.
- Mix 1 teaspoon of dishwashing liquid with 1 cup of cold water.
- Scrub with the mixture using a toothbrush. Don't get too much moisture on the surface or it will create further staining.
- Wipe with a damp cloth until the solution is removed.
- Absorb moisture by covering the area with paper towel. Place a book on top of the paper towel to assist with absorption.

On cotton/fabric

- Rinse under the tap using cold water.
- Sprinkle with bicarb.
- Leave for 20 minutes.
- Wash according to the fabric. Dry on the clothesline or clothes airer.

On granite/marble

- Absorb excess by sprinkling over the stain with bicarb.
- Wipe with a damp cloth. Alternatively, wipe with milk on a cloth.

LIME SCALE

In kettle

- Empty the kettle. Add 2 tablespoons of uncooked rice, 2 tablespoons of bicarb and 2 tablespoons of white vinegar.
- Cover the openings with your hands and shake for 1 minute.
- Rinse thoroughly with water.
- Alternatively, add 1 teaspoon of citric acid powder, fill with water and bring to the boil. Allow the water to cool.
- Remove and rinse thoroughly.
- Alternatively, fill the kettle with 1 cup of white vinegar or ½ cup of lemon juice.
- Leave for 1 hour.
- Add water and boil.
- Discard the water, refill the kettle with clean water and boil again.

On ceramic

- Sprinkle with bicarb.
- Spray with white vinegar.
- While the mixture is fizzing, rub with rolled up pantyhose.
- Rinse with a damp cloth.

On outdoor tiles

- Wash with white vinegar on a broom.
- If this doesn't work, it's glass cancer, which means the surface has been damaged.
- Clean and alleviate by wiping with sweet almond oil on a stiff broom.
- Polish with a cloth.
- Seal with a good-quality tile sealer.

On polycarbonate bath

- Wet the stained area with water and sprinkle with talcum powder.
- Put on rubber gloves and apply *CLR* or *Ranex*. Don't get *CLR* or *Ranex* on your skin because it can cause irritation. Leave for 10 minutes.
- Still wearing gloves, neutralise the chemicals by wiping with white vinegar on a cloth.

LINEN

For brown/yellow marks

- Place a small mountain of uniodised salt over each mark.
- Squeeze drops of fresh lemon juice over each mountain of salt until it's moist but doesn't collapse. Stop squeezing before the juice hits the bottom of the salt.
- Leave for 20 minutes. If you can, leave in sunshine.
- Wash according to the fabric. Dry on the clothesline or clothes airer.

For tea/coffee marks

- Wipe with glycerine and leave overnight.
- Scribble with a cake of bathroom soap run under cold water. Rub the fabric against itself using your hands.
- Wash according to the fabric. Dry on the clothesline or clothes airer.

HOW TO MAKE ACID-FREE DRAWER LINERS

Fill a spray pack with warm water, add 1 tea bag and allow to sit for 3 minutes. Remove the tea bag and add 2 drops of oil of cloves and your favourite perfume or essential oil to the bottle. Spray over acid-free paper (available from newsagencies and removalists). Allow the paper to dry, cut to size and place in drawers and cupboards. Replace each year.

TIPS

For drawers that stick when opening and closing, rub a cake of bathroom soap or a candle along the wooden runners. If the runners are made of plastic, polish with Gumption. *If you still have a problem, your drawers could be uneven and need repairs.*

When moving house, rather than writing on boxes, make removable labels. Removalists' boxes in reasonable condition can be refunded.

HOW TO SORT THE LINEN CUPBOARD

Remove items from the linen cupboard and vacuum the shelves. Shake and refold items and place the most-used ones at eye level. Store linen according to the room it's used in so you can quickly grab one pile rather than sorting through everything. The fewer the folds in the linen the better. Roll towels. When storing precious items, use acid-free paper to prevent yellowing (see '*How to Make Acid-Free Drawer Liners*'). Deter bugs by leaving bath salts and soaps inside the cupboard.

LINT

On fabric

- Put on rubber gloves and wash your gloved hands with a cake of bathroom soap and water.
- Shake hands dry.
- Wipe over the garment. The lint will stick to the gloves.
- Alternatively, apply sticky tape and quickly lift off.

TIPS

For garments covered in lint, wash in the washing machine and add pantyhose. The lint will stick to the pantyhose.

To remove the static charge in clothes, place 1 teaspoon of cheap hair conditioner in a 1-litre spray pack of water and lightly mist over the clothes as they dry.

LIP BALM

On carpet/upholstery

- Remove excess by blotting with paper towel.
- If the lip balm isn't coloured, massage with a couple of drops of dishwashing liquid on your fingertips until the liquid feels like jelly.
- Wipe with a damp cloth until dishwashing liquid is removed.
- If the lip balm is coloured, wipe with white spirits on a cotton ball.
- Massage with a couple of drops of dishwashing liquid on your fingertips until the liquid feels like jelly.
- Wipe with a damp cloth until dishwashing liquid is removed.
- If the lip balm contains wax, add 2 drops of tea tree oil to the dishwashing liquid and massage.
- In all cases, absorb moisture by covering the area with paper towel. Place a book on top of the paper towel to assist with absorption.

On cotton/fabric (not silk/wool)

- Remove excess under the tap using cold water.
- If the lip balm doesn't contain colour, massage with a couple of drops of dishwashing liquid on your fingertips until the liquid feels like jelly.
- If the lip balm is coloured, wipe with white spirits on a cotton ball. Massage with a couple of drops of dishwashing liquid on your fingertips until the liquid feels like jelly.
- If it contains wax, add 2 drops of tea tree oil to the dishwashing liquid and massage with your fingertips.

- In all cases, rinse under blood-heat (body temperature) water.
- Wash according to the fabric. Dry on the clothesline or clothes airer.

On silk/wool

- If the lip balm is coloured, wipe with white spirits on a cotton ball. Hand wash in 1 teaspoon of cheap shampoo and blood-heat (body temperature) water.
- If the lip balm contains wax, add 2 drops of tea tree oil to the cheap shampoo.
- In all cases, rinse in 1 teaspoon of cheap hair conditioner and blood-heat water.
- Gently wring and dry flat on a towel in the shade. Ensure silk is dried away from the wind so the fibres don't tangle and leave a dusty look.

LIPSTICK

On carpet/upholstery

- Remove excess by blotting with paper towel.
- Wipe with white spirits on a cotton ball.
- Sprinkle with unprocessed wheat bran.
- Scrub backwards and forwards with a brush or broom.
- When dry, vacuum.

On cotton/fabric (not silk/wool)

- Blot with white spirits on a cotton bud or cotton ball.
- Alternatively, wipe with 2 drops of glycerine on a cotton ball. Leave for 90 minutes.
- In both cases, wash according to the fabric. Dry on the clothesline or clothes airer.

On glass

- Wipe with white vinegar on a cloth.

On silk/wool

- Wipe with 2 drops of glycerine on a cloth. Leave for 90 minutes.
- Hand wash in 1 teaspoon of cheap shampoo and blood-heat (body temperature) water.
- Rinse in 1 teaspoon of cheap hair conditioner and blood-heat water.
- Gently wring and dry flat on a towel in the shade. Ensure silk is dried away from the wind so the fibres don't tangle and leave a dusty look.

On stone

- Scrub with white spirits on a toothbrush.
- If stubborn, mix plaster of Paris and water to the consistency of peanut butter.
- To each cup of mixture, add 1 teaspoon of white spirits.
- Spread 5 mm to 1 cm thick over the stain.
- Allow to dry completely. If it feels cold on the back of your hand, it's not dry.
- When dry, brush away.

LIQUID PAPER

(see 'Correction Fluid')

LIQUID SHOE POLISH

(see 'Shoe Polish')

LIQUORICE

(see 'Lollies')

LOLLIES

On carpet/upholstery

- Remove excess by lifting with a plastic comb or by blotting with paper towel.
- Place white vinegar on a cloth and wring tightly so it's damp but not wet. Blot over the mark. Leave for 10 minutes if the stain contains liquorice.
- To remove colouring, expose to sunlight or ultraviolet light. (If using ultraviolet light, protect areas around the stain with cardboard.) Check every 2 hours.
- In all cases, absorb moisture by covering the area with paper towel. Place a book on top of the paper towel to assist with absorption.

On cotton/fabric

- Remove excess under the tap using cold water.
- Blot with or soak in white vinegar. Leave for 10 minutes if the stain contains liquorice. Hang in the sunshine until the stain fades before washing.
- Wash according to the fabric. Dry on the clothesline or clothes airer.

LOTION

Lotions have various bases. Consult the label.

On carpet/upholstery

- Remove excess by blotting with paper towel.
- For water-based lotions, scribble with a cake of bathroom soap run under blood-heat (body temperature) water. Massage with your fingertips until the stain is loosened. Wipe with a damp cloth. Repeat, if needed.

- If there's a grey stain, massage with a couple of drops of dishwashing liquid on your fingertips until the liquid feels like jelly. Wipe with a damp cloth until dishwashing liquid is removed.
- For antibacterial lotions, mix 1 teaspoon of grated bathroom soap, 1 teaspoon of dishwashing liquid and 1 tablespoon of boiling water. Allow the soap and dishwashing liquid to dissolve. Massage 2 drops of the solution into the stain with your fingertips until the liquid feels like jelly. Wipe with a cold, damp cloth followed by a dry cloth hand over hand, as though stroking a cat.
- For wax-based lotions, mix 2 drops of tea tree oil with 2 drops of dishwashing liquid and massage with your fingertips until the liquid feels like jelly. Wipe with a cold, damp cloth. Repeat, if needed.
- For liniment, wring a cloth in white vinegar, place over the stain and stand or sit on it for 5 seconds. Remove.
- In all cases, absorb moisture by covering the area with paper towel. Place a book on top of the paper towel to assist with absorption.

On cotton/fabric

- Remove excess under the tap using blood-heat (body temperature) water.
- For water-based lotions, scribble with a cake of bathroom soap. Massage with your fingertips until the stain is loosened.
- If there's a grey stain, massage with a couple of drops of dishwashing liquid on your fingertips until the liquid feels like jelly.

- For antibacterial lotions, mix 1 teaspoon of grated bathroom soap, 1 teaspoon of dishwashing liquid and 1 tablespoon of boiling water. Allow the soap and dishwashing liquid to dissolve. Massage 2 drops of the solution into the stain with your fingertips until the liquid feels like jelly.
- For wax-based lotions, mix 2 drops of tea tree oil with 2 drops of dishwashing liquid and massage with your fingertips until the liquid feels like jelly.
- For liniment, blot with or soak in white vinegar.
- In all cases, wash according to the fabric. Dry on the clothesline or clothes airer.

LOUNGE

(see 'Couch')

LUBRICANT

On carpet/upholstery

- Absorb excess by blotting with paper towel.
- For gelatine-based lubricant (stain has a dark outer edge), scribble with a cake of bathroom soap run under cold water.
- Scrub with a toothbrush in all directions – north, south, east and west.
- Wipe with a damp cloth.
- Absorb moisture by covering the area with paper towel. Place a book on top of the paper towel to assist with absorption.
- For oil-based lubricant, remove excess then massage with a couple of drops of dishwashing liquid on your fingertips until the liquid feels like jelly.

- Wipe with a damp cloth until dishwashing liquid is removed.
- Absorb moisture by covering the area with paper towel.
- For silicone-based lubricant, remove excess then spray with 1 teaspoon of lavender oil in a 1-litre spray pack of water and wipe with pantyhose.
- Wipe with a damp cloth and dry cloth hand over hand, as though stroking a cat.
- Absorb moisture by covering the area with paper towel. Place a book on top of the paper towel to assist with absorption.

On cotton/fabric

- Remove excess under the tap using cold water.
- To remove gelatine-based lubricant (stain has a dark outer edge), scribble with a cake of bathroom soap run under cold water.
- To remove oil-based lubricant, massage with a couple of drops of dishwashing liquid on your fingertips until the liquid feels like jelly.
- For silicone-based lubricant, wipe with 2 drops of lavender oil.
- In all cases, wash according to the fabric. Dry on the clothesline or clothes airer.

On mattress

- Absorb excess by blotting with paper towel.
- Sprinkle with talcum powder.
- If it contains silicone, spray with 1 teaspoon of lavender oil in a 1-litre spray pack of water.
- Massage with a couple of drops of dishwashing liquid on your fingertips until the liquid feels like jelly.

- Wipe with a damp cloth.
- Vacuum.
- If damp, dry with a hair dryer.

LYCRA

(see 'Sportswear')

M

MAKE-UP

(see also 'Lipstick', 'Mascara')

Oil-Based (Foundation, Concealer etc.)

On carpet/upholstery (not leather)

- Remove excess by blotting with paper towel.
- Massage with a couple of drops of dishwashing liquid on your fingertips until the liquid feels like jelly.
- Wipe with a damp cloth until the dishwashing liquid is removed.
- If there's colour, wipe with white spirits on a cotton bud and then wipe with white vinegar on a cloth.
- In all cases, absorb moisture by covering the area with paper towel. Place a book on top of the paper towel to assist with absorption.

On cotton/fabric

- Remove excess under the tap using blood-heat (body temperature) water.
- Massage with a couple of drops of dishwashing liquid on your fingertips until the liquid feels like jelly.
- Rinse with blood-heat water.
- If there's colour, wipe with white spirits on a cloth.
- Mix *Vanish NapiSan Oxi Action* and water to form a paste the consistency of spreadable butter and leave on the stain for 20 minutes. Don't use on wool or silk.
- For wool and silk, wash in 1 teaspoon of cheap shampoo and blood-heat (body temperature) water.
- In all cases, wash according to the fabric. Dry on the clothesline or clothes airer. Dry wool and silk flat on a towel in the shade.

- Alternatively, remove excess then massage with equal parts methylated spirits and dishwashing liquid on your fingertips. Wash according to the fabric. Dry on the clothesline or clothes airer.

On leather

- Massage with a couple of drops of dishwashing liquid on your fingertips until the liquid feels like jelly. Or wipe with saddle soap.
- Wipe with a damp cloth.
- Sprinkle with talcum powder.
- When dry, brush off.
- Wipe with leather conditioner. Make your own – see **Household formulas**.

On polycarbonate/porcelain

- Wipe with equal parts dishwashing liquid and glycerine on rolled up pantyhose until the make-up smears.
- Wipe with paper towel.
- Rinse with hot water.

On stone

- Wipe with dishwashing liquid on a cloth.
- If stubborn, mix plaster of Paris and water to the consistency of peanut butter.
- To each cup of mixture, add 1 teaspoon of dishwashing liquid.
- Spread 5 mm to 1 cm thick over the stain.
- Allow to dry completely. If it feels cold on the back of your hand, it's not dry.
- When dry, brush away.

Powder-Based (Eye Shadow, Blush etc.)

On carpet/upholstery

- Vacuum as much as possible.
- For residue, cut a cake of bathroom soap in half lengthways and round the edges. Dampen it and use like a rolling pin over the powder. The powder will stick to the soap. Clear it from the soap under water as you go.
- Alternatively, after vacuuming, put on rubber gloves and wash your gloved hands with a cake of bathroom soap and water. Shake your hands dry. When dry, wipe over the powder. The powder will stick to the rubber.
- In both cases, absorb moisture by covering the area with paper towel. Place a book on top of the paper towel to assist with absorption.

On cotton/fabric

- Rinse under the tap with cold water. The make-up stain should come out.
- For residue, cut a cake of bathroom soap in half lengthways and round the edges to create a soap sausage. Dampen it and use like a rolling pin over the powder. The powder will stick to the soap. Clear it from the soap under water as you go.
- In all cases, wash according to the fabric. Dry on the clothesline or clothes airer.

MANGO

On carpet/upholstery

- Remove excess by lifting with a plastic comb or by blotting with paper towel.

- Place white vinegar on a cloth and wring tightly so it's damp but not wet. Blot over the mark.
- Place the vinegar cloth in one hand and a dry cloth in the other and wipe hand over hand, as though stroking a cat, until the stain is removed.
- Absorb excess by covering with paper towel. Place a book on top.

On cotton/fabric

- Remove excess under the tap using cold water.
- Blot with or soak in white vinegar. Alternatively, soak in ½ lid of *Vanish NapiSan Oxi Action* and 9 litres of water for 20 minutes. Don't use on wool, silk or leather.
- Wash according to the fabric. Dry on the clothesline or clothes airer.

MAPLE SYRUP

On carpet/upholstery

- Remove excess by blotting with paper towel.
- Scribble with a cake of bathroom soap run under blood-heat (body temperature) water.
- Scrub with a toothbrush or pantyhose in all directions – north, south, east and west.
- Blot with equal parts white vinegar and water on a cloth.
- Absorb moisture by covering the area with paper towel. Place a book on top of the paper towel to assist with absorption.
- When almost dry, repeat.
- If a shadow returns in a couple of weeks, repeat again.

On cotton/fabric (not wool)

- Remove excess under the tap using cold water.
- Scribble with a cake of bathroom soap run under blood-heat (body temperature) water. Rub the fabric against itself using your hands.
- Rinse in equal parts white vinegar and water.
- Wash according to the fabric. Dry on the clothesline or clothes airer.

On stone

- Wipe with a cake of bathroom soap and blood-heat (body temperature) water on a cloth.
- Mix plaster of Paris and water to the consistency of peanut butter.
- To each cup of mixture, add 1 teaspoon of grated soap.
- Spread 5 mm to 1 cm thick over the stain.
- Allow to dry completely. If it feels cold on the back of your hand, it's not dry.
- When dry, brush away.

On wool

- Scribble with a cake of bathroom soap and blood-heat (body temperature) water.
- Massage with a little cheap shampoo on your fingertips.
- Rinse in equal parts white vinegar and blood-heat water.
- Rinse in 1 teaspoon of cheap hair conditioner and blood-heat water.
- Gently wring and dry flat on a towel in the shade.

MARBLE

For chips

- Find a candle in a colour that matches the marble.
- Melt the candle wax over the chips.
- Buff with pantyhose or silk to make it flat.
- Seal or polish the marble with liquid polish wax *CeraFluida*.

To clean

- Dampen pantyhose with a cake of bathroom soap and water. Roll them into a ball and wipe over the surface.
- For heavy staining, mix plaster of Paris and water to the consistency of peanut butter.
- To each cup of mixture, mix in 1 teaspoon of grated soap.
- Spread 5 mm to 1 cm thick over the stain.
- Allow to dry completely. If it feels cold on the back of your hand, it's not dry.
- When dry, brush away.

TIP

To prevent staining on marble, apply marble floor wax at least once a month.

MARGARINE

(see 'Butter')

MARMALADE

(see 'Jam')

MASCARA

On carpet/upholstery

- Remove excess by lifting with a plastic comb or by blotting with paper towel.
- For waterproof mascara, wipe with white spirits on a cotton ball. For non-waterproof mascara, wipe with methylated spirits on a cotton ball.
- Wipe with a damp cloth and dry cloth hand over hand, as though stroking a cat.
- Absorb moisture by covering the area with paper towel. Place a book on top of the paper towel to assist with absorption.

On cotton/fabric

- For waterproof mascara, put a dry cotton ball behind the stain. Wipe the stain with white spirits on a cotton ball.
- For non-waterproof mascara, put a dry cotton ball behind the stain. Wipe the stain with methylated spirits on a cotton ball.
- Wash according to the fabric. Dry on the clothesline or clothes airer.

MASSAGE OIL

On carpet/upholstery

- Remove excess by blotting with paper towel.
- Mix equal parts tea tree oil and dishwashing liquid.
- Massage with the mixture on your fingertips until the liquid feels like jelly.
- Wipe with a damp cloth until the mixture is removed.

- Absorb moisture by covering the area with paper towel. Place a book on top of the paper towel to assist with absorption.

On cotton/fabric

- Remove excess by washing under the tap.
- Mix equal parts tea tree oil and dishwashing liquid.
- Massage with the mixture on your fingertips until the liquid feels like jelly.
- Wash according to the fabric. Dry on the clothesline or clothes airer.

MATTRESS

For spot stains

- Scribble with a cake of bathroom soap run under cold water.
- Scrub with a nylon brush until the soap becomes foamy.
- Sprinkle with talcum powder and leave until absorbed.
- Whack with a tennis racquet, cricket bat or equivalent.
- When dry, vacuum.

To clean

- Sprinkle with equal parts talcum powder and bicarb.
- Whack with a tennis racquet, cricket bat or equivalent.
- Vacuum.

TIP

It's always best to use a mattress and pillow protectors and to wash them regularly.

MAYONNAISE

On carpet/upholstery

- Remove excess by lifting with a plastic comb or by blotting with paper towel.
- Massage with a couple of drops of dishwashing liquid on your fingertips until the liquid feels like jelly. For whole-egg mayonnaise, scribble with a cake of bathroom soap run under cold water first.
- Wipe with a damp cloth until the dishwashing liquid is removed.
- For colour residue, remove excess then scrub with 2 drops of glycerine on a toothbrush. Leave for 90 minutes. Tightly wring a cloth in white vinegar, fold the cloth flat and polish out the glycerine without pushing it into the back of the carpet or upholstery.
- In all cases, absorb moisture by covering the area with paper towel. Place a book on top of the paper towel to assist with absorption.

On cotton/fabric (not wool)

- Remove excess under the tap using cold water.
- Massage with a couple of drops of dishwashing liquid on your fingertips until the liquid feels like jelly. For whole-egg mayonnaise, scribble with a cake of bathroom soap run under cold water first.
- Rinse under blood-heat (body temperature) water.
- For colour residue, remove excess then scrub with 2 drops of glycerine on a toothbrush. Leave for 90 minutes. Blot with white vinegar.
- In all cases, wash according to the fabric. Dry on the clothesline or clothes airer.

On wool

- Remove excess under the tap using blood-heat (body temperature) water.
- Massage with 1 teaspoon of cheap shampoo and blood-heat water.
- Rinse in blood-heat water.
- Rinse in 1 teaspoon of cheap hair conditioner and blood-heat water.
- Gently wring and dry flat on a towel in the shade.

MEAT JUICE

(Cooked/raw)

On carpet/upholstery

- Remove excess by blotting with paper towel.
- Scribble with a cake of bathroom soap run under cold water.
- Wipe with a damp cloth.
- Absorb moisture by covering the area with paper towel. Place a book on top of the paper towel to assist with absorption.

On cotton/fabric

- Remove excess under the tap using cold water.
- Scribble with a cake of bathroom soap. Rub the fabric against itself using your hands.
- Rinse using cold water.
- Wash according to the fabric. Dry on the clothesline or clothes airer.

On timber/stone

- Remove excess by blotting with paper towel.
- Mix plaster of Paris and water to the consistency of peanut butter.
- To every cup of mixture, add 1 teaspoon of grated bathroom soap.
- Spread mixture 5 mm to 1 cm thick over the stain.
- Allow to dry completely. If it feels cold on the back of your hand, it's not dry.
- When dry, sweep away with a broom. Repeat, if needed.

MEAT PIE

On carpet/upholstery (not leather)

- Remove excess by lifting with a plastic comb or by blotting with paper towel.
- Scribble with a cake of bathroom soap run under cold water.
- Massage with a couple of drops of dishwashing liquid on your fingertips until the liquid feels like jelly.
- Wipe with a damp cloth until the dishwashing liquid is removed.
- Absorb moisture by covering the area with paper towel. Place a book on top of the paper towel to assist with absorption.

On cotton/fabric

- Remove excess under the tap using cold water.
- Scribble with a cake of bathroom soap run under cold water.
- Massage with a couple of drops of dishwashing liquid on your fingertips until the liquid feels like jelly.

- Rinse under blood-heat (body temperature) water.
- Wash according to the fabric. Dry on the clothesline or clothes airer.

On leather

- Remove excess with a cold, damp cloth.
- Massage with saddle soap on your fingertips.
- Wipe with a damp cloth.
- Sprinkle with bicarb.
- When dry, brush off.
- Wipe with leather conditioner. Make your own – see **Household formulas**.

MEDICINE

On carpet/upholstery

- Remove excess by blotting with paper towel.
- Scribble with a cake of bathroom soap run under cold water.
- Massage with a couple of drops of dishwashing liquid on your fingertips until the liquid feels like jelly.
- Wipe with a damp cloth until the dishwashing liquid is removed.
- If there's residue, scrub with 2 drops of glycerine on a toothbrush. Leave for 90 minutes. Tightly wring a cloth in white vinegar, fold the cloth flat and polish out the glycerine without pushing it into the back of the carpet or upholstery.
- To remove colouring, follow instructions above then expose to sunlight or ultraviolet light. (If using ultraviolet light, protect areas around the stain with cardboard.) Check every 2 hours.

- In all cases, absorb moisture by covering the area with paper towel. Place a book on top of the paper towel to assist with absorption.

On cotton/fabric

- Remove excess under the tap using cold water.
- Scribble with a cake of bathroom soap run under cold water.
- Massage with a couple of drops of dishwashing liquid on your fingertips until the liquid feels like jelly.
- If there's residue, scrub with 2 drops of glycerine on a toothbrush. Leave for 90 minutes. Blot with white vinegar and hang in sunshine until the stain fades before washing.
- Wash according to the fabric. Dry on the clothesline or clothes airer.

MICE

To deter

- Buy dehydrated snake poo online – python poo is preferable to viper poo.
- Scatter it in the ceiling or under the house. The poo is a small pellet; humans can't smell it and it lasts for about 1 year.
- Alternatively, scatter with naphthalene flakes or camphor. (Note: These are less potent than snake poo.)

⚠ WARNING

Do not use naphthalene flakes if you have children under 3 years of age.

- For large areas, mix 1 teaspoon of dehydrated snake poo and 1 litre of water in a spray pack and spray under the house.

MICROWAVE

To clean

- Mix 2 tablespoons of bicarb, 2 tablespoons of white vinegar and 1 cup of water in a microwave-safe bowl (2-litre volume).
- Place the bowl in the microwave and heat until the mixture comes to the boil, but doesn't boil over, and the interior is covered in steam.
- Wipe every surface of the microwave, including the back grille, with a cloth wrung out in the mixture.
- Remove the filter pad inside the grille and place it in the solution. Rub gently with your fingertips until clean. No need to rinse.
- Allow the filter pad to dry before returning. This will reduce smells.

TIP

Create a Christmas fragrance by heating orange peel in the microwave on high for 1 minute. Or mix 1 teaspoon of vanilla extract and 4 tablespoons of water in a bowl and heat in the microwave for 1 minute.

MILDEW

(see 'Mould')

MILK

On carpet/upholstery

- Remove excess by blotting with paper towel.
- Scribble with a cake of bathroom soap run under cold water.
- Scrub with a toothbrush or pantyhose in every direction – north, south, east and west.
- Wipe with a damp cloth.
- Absorb moisture by covering the area with paper towel. Place a book on top of the paper towel to assist with absorption.

On cotton/fabric (not wool)

- Remove excess under the tap using cold water.
- Scribble with a cake of bathroom soap. Rub the fabric against itself using your hands.
- Rinse using cold water.
- Wash according to the fabric. Dry on the clothesline or clothes airer.

On stone

- Wipe with a cake of bathroom soap run under cold water.
- If stubborn, mix plaster of Paris and water to the consistency of peanut butter.
- To each cup of mixture, add 1 teaspoon of grated bathroom soap.
- Spread 5 mm to 1 cm thick over the stain.
- Allow to dry completely. If it feels cold on the back of your hand, it's not dry.
- When dry, brush away.

On wool

- Scribble with a cake of bathroom soap run under blood-heat (body temperature) water.
- Massage with a little cheap shampoo on your fingertips.
- Rinse in blood-heat water.
- Rinse in 1 teaspoon of cheap hair conditioner and blood-heat water.
- Gently wring and dry flat on a towel in the shade.

MOISTURISER

On carpet/upholstery

- Remove excess by blotting with paper towel.
- Massage with a couple of drops of dishwashing liquid on your fingertips until the liquid feels like jelly. To remove moisturiser with a waxy base (check the label), mix 1 teaspoon of tea tree oil with 1 teaspoon of dishwashing liquid and massage using your fingertips.
- Wipe with a damp cloth until the liquid is removed.
- Absorb moisture by covering the area with paper towel. Place a book on top of the paper towel to assist with absorption.

On cotton/fabric (not wool)

- Remove excess under the tap using cold water.
- Massage with a couple of drops of dishwashing liquid on your fingertips until the liquid feels like jelly. To remove moisturiser with a waxy base (check the label), mix 1 teaspoon of tea tree oil with 1 teaspoon of dishwashing liquid and massage using your fingertips.
- Wash according to the fabric. Dry on the clothesline or clothes airer.

On wool

- Scribble with a cake of bathroom soap run under blood-heat (body temperature) water.
- Massage with a little cheap shampoo on your fingertips.
- Rinse in blood-heat water.
- Rinse in 1 teaspoon of cheap hair conditioner and blood-heat water.
- Gently wring and dry flat on a towel in the shade.

MOLASSES

(see 'Maple Syrup')

MOSQUITOES

To deter

- Mix 1 teaspoon of lavender oil in a 1-litre spray pack of water and lightly mist around the area. It can also be used as a personal insecticide.
- Wipe chairs and tables with 2 drops of lavender oil on a cloth.
- Plant lavender, basil, pennyroyal, pyrethrum daisy, *Pelargonium citrosum* (citronella plant) and tansy around entertainment areas.
- Alternatively, place freshly chopped mint in a vase.

MOTHS

In pantries

- For pantry moths, place bay leaves at 50-cm intervals along shelves and inside containers that hold carbohydrates such as pasta and rice. It will take 3 weeks to get rid of the moths.

- For a serious problem, add 1 teaspoon of bay oil to 1 litre of water in a spray pack. Spray over surfaces and wipe with a cloth.
- Alternatively, wipe shelves with 1 drop of oil of pennyroyal on a cloth.

⚠ WARNING

Oil of pennyroyal can be harmful to pregnant women and pregnant pets.

In wardrobes

- To deter silverfish, mould and moths, place 1 camphor ball, 4 cloves, 2 drops of lavender oil and 2 drops of eucalyptus oil in a small muslin bag. (You could also use 6 cedar chips in place of the cloves or eucalyptus oil.) Tie it off and hang in your wardrobe. Replace eucalyptus and lavender oils every 2 months. Replace the rest yearly.

MOTOR OIL

(see 'Engine Grease')

MOULD

In wardrobes

- Wipe interior walls with 1/4 teaspoon of oil of cloves in a 250-ml bottle of baby oil on a cloth. Relabel the bottle.
- To absorb moisture, tie 6 sticks of white blackboard chalk together with string or ribbon and leave inside the wardrobe to absorb moisture. When the chalk sticks are wet, place them in the sun until they dry out. You can use them over and over again.

- To prevent mould from reoccuring (and to also deter silverfish and moths), place 1 camphor ball, 4 cloves, 2 drops of lavender oil and 2 drops of eucalyptus oil in a small muslin bag. (You could also use 6 cedar chips in place of the cloves or eucalyptus oil.) Tie it off and hang in your wardrobe. Replace eucalyptus and lavender oils every 2 months. Replace the rest yearly.
- For serious continuous damp, seek professional advice.

On carpet/upholstery (not leather/suede)

- Remove excess by vacuuming.
- Mix 1/4 teaspoon of oil of cloves in 1 litre of water in a spray pack.
- Lightly spray over the area.
- Sprinkle with uniodised salt.
- Scrub with a clean broom.
- Vacuum.

On cotton/fabric (not polyester satin/silk)

- Remove excess under the tap using cold water.
- Soak in 1/2 lid of *Vanish NapiSan Oxi Action* and 9 litres of blood-heat (body temperature) water for 20 minutes. Don't use on wool, silk or leather. (See also 'On Delicates', below.)
- If mould remains, add 1 kg of uniodised salt to a 9-litre bucket of water. Soak fabric overnight.
- Remove, gently wring but don't rinse, and hang in the shade to dry. A salt crust will form.
- Brush the salt off and the mould will come off with it.
- Wash according to the fabric. Dry on the clothesline or clothes airer.

On delicates

- Wipe with methylated spirits on a cloth.
- Add 1 cup of uniodised salt to a 9-litre bucket of blood-heat (body temperature) water.
- Immerse the garments and soak overnight (salt water won't damage delicates).
- Gently wring but don't rinse the items, hang to dry (shade is best) and a salty crust will form.
- When dry, brush the crust off with a soft brush and the mould will come away with it.
- Rinse in 1 teaspoon of cheap shampoo and blood-heat water.
- Gently wring and dry flat on a towel in the shade.

On leather

- Mix ¼ teaspoon of oil of cloves in a 250-ml bottle of baby oil. Shake the bottle and relabel it.
- Wipe the mixture with a cloth in even, parallel strokes across the entire panel of leather.

On polyester satin

- Aim a hair dryer at the satin until warm.
- Rub a clothes brush in the direction of the watery-looking part of the satin.
- If any mould remains, cover with uniodised salt and brush backwards and forwards with a clothes brush. The salt does the cleaning.

On silicone

- If mould is on the surface of the silicone, sprinkle with bicarb, spray with white vinegar and scrub with a toothbrush.

- If mould has penetrated the silicone, you may have to replace it. Test first by spraying with ¼ teaspoon of oil of cloves in 1 litre of water in a spray pack. Spray over the area and leave for 24 hours.
- To replace silicone, remove the old silicone with a special silicone remover or a very sharp knife. Then replace with new silicone or candle wax.

On silk

- Place coarse uniodised salt in the toe of pantyhose and tie off.
- Rub over the stain – with the grain of the silk – until the mould comes off.
- Hang in sunshine. Ensure it is dried away from the wind so the fibres don't tangle and leave a dusty look.

On suede

- Mix ¼ teaspoon of oil of cloves and 1 litre of water in a spray pack.
- Lightly mist over the suede.
- Leave in the shade to dry.
- Brush the mould off with a stiff brush. If any mould remains, repeat.

On timber

- For French polish or unsealed timber, wipe with ¼ teaspoon of oil of cloves in a 250-ml bottle of baby oil on a cloth. Relabel the bottle.
- For sealed timber, mix ¼ teaspoon of oil of cloves in 1 litre of water in a spray pack. Lightly spray and wipe with a damp cloth.

MOUTHWASH

On cotton/fabric

- Remove excess under the tap using cold water.
- Blot with or soak in white vinegar.
- If the mouthwash contains colour, soak in white vinegar and hang in sunshine until the colour fades.
- Wash according to the fabric. Dry on the clothesline or clothes airer.

On marble

- Remove excess by blotting with paper towel.
- Mix plaster of Paris and water to the consistency of peanut butter.
- Spread 5 mm to 1 cm thick over the stain.
- Allow to dry completely. If it feels cold on the back of your hand, it's not dry.
- When dry, brush away.

MUCOUS

On carpet/upholstery

- Remove excess by blotting with paper towel.
- Scribble with a cake of bathroom soap run under cold water.
- Massage with a couple of drops of dishwashing liquid on your fingertips until the liquid feels like jelly.
- Wipe with a damp cloth until the dishwashing liquid is removed.
- Absorb moisture by covering the area with paper towel. Place a book on top of the paper towel to assist with absorption.

On cotton/fabric

- Remove excess under the tap using cold water.
- Scribble with a cake of bathroom soap.
- Massage with a couple of drops of dishwashing liquid on your fingertips until the liquid feels like jelly.
- Rinse under blood-heat (body temperature) water.
- Wash according to the fabric. Dry on the clothesline or clothes airer.

MUD

On carpet/upholstery

- Allow the mud to dry or it will smear. Vacuum.
- For black mud, scribble with a cake of bathroom soap run under cold water.
- Wipe with a damp cloth until the soap is removed.
- Absorb moisture by covering the area with paper towel. Place a book on top of the paper towel to assist with absorption.
- For red mud, wipe with white spirits on a cloth.
- Sprinkle with talcum powder. Vacuum.
- If mud is on the surface, sprinkle with equal parts unprocessed wheat bran and bicarb. Scrub with a brush to loosen. Vacuum.

On cotton/fabric

- Remove excess under the tap using cold water.
- Soak in ½ lid of *Vanish NapiSan Oxi Action* and 9 litres of water for 20 minutes. Don't use on wool or silk. For wool and silk, scribble with a cake of bathroom soap run under cold water.

- Wash according to the fabric. Dry on the clothesline or clothes airer.

MULBERRY

(see 'Berry')

MUSTARD

On carpet/upholstery

- Remove excess by lifting with a plastic comb or by blotting with paper towel.
- Massage with a couple of drops of dishwashing liquid on your fingertips until the liquid feels like jelly.
- Wipe with a damp cloth until the dishwashing liquid is removed.
- If there are yellow marks, wipe with 2 drops of lavender oil on a cloth.
- Absorb moisture by covering the area with paper towel. Place a book on top of the paper towel to assist with absorption.

On cotton/fabric

- Remove excess under the tap using cold water.
- Massage with a couple of drops of dishwashing liquid on your fingertips until the liquid feels like jelly.
- Rinse using cold water.
- If there are yellow marks, wipe with 2 drops of lavender oil on a cloth.
- Wash according to the fabric. Dry on the clothesline or clothes airer.

On stone

- Massage with a couple of drops of dishwashing liquid on your fingertips until the liquid feels like jelly.
- Wipe with a damp cloth.
- If there are yellow marks, rub with 2 drops of lavender oil on a cloth.
- If stubborn, mix plaster of Paris and water to the consistency of peanut butter.
- To each cup of mixture, add 1 teaspoon of dishwashing liquid.
- Spread 5 mm to 1 cm thick over the stain.
- Allow to dry completely. If it feels cold on the back of your hand, it's not dry.
- When dry, brush away.

MYSTERY STAINS

If you don't know what the stain is, use this guide.

Proteins

- These have a dark ring around the edge and include blood, semen, seeds, nuts, meat, cheese, milk, other dairy and fish.
- To remove, use cold water and scribble with a cake of bathroom soap. For fabrics, rub the fabric against itself to loosen the stain. Wash according to the fabric. Don't use blood-heat (body temperature) or hot water, or you'll set the stain.

Carbohydrates

- These are darker in the centre, lighter around the edge and feel stiff. They include sugar, fruit, fruit juice, cakes, biscuits, lollies, soft drink, alcohol, honey and many plants. They also include starches, such as potato, rice, corn, ground corn, wheat-based products (pasta, couscous etc.), floury grain foods and wallpaper paste.
- To remove sugar stains, use blood-heat (body temperature) water and scribble with a cake of bathroom soap. For fabrics, rub the fabric against itself to loosen the stain. Wash according to the fabric.
- To remove starchy stains, use cold water and scribble with a cake of bathroom soap. For fabrics, rub the fabric against itself to loosen the stain. Wash according to the fabric. If in doubt, use cold water first.

Fats/oils

- These spread evenly across a surface, feel greasy between your fingers and, if you wash the stained garment, continue to spread. It's why a greasy chip mark on your T-shirt gets bigger every time you wash it. Stains include cooking oils (lighter in colour) and mechanical oils (darker in colour and more viscous).
- To remove lighter oils, massage with dishwashing liquid on your fingertips until the liquid feels like jelly. This means the oil has been emulsified and is water soluble. Wipe with a damp cloth.
- For darker or thicker oils, such as engine grease, use baby oil to dilute the stain before emulsifying with dishwashing liquid. Wipe with a damp cloth.

Pigments

- These include ink, paint, dye, rust and oxide and each requires a different solution.
- For ink stains, place rotten milk solids over the stain. The ink will be absorbed into the solids. Alternatively, rub with white spirits on a cotton bud.
- Permanent pen markers contain their own solvent, so write over the mark, and while it's wet, wipe with white spirits on a cotton bud.
- For children's or artists' watercolour paint, blot with water on a cloth until removed.
- For water-based paint, use methylated spirits on a cotton bud or cotton ball. For oil-based paint, use white spirits or turpentine on a cotton bud or cotton ball.
- For fresh vinyl-based paint, blot with a couple of drops of dishwashing liquid on a damp, cold cloth.
- For old vinyl-based paint, blot with methylated spirits on a cloth.
- To remove rust from hard surfaces, use *CLR* or *Ranex*. Always wear rubber gloves. Don't get *CLR* or *Ranex* on your skin because it can cause irritation. To remove rust from absorbent surfaces, use lemon juice and salt.
- For a vegetable-based stain, wipe with white vinegar on a cloth.
- For an oxide stain, wipe with 2 drops of glycerine on a cloth and remove any remaining colour by exposing the stain to ultraviolet light. Protect the area around the ultraviolet light with cardboard.

Resins

- These include sap, chewing gum, shellac, silicone, wax and glue and feel sticky to touch.

- For plant-based resins, such as tree sap, wipe with glycerine or tea tree oil.
- The solvent for shellac is methylated spirits applied with a cloth.
- For superglue, remove with superglue remover or acetone.
- For craft and PVA glues (which go on white and dry clear), use steam.
- For two-part epoxy glues (e.g. *Araldite*), remove with acetone.
- For gums and paper glues, wipe with a damp cloth.
- For contact adhesives, remove with tea tree oil.
- Glues used in children's crafts are made of carbohydrates, so use blood-heat (body temperature) water and a cake of bathroom soap and scribble over the stain.
- To remove silicone, carefully cut it off with a utility knife.

NAIL POLISH

On carpet

- Wrap a fine-toothed metal comb in a tissue so the teeth come through the tissue. Don't use a plastic comb because acetone, the solvent, will melt it.
- Wedge the comb underneath the stain and rub the stain with acetone on a cotton ball. Acetone can affect carpet so make sure it doesn't penetrate the base.
- Replace the tissue when wet.
- It's a slow process and may need to be repeated a few times.
- To remove the smell of acetone, wipe with equal parts methylated spirits or white vinegar and water on a tightly wrung cloth.
- Absorb moisture by covering the area with paper towel. Place a book on top of the paper towel to assist with absorption.

On cotton/fabric

- Hold a clean cotton ball behind the stain. Wipe with acetone on a cotton ball.
- Rub in a circular motion from the outside to the inside of the stain.
- Repeat until the nail polish colour is removed, replacing the cotton balls as you go.
- Wash according to the fabric. Dry on the clothesline or clothes airer.

On leather

- Make a ring of talcum powder around the nail polish mark to protect the leather around the stain.

- Wipe with acetone on a cotton bud, then wipe straight off with a clean cotton bud.
- Repeat until the nail polish is removed.
- To neutralise the acetone, wipe with white vinegar on a cotton bud.
- Sprinkle with talcum powder.
- When it dries, brush away with the back of your hand.
- Wipe with leather conditioner. Make your own – see **Household formulas**.

On timber

- For a polyurethane finish, wipe over only the nail polish with acetone on a cotton bud. Work quickly, using as little pressure and acetone as possible.
- When the colour is removed, wipe with white vinegar on a cloth.
- If the surface is dulled, polish with a little *Brasso* on a cloth.
- For oil-based varnish, shellac or wax-based surfaces, use the same technique but polish with a little beeswax rather than *Brasso*.
- Acetone can affect acrylic surfaces so you may need to reapply the acrylic.

On upholstery (not leather)

- Blot with acetone on a cotton bud.
- When removed, wipe with a little methylated spirits or white vinegar on a cotton bud. Do this quickly because acetone can damage the upholstery.

NAPPY

To clean

- Fill a bucket with nappy soaker (diluted with water according to the label).
- Fill another bucket with hot water and 1 teaspoon of tea tree oil.
- Shake the solids from the nappy into the toilet.
- Rinse the nappy under water.
- Place nappies in the first bucket and leave for 12 hours.
- Place nappies in the second bucket and leave for 20 minutes.
- Wash in the washing machine with hot water and 1 teaspoon of *Vanish NapiSan Oxi Action*.
- Add ½ cup of white vinegar to the rinse water (in the fabric conditioner slot).
- Dry in the sun.

NAPPY RASH CREAM

On carpet/upholstery

- Remove excess by lifting with a plastic comb or by blotting with paper towel.
- For lanolin-based cream, massage with a couple of drops of dishwashing liquid on your fingertips until the liquid feels like jelly. For zinc-based cream, sprinkle with talcum powder and scrub with pantyhose first.
- Mix 1 teaspoon of tea tree oil with 1 cup of cold water and wipe on with a cloth.
- Absorb moisture by covering the area with paper towel. Place a book on top of the paper towel to assist with absorption.

NEOPRENE

(see 'Wetsuit')

NEW CLOTHING

Always wash new clothes before wearing them to remove chemicals and fabric dressing.

To clean in a front-loading washing machine

- Use 1/8 of the recommended quantity of laundry detergent and 2 tablespoons of bicarb in the washing slot and 2 tablespoons of white vinegar in the fabric conditioner slot. Best temperature is 37°C – blood-heat water.
- After washing, hang clothing in sunshine to help break down the chemicals used in the fabric dressing. Don't use the dryer.

To clean in a top-loading washing machine

- Combine 1/4 of the recommended quantity of laundry detergent with 2 tablespoons of bicarb in the washing slot and 2 tablespoons of white vinegar in the fabric conditioner slot. Best temperature is 37°C – blood-heat (body temperature) water.
- After washing, hang clothing in sunshine to help break down the chemicals used in the fabric dressing. Don't use the dryer.

NEWSPAPER INK

On carpet/upholstery

- For surface marks, sprinkle with uniodised salt and scrub with a stiff brush.

- For deeper marks, blot with white vinegar on a cloth.
- For marks on large areas, place 1 cup of unprocessed wheat bran in a large bowl. Add drops of white vinegar one at a time, stirring as you go, until the mixture resembles breadcrumbs. It shouldn't be wet. Place in the toe of pantyhose and tie off.
- Rub the pantyhose across the surface as though using an eraser.
- If the ink is wet, rot some full cream milk in the sun and place the rotten milk solids over the stain. Leave until the ink is absorbed into the solids. Remove the solids by lifting with a plastic comb and wipe with a damp cloth.
- In all cases, absorb moisture by covering the area with paper towel. Place a book on top of the paper towel to assist with absorption.

On cotton/fabric

- Blot with or soak in white vinegar.
- Wash according to the fabric. Dry on the clothesline or clothes airer.

NOODLES

The stain is likely to be from oil.

On carpet/upholstery

- Remove excess by lifting with a plastic comb or by blotting with paper towel.
- Massage with a couple of drops of dishwashing liquid on your fingertips until the liquid feels like jelly.
- Wipe with a damp cloth until the dishwashing liquid is removed.

- For vegetable dye, blot with white vinegar on a cloth and expose to sunlight or ultraviolet light. (If using ultraviolet light, protect areas around the stain with cardboard.) Check every 2 hours.
- Absorb moisture by covering the area with paper towel. Place a book on top of the paper towel to assist with absorption.

On cotton/fabric

- Remove excess under the tap using cold water.
- Massage with a couple of drops of dishwashing liquid on your fingertips until the liquid feels like jelly.
- Rinse under blood-heat (body temperature) water.
- For vegetable dye, blot with white vinegar and hang in sunshine until the stain fades before washing.
- Wash according to the fabric. Dry on the clothesline or clothes airer.

NUTELLA

The stain is from protein, fat and sugar.

On carpet/upholstery

- Remove excess by lifting with a plastic comb or by blotting with paper towel.
- Scribble with a cake of bathroom soap run under cold water.
- Massage with a couple of drops of dishwashing liquid on your fingertips until the liquid feels like jelly.
- Wipe with a damp cloth until the dishwashing liquid is removed.

- Place white vinegar on a cloth and wring tightly so it's damp but not wet. Blot over the mark.
- Absorb moisture by covering the area with paper towel. Place a book on top of the paper towel to assist with absorption.

On cotton/fabric

- Remove excess under the tap using cold water.
- Scribble with a cake of bathroom soap run under cold water.
- Massage with a couple of drops of dishwashing liquid on your fingertips until the liquid feels like jelly.
- Blot with or soak in white vinegar.
- Wash according to the fabric. Dry on the clothesline or clothes airer.

ODOUR

For fish

- After cleaning, place equal parts dry mustard and bicarb on a tray inside the fridge.

In car

- Sprinkle bicarb over the upholstery.
- Leave for 20 minutes.
- Vacuum.
- Add 2 drops of lavender oil to a damp tea bag and place it over the air-conditioning intake vent.

In fridge

- Fill a small divided dish with vanilla essence on one side and bicarb on the other and place in the fridge.
- Don't forget to locate the source of the smell and remove it.

In shoes

- Mix 2 tablespoons of bicarb, 2 tablespoons of talcum powder, 1 drop of tea tree oil, 1 drop of oil of cloves and 1 drop of lavender oil.
- Place the mixture in the centre of a small piece of muslin or cotton voile and tie with string or ribbon to enclose. Alternatively, place in the toe of pantyhose.
- Pat in smelly shoes and on smelly feet. This also kills tinea.

On carpet/upholstery

- Sprinkle with bicarb. If you like scent, add a couple of drops of lavender oil.

- Sweep backwards and forwards over the surface with a brush.
- Leave for 20 minutes.
- Vacuum.

Overpowering perfume

- Mix 1 cup of cold black tea, 2 cups of cold water and 1/4 teaspoon of lavender oil in a spray pack.
- Spray over hard surfaces and wipe with a cloth.
- Lightly mist over upholstery.

OIL

(see 'Cooking Oil' or 'Engine Grease')

OINTMENT

On carpet/upholstery

- Remove excess by lifting with a plastic comb or by blotting with paper towel.
- For water-based ointments, scribble with a cake of bathroom soap run under blood-heat (body temperature) water. Massage with your fingertips until the stain is loosened. Wipe with a damp cloth. Repeat, if needed.
- For grey staining, massage with a couple of drops of dishwashing liquid on your fingertips until the liquid feels like jelly. Wipe with a damp cloth until the dishwashing liquid is removed.
- For antibacterial ointments, combine 1 teaspoon of grated bathroom soap, 1 teaspoon of dishwashing liquid and 1 tablespoon of boiling water and mix until the soap dissolves. Massage 2 drops of the solution into the stain using your fingertips until the solution feels like jelly.

Wipe with a cold, damp cloth followed by a dry cloth hand over hand, as though stroking a cat.

- For wax-based ointments, mix 2 drops of tea tree oil and 2 drops of dishwashing liquid and massage with your fingertips until the liquid feels like jelly. Wipe with a cold, damp cloth. Repeat, if needed.
- For liniment, wring a cloth in white vinegar, place over the stain and stand or sit on it for 5 seconds. Remove.
- In all cases, absorb moisture by covering the area with paper towel. Place a book on top of the paper towel to assist with absorption.

On cotton/fabric (not wool)

- Remove excess under the tap using blood-heat (body temperature) water.
- For water-based ointments, scribble with a cake of bathroom soap. Massage with your fingertips until the stain is loosened.
- For grey staining, massage with a couple of drops of dishwashing liquid on your fingertips until the liquid feels like jelly.
- For antibacterial ointments, mix together 1 teaspoon of grated bathroom soap, 1 teaspoon of dishwashing liquid and 1 tablespoon of boiling water. Allow the mixture to dissolve. Massage 2 drops of the solution into the stain with your fingertips until the solution feels like jelly.
- For wax-based ointments, mix 2 drops of tea tree oil with 2 drops of dishwashing liquid and massage with your fingertips until the liquid feels like jelly.
- For liniment, blot with or soak in white vinegar.
- In all cases, wash according to the fabric. Dry on the clothesline or clothes airer.

On wool

- Scribble with a cake of bathroom soap run under blood-heat (body temperature) water.
- Massage with a little cheap shampoo on your fingertips.
- Rinse in blood-heat water.
- Rinse in 1 teaspoon of cheap hair conditioner and blood-heat water.
- Gently wring and dry flat on a towel in the shade.

OLIVE OIL

(see 'Cooking Oil')

ORANGE JUICE

On carpet/upholstery

- For a fresh stain, remove excess by blotting with paper towel. Tightly wring a cloth in white vinegar and blot over the mark.
- For an old stain, wipe with 2 drops of glycerine on a toothbrush. Tightly wring a cloth in white vinegar, fold the cloth flat and polish out the glycerine without pushing it into the back of the carpet or upholstery.
- To remove dye, expose to sunlight or ultraviolet light. (If using ultraviolet light, protect areas around the stain with cardboard.) Check every 2 hours.
- In all cases, absorb moisture by covering the area with paper towel. Place a book on top of the paper towel to assist with absorption.

On cotton/fabric (not wool)

- Remove excess under the tap using cold water.
- Blot with or soak in white vinegar until the stain is removed. Alternatively, soak in ½ lid of *Vanish NapiSan Oxi Action* and 9 litres of water for 20 minutes. Don't use on wool, silk or leather.
- Wash according to the fabric. Dry in sunshine.

On wool

- Blot with or soak in white vinegar on a cloth.
- Massage with a little cheap shampoo on your fingertips.
- Rinse in blood-heat (body temperature) water.
- Rinse in 1 teaspoon of cheap hair conditioner and blood-heat water.
- Gently wring and dry flat on a towel in the shade. If there's an orange residue, dry in sunshine.

ORANGE OIL

(see 'Essential Oils')

OVEN

To clean

- Remove oven racks, rack supports, element and light cover.
- Place in the sink with a little dishwashing liquid and hot water.
- In a cold oven, sprinkle surfaces with bicarb, spray white vinegar on top and scrub with a nylon brush or rolled up pantyhose as the mixture fizzes.

- To clean the sides of the oven, dip one damp sponge in bicarb and dip another sponge in white vinegar. Press both sponges together with the white vinegar sponge on top and wipe over the sides of the oven.
- Rinse with a damp cloth.
- If there are stubborn stains or burns, reapply the bicarb and white vinegar several times and scrub with a nylon brush.
- Place a small mirror at the bottom of the oven to help you scrub the top of the oven. Remove when finished.

OYSTER

On carpet/upholstery

- Remove excess by lifting with a plastic comb or by blotting with paper towel.
- For natural oysters, scribble with a cake of bathroom soap run under cold water.
- Scrub with a toothbrush in all directions – north, south, east and west.
- Wipe with a damp cloth.
- To remove oily sauces, massage with a couple of drops of dishwashing liquid on your fingertips until the liquid feels like jelly.
- Wipe with a damp cloth until the dishwashing liquid is removed.
- To remove coloured sauces, wipe with white vinegar on a cloth.
- In all cases, absorb moisture by covering the area with paper towel. Place a book on top of the paper towel to assist with absorption.

On cotton/fabric

- Remove excess under the tap using cold water.
- For natural oysters, scribble with a cake of bathroom soap run under cold water. Rub the fabric against itself using your hands.
- To remove oily sauces, massage with a couple of drops of dishwashing liquid on your fingertips until the liquid feels like jelly.
- To remove coloured sauces, blot with or soak in white vinegar.
- In all cases, wash according to the fabric. Dry on the clothesline or clothes airer.

P

PAINT

There are three main types of paint: children's paint, vinyl-based paint and oil-based paint. In all cases, it's easier to remove the earlier you get to it.

On carpet/upholstery (not leather)

- Remove excess by lifting with a plastic comb or by blotting with paper towel. Try not to spread it.
- For children's and artists' watercolour paint, blot with water on a cloth until removed.
- For fresh vinyl-based paint, blot with a couple of drops of dishwashing liquid on a damp, cold cloth.
- For old vinyl-based paint, soak a cloth with methylated spirits and place it over the stain. Cover in plastic wrap. Leave for 1 hour.
- For water-based paint, use methylated spirits on a cotton bud or cotton ball.
- For both fresh and old oil-based paint, blot with white spirits or turpentine on a cloth. Then neutralise by wiping with white vinegar on a cloth.
- In all cases, absorb moisture by covering the area with paper towel. Place a book on top of the paper towel to assist with absorption.

On concrete/sandstone

- Remove excess by lifting with a plastic comb or blotting with paper towel.
- For children's and artists' watercolour paint, scrub with water on a brush. If stubborn, add a couple of drops of dishwashing liquid.

- For vinyl-based paint, soak a cloth in methylated spirits and place it over the stain. Cover in plastic wrap. Leave for 1 hour.
- If the paint comes away easily, scrub with methylated spirits on a stiff brush.
- If it doesn't come away, soak again with a cloth soaked in methylated spirits. Cover in plastic wrap. Leave for 1 hour. Then scrub again with methylated spirits on a stiff brush.
- For very old vinyl-based paint, use methyl ethyl ketone, or MEK. You must wear gloves and a mask. Apply with a bristle brush.

⚠ WARNING

MEK is very toxic.

- For oil-based paint, soak a cloth in white spirits or turpentine and place over the stain. Leave for 10 minutes. Scrub with a stiff brush.

On cotton/fabric

- For children's and artists' watercolour paint, rinse off using cold water. If stubborn, rub the fabric with 2 drops of dishwashing liquid until removed.
- For vinyl-based paint, place a clean cotton ball behind the stain, then wipe with methylated spirits on a cotton ball.
- For water-based paint, use methylated spirits on a cotton bud or cotton ball.
- For oil-based paint, place a clean cotton ball behind the stain, then wipe with white spirits or turpentine on a cotton ball.

- In all cases, wipe in a circular motion from the outside to the inside of the stain.
- If stubborn, soak in the appropriate solvent.
- In all cases, wash according to the fabric. Dry on the clothesline or clothes airer.

On leather

- For children's and artists' watercolour paint, wipe with a damp cloth.
- For acrylic, water-based or vinyl-based paint, apply methylated spirits on a cotton bud. Spin the bud over only the stained area.
- For oil-based paint, wipe with white spirits or turpentine on a cotton bud. Spin the bud over only the stained area. Sprinkle with talcum powder. When dry, brush off.
- In all cases, wipe with leather conditioner. Make your own – see **Household formulas**.

PAN

(see 'Pot or Pan')

PAPAYA

Dried/glacé

On carpet/upholstery

- Remove excess by lifting with a plastic comb or by blotting with paper towel.
- Scribble with a cake of bathroom soap run under blood-heat (body temperature) water.
- Scrub with a toothbrush or pantyhose in all directions – north, south, east and west.

- Blot with equal parts white vinegar and water on a cloth.
- Absorb moisture by covering the area with paper towel. Place a book on top of the paper towel to assist with absorption.
- When almost dry, repeat.
- If a shadow returns in a couple of weeks, repeat again.

On cotton/fabric

- Remove excess under the tap using cold water.
- Scribble with a cake of bathroom soap run under blood-heat (body temperature) water. Rub the fabric against itself using your hands.
- Rinse in equal parts white vinegar and water.
- Wash according to the fabric. Dry on the clothesline or clothes airer.

Fresh

On carpet/upholstery

- Remove excess by lifting with a plastic comb or by blotting with paper towel.
- Wipe with 2 drops of glycerine on a cotton ball or toothbrush.
- Sprinkle with talcum powder.
- When dry, vacuum.
- Alternatively, remove excess then wipe with white vinegar on a cloth.
- Absorb moisture by covering the area with paper towel. Place a book on top of the paper towel to assist with absorption.

On cotton/fabric

- Remove excess under the tap using cold water.
- Blot with or soak in white vinegar until the stain is removed.
- If stubborn, wipe with 2 drops of glycerine before blotting with white vinegar.
- Wash according to the fabric. Dry on the clothesline or clothes airer.

PARAFFIN WAX

On carpet/upholstery

- For hard paraffin wax, put ice cubes in a zip-lock bag and place on top of the wax. When the wax is chilled, remove it by lifting with a plastic comb.
- Vacuum.
- Wipe with 2 drops of tea tree oil on a cotton ball or cloth.
- For soft paraffin wax, massage with equal parts dishwashing liquid and tea tree oil on your fingertips until the liquid feels like jelly.
- Wipe with a damp cloth until removed.
- In both cases, absorb moisture by covering the area with paper towel. Place a book on top of the paper towel to assist with absorption.

On cotton/fabric

- For hard paraffin wax, place in the freezer for 15 minutes. Or place ice cubes on top of the wax.
- When the wax is chilled, remove as much as possible by rubbing the fabric with the wax on it against itself or scraping the wax off with a plastic comb.
- Rub 2 drops of tea tree oil over the wax residue.

- For soft paraffin wax, massage with equal parts dishwashing liquid and tea tree oil on your fingertips until the liquid feels like jelly.
- In both cases, wash according to the fabric. Dry on the clothesline or clothes airer.

On timber

- Rub with 2 drops of tea tree oil on a cloth.
- For French polish, dampen some silk and heat in the microwave in 10-second bursts. Rub over the wax until flush or even. This cuts through the wax without damaging the surface.

PASTA SAUCE

On carpet/upholstery

- Remove excess by lifting with a plastic comb or by blotting with paper towel.
- For cream sauces, scribble with a cake of bathroom soap run under cold water. Massage with a couple of drops of dishwashing liquid on your fingertips until the liquid feels like jelly. Wipe with a damp cloth until dishwashing liquid is removed.
- For green sauces, wipe with white spirits on a cloth. Place white vinegar on a cloth and wring tightly so it's damp but not wet. Blot over the mark.
- For tomato sauces, tightly wring a cloth in white vinegar and blot.
- To remove food colouring, expose to sunlight or ultraviolet light. (If using ultraviolet light, protect areas around the stain with cardboard.) Check every 2 hours.

- In all cases, absorb moisture by covering the area with paper towel. Place a book on top of the paper towel to assist with absorption.

On cotton/fabric

- Remove excess under the tap using cold water.
- For cream sauces, scribble with a cake of bathroom soap run under cold water. Massage with a couple of drops of dishwashing liquid on your fingertips until the liquid feels like jelly. Rinse using cold water.
- For green sauces, wipe with white spirits, then blot with or soak in white vinegar.
- For tomato sauces, blot with or soak in white vinegar. Massage with a couple of drops of dishwashing liquid on your fingertips until the liquid feels like jelly.
- In all cases, wash according to the fabric. Dry on the clothesline or clothes airer.

PÂTÉ

On carpet/upholstery

- Remove excess by lifting with a plastic comb or by blotting with paper towel.
- Scribble with a cake of bathroom soap run under cold water.
- Massage with a couple of drops of dishwashing liquid on your fingertips until the liquid feels like jelly.
- Wipe with a damp cloth until dishwashing liquid is removed.
- Absorb moisture by covering the area with paper towel. Place a book on top of the paper towel to assist with absorption.

On cotton/fabric

- Remove excess under the tap using cold water.
- Scribble with a cake of bathroom soap run under cold water.
- Massage with a couple of drops of dishwashing liquid on your fingertips until the liquid feels like jelly.
- Wash according to the fabric. Dry on the clothesline or clothes airer.

PAVLOVA

On carpet/upholstery

- Remove excess by lifting with a plastic comb or by blotting with paper towel.
- Mix ½ teaspoon of dishwashing liquid in cold water to generate a sudsy mix.
- Scrub with only the suds on a toothbrush in all directions – north, south, east and west.
- Massage with a couple of drops of dishwashing liquid on your fingertips until the liquid feels like jelly.
- Wipe with a damp cloth until dishwashing liquid is removed.
- Absorb moisture by covering the area with paper towel. Place a book on top of the paper towel to assist with absorption.
- Alternatively, remove excess then wipe with white spirits on a cotton ball.
- Sprinkle with talcum powder.
- When dry, vacuum.
- Also consult relevant fruits (e.g. 'Berry', 'Kiwi Fruit'), if needed.

On cotton/fabric

- Remove excess under the tap using blood-heat (body temperature) water.
- Massage with a little dishwashing liquid on your fingertips until the liquid feels like jelly.
- Rinse in blood-heat water.
- Wash according to the fabric. Dry on the clothesline or clothes airer.
- Also consult relevant fruits (e.g. 'Berry', 'Kiwi Fruit'), if needed.

PEACH

On carpet/upholstery

- Remove excess by lifting with a plastic comb or by blotting with paper towel.
- Wipe with 2 drops of glycerine on a cotton ball or toothbrush.
- Spray with *Vanish Preen Oxi Action Carpet Stain Remover.*
- When dry, vacuum.
- Alternatively, remove excess then wipe with white vinegar on a cloth.
- Absorb moisture by covering the area with paper towel. Place a book on top of the paper towel to assist with absorption.

On cotton/fabric

- Remove excess under the tap using cold water.
- Blot with or soak in white vinegar until the stain is removed.

- If stubborn, wipe with 2 drops of glycerine, then soak in white vinegar again.
- Wash according to the fabric. Dry on the clothesline or clothes airer.

PEANUT BUTTER

On carpet/upholstery

- Remove excess by lifting with a plastic comb or by blotting with paper towel.
- Massage with a couple of drops of dishwashing liquid on your fingertips until the liquid feels like jelly.
- Wipe with a damp cloth until dishwashing liquid is removed.
- Absorb moisture by covering the area with paper towel. Place a book on top of the paper towel to assist with absorption.

On cotton/fabric

- Remove excess by lifting with a plastic comb.
- Massage with a couple of drops of dishwashing liquid on your fingertips until the liquid feels like jelly.
- Rinse with blood-heat (body temperature) water.
- Wash according to the fabric. Dry on the clothesline or clothes airer.

On granite/marble/timber

- Mix plaster of Paris and water to the consistency of peanut butter.
- To each cup of mixture, add 1 teaspoon of dishwashing liquid.
- Spread 5 mm to 1 cm thick over the stain.

- Allow to dry completely. If it feels cold on the back of your hand, it's not dry.
- When dry, brush off with a broom or brush.

PEAR

On carpet/upholstery

- Remove excess by lifting with a plastic comb or by blotting with paper towel.
- Wipe with 2 drops of glycerine on a toothbrush.
- Leave for 90 minutes.
- Tightly wring a cloth in white vinegar, fold the cloth flat and polish out the glycerine without pushing it into the back of the carpet or upholstery.
- Absorb moisture by covering the area with paper towel. Place a book on top of the paper towel to assist with absorption.

On cotton/fabric

- Remove excess under the tap using cold water.
- Wipe with 2 drops of glycerine on your fingertips.
- Leave for 90 minutes.
- Wash according to the fabric. Dry on the clothesline or clothes airer.

PEAS

On carpet/upholstery

- Remove excess by lifting with a plastic comb or by blotting with paper towel.
- Wipe with 2 drops of glycerine on a cloth. Leave for 90 minutes.

- For a green stain, expose to sunlight or ultraviolet light. (If using ultraviolet light, protect areas around the stain with cardboard.) Check every 2 hours.
- Wipe with a damp cloth.
- Absorb moisture by covering the area with paper towel. Place a book on top of the paper towel to assist with absorption.

On cotton/fabric

- Remove excess under the tap using cold water.
- Wipe with 2 drops of glycerine on a cloth. Leave for 90 minutes.
- Blot with or soak in white vinegar until the stain is removed.
- Wash according to the fabric. Dry on the clothesline or clothes airer.

On timber

- For a polyurethane finish, polish with equal parts glycerine and talcum powder on a cloth.
- For a shellac finish, wipe with beeswax on a cloth.
- To remove a green stain, expose to sunlight or ultraviolet light. (If using ultraviolet light, protect areas around the stain with cardboard.) Check every 2 hours.

PEN

(see also 'Fluorescent Pen')

There are several types of ink used in pens. Test the solvent using a cotton bud.

Ballpoint Pen/Bottled Ink (Non-gel)

On carpet/upholstery (not leather)

- Rot some full cream milk in the sun.
- Place the rotten milk solids on the stain and rub in circles with your hands.
- When the ink is absorbed, remove and wipe stain with a damp cloth.
- Scribble with a cake of bathroom soap run under blood-heat (body temperature) water.
- Wipe with a damp cloth.
- Absorb moisture by covering the area with paper towel. Place a book on top of the paper towel to assist with absorption.
- Alternatively, wipe with white spirits on a cloth or cotton bud.
- Sprinkle with talcum powder.
- When dry, vacuum.

On cotton/fabric

- Rot some full cream milk in the sun. Place the rotten milk solids over the stain. For red ink, wipe with white spirits on a cotton ball first.
- Leave until the ink is absorbed into the solids.
- Remove the solids under cold water.
- Scribble with a cake of bathroom soap run under blood-heat (body temperature) water. Rub the fabric against itself using your hands.
- Wash according to the fabric. Dry on the clothesline or clothes airer.

On leather

- Wipe over the mark with white spirits on a cotton bud. If there's a watermark, wipe with white spirits in even, parallel strokes over the entire panel of leather.
- Sprinkle evenly with talcum powder.
- When dry, brush with a soft brush.
- Wipe with leather conditioner. Make your own – see **Household formulas**.

On stone

- Rot some full cream milk in the sun.
- Place the milk solids over the stain.
- Leave until the ink bleeds into the solids.
- Remove with a damp cloth.

On timber

- Wipe with white spirits on a cotton bud.
- Alternatively, rot some full cream milk in the sun. Place the solids over the stain until the ink is absorbed.
- In both cases, wipe with a damp cloth.

Felt Pen

- For children's felt pen, wipe with methylated spirits on a cotton bud or cotton ball.
- For adults' felt pen, wipe with white spirits on a cotton bud or cotton ball. Work from the outside to the inside of the stain.

Gel Pen

- To identify a gel pen, look to see if there's a ball of clear liquid at the end of the gel in the plastic tube.
- Wipe with methylated spirits on a cotton bud.

Liquid Marker

On carpet/upholstery

- The solvent is either methylated spirits or white spirits.
- Test by wiping with the solvent on a cotton bud. If marker colour comes away, that's the solvent.
- Wipe the solvent in circles on a cotton ball. Keep replacing the ball until the stain is removed.
- Sprinkle with talcum powder.
- When dry, vacuum.

On cotton/fabric

- The solvent is either methylated spirits or white spirits.
- Test by wiping with the solvent on a cotton bud. If marker colour comes away, that's the solvent.
- Blot with or soak in the solvent.
- Wash according to the fabric. Dry on the clothesline or clothes airer.

On timber

- Write over the mark using the same pen.
- Wipe with white spirits on a cotton bud.

Permanent Marker

- Permanent marker contains its own solvent, so draw over the mark with the same permanent marker.
- Wipe with white spirits on a cotton bud or cotton ball.
- Sprinkle with talcum powder.

Texta

- Wipe with methylated spirits on a cotton bud or cotton ball.

Whiteboard Marker

- Wipe with methylated spirits on a cotton bud or cotton ball.

PENCIL

(Lead; see also 'Coloured Pencil')

On carpet/upholstery

- Rub with a soft pencil eraser.
- Wipe with white spirits on a cloth.
- If stubborn, wring a cloth in white spirits and place over the mark. Leave for 30 minutes.
- Sprinkle with talcum powder.
- When dry, vacuum.

On cotton/fabric

- Rub with a soft pencil eraser.
- Wipe with white spirits on a cloth.
- If stubborn, wring a cloth in white spirits and place over the mark. Leave for 30 minutes.
- Wash according to the fabric. Dry on the clothesline or clothes airer.

On stone

- Rub with a pencil eraser.
- If stubborn, mix plaster of Paris and water to the consistency of peanut butter.

- To each cup of mixture, add 1 teaspoon of white spirits.
- Spread 5 mm to 1 cm thick over the stain.
- Allow to dry completely. If it feels cold on the back of your hand, it's not dry.
- When dry, brush away.

On walls

- Rub with a pencil eraser. Wipe with a damp cloth.
- Alternatively, wipe stain with a slice of brown bread.

PERFUME

On carpet/upholstery

- Absorb excess by blotting with paper towel.
- Lightly brush with 2 drops of glycerine on a toothbrush. Leave for 90 minutes.
- Tightly wring a cloth in white vinegar, fold the cloth flat and polish out the glycerine without pushing it into the back of the carpet or upholstery.
- Absorb moisture by covering the area with paper towel. Place a book on top of the paper towel to assist with absorption.

On cotton/fabric

- Soak in ½ lid of *Vanish NapiSan Oxi Action* and 9 litres of cold water for 30 minutes. Don't use on wool or silk. For wool and silk, blot with or soak in white vinegar. Rinse in 1 teaspoon of cheap shampoo and blood-heat (body temperature) water.
- Wash according to the fabric. Dry on the clothesline or clothes airer.

On stone

- Wipe with glycerine on a cloth.
- If stubborn, mix plaster of Paris and water to the consistency of peanut butter.
- To each cup of mixture, add 1 teaspoon of glycerine.
- Spread 5 mm to 1 cm thick over the stain.
- Allow to dry completely. If it feels cold on the back of your hand, it's not dry.
- When dry, brush away.

On timber

- Absorb excess by blotting with paper towel.
- Wipe with a paste of bicarb and water on a cloth.
- Wipe with a damp cloth.
- If bleached, leave a damp tea bag over the timber.
- If perfume has removed the sealant, you'll need to revarnish the timber.

PERMANENT MARKER

(see 'Pen')

PERSPIRATION

(see 'Body Odour/Perspiration')

PESTO

On carpet/upholstery

- Remove excess by lifting with a plastic comb or by blotting with paper towel.
- Sprinkle with bicarb or talcum powder to absorb the oil. Vacuum.

- Massage with a couple of drops of dishwashing liquid on your fingertips until the liquid feels like jelly.
- Wipe with a damp cloth until dishwashing liquid is removed.
- For a green stain, brush with 2 drops of glycerine on a toothbrush. Leave for 90 minutes. Tightly wring a cloth in white vinegar, fold the cloth flat and polish out the glycerine without pushing it into the back of the carpet or upholstery.
- In all cases, absorb moisture by covering the area with paper towel. Place a book on top of the paper towel to assist with absorption.

On cotton/fabric

- Remove excess under the tap using blood-heat (body temperature) water.
- Massage with a couple of drops of dishwashing liquid on your fingertips until the liquid feels like jelly.
- For a green stain, remove excess then wipe with 2 drops of glycerine. Leave for 90 minutes. Blot with white vinegar.
- In all cases, wash according to the fabric. Dry on the clothesline or clothes airer.

PETS

(see 'Cat Hair', 'Cat Urine', 'Dog Hair', 'Dog Poo' or 'Dog Urine')

PETROL

On carpet/upholstery (not leather)

- Put on rubber gloves to protect your hands from the petrol.

- Wipe with white spirits on a cotton ball or cloth.
- Sprinkle with talcum powder.
- When dry, vacuum.
- Mix 1 teaspoon of dishwashing liquid in cold water to generate suds.
- Scrub with only the suds on a toothbrush in all directions – north, south, east and west.
- Wipe with a damp cloth.
- Absorb moisture by covering the area with paper towel. Place a book on top of the paper towel to assist with absorption.

On cotton/fabric

- Put on rubber gloves to protect your hands from the petrol.
- Massage with a couple of drops of dishwashing liquid on your fingertips until the liquid feels like jelly.
- Rinse under blood-heat (body temperature) water.
- Sprinkle with talcum powder.
- If staining remains, soak in white vinegar for 30 minutes.
- Wash according to the fabric. Dry on the clothesline or clothes airer.

On leather

- Put on rubber gloves to protect your hands from the petrol.
- Wipe with white spirits on a cotton ball. Wipe in even, parallel strokes over the entire panel of leather.
- Sprinkle with talcum powder.
- When dry, brush off.
- Wipe with leather conditioner. Make your own – see **Household formulas**.

On pavers

- Put on rubber gloves to protect your hands from the petrol.
- Mix plaster of Paris and water to the consistency of peanut butter.
- To every cup of mixture, add 1 teaspoon of dishwashing liquid.
- Spread 5 mm to 1 cm thick over the stain.
- Allow to dry completely. If it feels cold on the back of your hand, it's not dry.
- When dry, brush off.

PETROLEUM JELLY

On carpet/upholstery

- Remove excess by lifting with a plastic comb or by blotting with paper towel.
- Massage with a couple of drops of dishwashing liquid on your fingertips until the liquid feels like jelly.
- Wipe with a damp cloth until dishwashing liquid is removed.
- Absorb moisture by covering the area with paper towel. Place a book on top of the paper towel to assist with absorption.

On cotton/fabric (not wool)

- Remove excess by blotting with a cloth.
- Massage with a couple of drops of dishwashing liquid on your fingertips until the liquid feels like jelly.
- Wash according to the fabric. Dry on the clothesline or clothes airer.

On wool

- Massage with 1 teaspoon of cheap shampoo using your fingertips.
- Rinse in 1 teaspoon of cheap hair conditioner and blood-heat (body temperature) water.
- Rinse under blood-heat water.
- Gently wring and dry flat on a towel in the shade.

TIP

Waterproof leather shoes by wiping with petroleum jelly and placing in the sunshine for half an hour.

PIANO

To clean

- Wipe with furniture polish. Make your own – see **Household formulas**.
- Clean plastic keys with 2 drops of glycerine on a cloth.
- Clean ivory keys (which have slightly uneven parallel lines along them) with sweet almond oil on a cloth. If noticeably dirty, wipe with methylated spirits first. If the keys are really dirty, use a small quantity of non-gel toothpaste mixed with water and apply carefully with a cotton bud, then apply sweet almond oil to protect the ivory from cracking.
- Clean ivorite keys (which have even parallel lines along them) with methylated spirits on a cloth.

PICKLE

On carpet/upholstery (not leather)

- Remove excess pickle by lifting with a plastic comb or by blotting with paper towel.
- Wipe with white vinegar on a cloth.
- For yellow marks, mix 1 teaspoon of 3 per cent hydrogen peroxide in 2 cups of water. Tightly wring a cloth in the mixture and blot over the mark.
- Absorb moisture by covering the area with paper towel. Place a book on top of the paper towel to assist with absorption.

On cotton/fabric (not wool)

- Remove excess under the tap using hot water.
- Blot with or soak in white vinegar until the stain is removed.
- For yellow marks, mix 1 teaspoon of 3 per cent hydrogen peroxide in 2 cups of water. Soak item for 30 minutes.
- Rinse under hot water.
- Wash according to the fabric. Dry on the clothesline or clothes airer.

On leather

- Remove excess by blotting with paper towel.
- Wipe only the stain with white vinegar on a cloth.
- Sprinkle with bicarb.
- When dry, brush off.
- Wipe with leather conditioner. Make your own – see **Household formulas**.

On wool

- Massage with 1 teaspoon of cheap shampoo using your fingertips.
- Rinse in 1 teaspoon of cheap hair conditioner and blood-heat (body temperature) water.
- Gently wring and dry flat on a towel in the shade.

PINEAPPLE

On carpet/upholstery

- Remove excess by blotting with paper towel.
- Place white vinegar on a cloth and wring tightly so it's damp but not wet. Blot over the mark.
- If staining remains, spray with *Vanish Preen Oxi Action Carpet Stain Remover.*
- Leave for 30 minutes.
- When dry, vacuum.

On cotton/fabric

- Remove excess under the tap using cold water.
- Blot with or soak in white vinegar.
- For brown marks, wipe with 2 drops of glycerine on a cloth. Leave for 90 minutes.
- Wash according to the fabric. Dry on the clothesline or clothes airer.

PIZZA

The stain is from protein, fats and tomato sauce.

On carpet/upholstery

- Remove excess by lifting with a plastic comb or by blotting with paper towel.

- Scribble with a cake of bathroom soap run under cold water.
- Wipe with a damp cloth.
- Massage with a couple of drops of dishwashing liquid on your fingertips until the liquid feels like jelly.
- Wipe with a damp cloth until dishwashing liquid is removed.
- To remove tomato sauce, tightly wring a cloth in white vinegar and blot over the mark.
- Absorb moisture by covering the area with paper towel. Place a book on top of the paper towel to assist with absorption.

On cotton/fabric

- Remove excess by lifting with a plastic comb or by blotting with paper towel.
- Scribble with a cake of bathroom soap run under cold water.
- Massage with a couple of drops of dishwashing liquid on your fingertips until the liquid feels like jelly.
- Rinse in blood-heat (body temperature) water.
- To remove tomato sauce, blot with or soak in white vinegar.
- Wash according to the fabric. Dry on the clothesline or clothes airer.

PLASTER

On carpet/upholstery

- Remove excess by scrubbing with a stiff brush or comb. Vacuum as you scrub.
- For old plaster, blot with white vinegar on a cloth. Scrub with a brush. Vacuum as you scrub.

On cotton/fabric

- Remove excess by scrubbing with a stiff brush.
- Blot with or soak in white vinegar.
- Wash according to the fabric. Dry on the clothesline or clothes airer.

PLASTICINE

On carpet/upholstery

- Remove excess by lifting with a plastic comb.
- Massage with 2 drops of dishwashing liquid and 2 drops of lavender oil on your fingertips until the mixture feels like jelly.
- Wipe with a damp cloth until dishwashing liquid is removed.
- Absorb moisture by covering the area with paper towel. Place a book on top of the paper towel to assist with absorption.

On cotton/fabric

- Remove excess under the tap using blood-heat (body temperature) water.
- Massage with 2 drops of dishwashing liquid and 2 drops of lavender oil on your fingertips until the mixture feels like jelly.
- Wash according to the fabric. Dry on the clothesline or clothes airer.

PLAY DOUGH

On carpet/upholstery

- Allow to dry. Scrub with a stiff brush and vacuum as you scrub.
- Scrub with a little uniodised salt on pantyhose or toothbrush.
- For large areas, sprinkle with unprocessed wheat bran.
- To remove colour, wipe with white vinegar on a cloth and expose to sunlight or ultraviolet light. (If using ultraviolet light, protect areas around the stain with cardboard.) Check every 2 hours.
- Vacuum thoroughly.
- Repeat until removed.

On cotton/fabric

- Allow to dry.
- Scrub with a little uniodised salt on pantyhose or toothbrush.
- To remove colour, blot with or soak in white vinegar. Hang in sunshine until the stain fades before washing.
- Wash according to the fabric. Dry on the clothesline or clothes airer.

PLUM

On carpet/upholstery

- Remove excess by blotting with paper towel.
- Place white vinegar on a cloth and wring tightly so it's damp but not wet. Blot over the mark.

- For a brown mark, wipe with 2 drops of glycerine on a toothbrush. Leave for 90 minutes. Scribble with a cake of bathroom soap run under cold water. Place equal parts white vinegar and water on a cloth and wring tightly so it's damp but not wet. Blot over the mark.
- Absorb moisture by covering the area with paper towel. Place a book on top of the paper towel to assist with absorption.

On cotton/fabric

- Remove excess under the tap using cold water.
- Blot with or soak in white vinegar until the stain is removed.
- For a brown mark, wipe with 2 drops of glycerine on a cloth. Leave for 90 minutes. Scribble with a cake of bathroom soap under cold water. Rub the fabric against itself using your hands.
- Wash according to the fabric. Dry on the clothesline or clothes airer.

POLISHED CONCRETE

To clean floor

- Sprinkle with a little bicarb. Spray with white vinegar.
- While fizzing, scrub with a broom.
- Wipe with an old T-shirt wrapped around a broom. Allow to dry.
- Apply carnauba wax with a polishing machine (available from hire companies or vacuum cleaner shops). Don't use beeswax because it's too soft.

To clean concrete benches

- Sprinkle with bicarb, spray with white vinegar and scrub with a nylon brush.
- For stains, mix plaster of Paris and water to the consistency of peanut butter. Place over the stain, allow to dry completely, then brush away.
- To seal, use liquid marble wax *CeraFluida*. Apply a small amount with a cloth and allow to dry.

POLLEN

On carpet/upholstery

- Remove excess by lifting with a plastic comb. Be careful not to spread the pollen.
- Rub with 2 drops of lavender oil on a cloth until removed.

On cotton/fabric

- Remove excess by lifting with a plastic comb. Don't spread the pollen.
- Put a dry cotton ball behind the stain, then blot the front of the stain with lavender oil on a cotton ball.
- Wash according to the fabric. Dry on the clothesline or clothes airer.

On hard surfaces

- Rub with 2 drops of lavender oil on rolled up pantyhose.

POMEGRANATE

On carpet/upholstery

- Remove excess by lifting with a plastic comb or by blotting with paper towel.

- Sprinkle with bicarb. It will turn blue.
- Vacuum.
- Place white vinegar on a cloth and wring tightly so it's damp but not wet. Blot over the mark.
- Absorb moisture by covering the area with paper towel. Place a book on top of the paper towel to assist with absorption.

On cotton/fabric

- Remove excess under the tap using cold water.
- Massage with a couple of drops of dishwashing liquid on your fingertips until the liquid feels like jelly.
- Rinse in cold water.
- Blot with or soak in white vinegar until the stain is removed.
- Wash according to the fabric. Dry in sunshine.

POO

(see 'Faeces'; see also 'Bat Poo', 'Bird Poo' or 'Dog Poo')

POPCORN

The stain is from the butter or margarine melted on top.

On carpet/upholstery

- Remove excess by lifting with a plastic comb or by blotting with paper towel.
- Massage with a couple of drops of dishwashing liquid on your fingertips until the liquid feels like jelly.
- Wipe with a damp cloth until dishwashing liquid is removed.

- Absorb moisture by covering the area with paper towel. Place a book on top of the paper towel to assist with absorption.

On cotton/fabric

- Remove excess under the tap using cold water.
- Massage with a couple of drops of dishwashing liquid on your fingertips until the liquid feels like jelly.
- Wash according to the fabric. Dry on the clothesline or clothes airer.

POSSUM

For urine

- Clean in the direction of the pee. If it has penetrated the ceiling, you'll need to get into the roof and spray the top side of the ceiling with white vinegar. Repeat 3 days later.

To deter

- Wipe access areas with naphthalene flakes. Or place 1 mothball in 1 litre of water in a spray pack and spray over access areas. Or smear *Vicks VapoRub* around access areas.

⚠ WARNING

Don't use mothballs or napthalene flakes if you have children under 3 years of age.

- Alternatively, consult a professional, who will find access points, remove the possums and block their re-entry. Or borrow a cat.

POTATO CHIPS

(Hot)

On carpet/upholstery

- Remove excess by lifting with a plastic comb or by blotting with paper towel.
- Massage with a couple of drops of dishwashing liquid on your fingertips until the liquid feels like jelly.
- Wipe with a damp cloth until the dishwashing liquid is removed.
- Absorb moisture by covering the area with paper towel. Place a book on top of the paper towel to assist with absorption.

On cotton/fabric

- Remove excess under the tap using cold water.
- Massage with a couple of drops of dishwashing liquid on your fingertips until the liquid feels like jelly.
- Wash according to the fabric. Dry on the clothesline or clothes airer.

TIP

If you don't have a sink plug, as a short-term solution, make one from potato. Measure by placing foil inside the plughole and cut the potato to size. The potato will expand in the plughole when you add water.

POT or PAN

For burns

- Sprinkle with bicarb, splash with white vinegar and, while fizzing, scrub with a nylon brush.

- For bad burns, cover with 1 cm of white vinegar and place in the freezer.
- When the vinegar is frozen, remove and allow to partially thaw. Then scrub with a nylon brush.
- If the pot won't fit in the freezer, sprinkle with bicarb followed by white vinegar and scrub with a nylon brush. Repeat until clean.

For rust

- Cut a potato in half and cover one of the cut ends with bicarb.
- Rub, cut end down, over the rust.

PRAM

To clean

- To clean plastic, mix 1 teaspoon of dishwashing liquid with 1 litre of water in a spray pack.
- Spray the mixture over the pram and scrub with a brush.
- Rinse with water on a cloth. Dry in sunshine.
- To clean canvas, mix 1 kg of uniodised salt and 1/4 teaspoon of oil of cloves in a 9-litre bucket of water. Allow to dissolve.
- Scrub with the mixture using a nylon brush.
- Leave in the sun until dry, then brush off the salt.
- To clean aluminium, wipe with a damp tea bag in the toe of pantyhose.

PRAWN

On carpet/upholstery

- Remove excess by lifting with a plastic comb or by blotting with paper towel.

- Scribble with a cake of bathroom soap run under cold water.
- Wipe with a damp cloth.
- Absorb moisture by covering the area with paper towel. Place a book on top of the paper towel to assist with absorption.

On cotton/fabric

- Remove excess under the tap using cold water.
- Scribble with a cake of bathroom soap run under cold water. Rub the fabric against itself using your hands.
- Wash according to the fabric. Dry on the clothesline or clothes airer.

PUMPKIN

On carpet/upholstery

- Remove excess by lifting with a plastic comb or by blotting with paper towel.
- Place white vinegar on a cloth and wring tightly so it's damp but not wet. Blot over the mark.
- To remove an orange stain, expose to sunlight or ultraviolet light. (If using ultraviolet light, protect areas around the stain with cardboard.) Check every 2 hours.
- Absorb moisture by covering the area with paper towel. Place a book on top of the paper towel to assist with absorption.

On cotton/fabric (not wool)

- Remove excess under the tap using cold water.
- Blot with or soak in white vinegar until the stain is removed.
- Wash according to the fabric. Dry in sunshine.

On wool

- Place equal parts white vinegar and cold water on a cloth and wring tightly so it's damp but not wet. Blot over the mark.
- If the stain has set, wipe with 2 drops of lavender oil on a cloth. Leave for 20 minutes.
- Wash in 1 teaspoon of cheap shampoo and blood-heat (body temperature) water.
- Rinse in blood-heat water.
- Gently wring and dry flat on a towel in the shade.

R

RAISINS

On carpet/upholstery

- Remove excess by lifting with a plastic comb or by blotting with paper towel.
- Mix equal parts white vinegar and blood-heat (body temperature) water.
- Scrub the mixture over the stain with a toothbrush or pantyhose in all directions – north, south, east and west.
- Absorb moisture by covering the area with paper towel. Place a book on top of the paper towel to assist with absorption.
- When almost dry, repeat.
- If a shadow returns in a couple of weeks, repeat again.

On cotton/fabric

- Remove excess under the tap using cold water.
- Blot with or soak in white vinegar.
- Wash according to the fabric. Dry on the clothesline or clothes airer.

RASPBERRY

(see 'Berry')

RED CABBAGE

On carpet/upholstery

- Remove excess by lifting with a plastic comb or by blotting with paper towel.
- Mix 1 teaspoon of dishwashing liquid in cold water to generate suds.

- Scrub with only the suds on a toothbrush in all directions – north, south, east and west.
- Wipe with a damp cloth.
- For a blue stain, expose to sunlight or ultraviolet light. (If using ultraviolet light, protect areas around the stain with cardboard.) Check every 2 hours.
- Absorb moisture by covering the area with paper towel. Place a book on top of the paper towel to assist with absorption.

On cotton/fabric

- Remove excess under the tap using cold water.
- Scribble with a cake of bathroom soap. Rub the fabric against itself using your hands.
- For a blue stain, wipe with white vinegar and hang in sunshine before washing.
- Wash according to the fabric. Dry on the clothesline or clothes airer.

RED WINE

(see 'Wine')

RELISH

On carpet/upholstery

- Remove excess by lifting with a plastic comb or by blotting with paper towel.
- Place white vinegar on a cloth and wring tightly so it's damp but not wet. Blot over the mark.
- For yellow stains, wipe with 2 drops of lavender oil on a cloth.

- To remove colouring, expose to sunlight or ultraviolet light. (If using ultraviolet light, protect areas around the stain with cardboard.) Check every 2 hours.
- In all cases, absorb moisture by covering the area with paper towel. Place a book on top of the paper towel to assist with absorption.

On cotton/fabric

- Remove excess under the tap using cold water.
- Blot with or soak in white vinegar until the stain is removed.
- For yellow stains, wipe with 2 drops of lavender oil on a cloth.
- Wash according to the fabric. Dry in sunshine.

RHUBARB

On carpet/upholstery

- Remove excess by lifting with a plastic comb or by blotting with paper towel.
- Wipe with methylated spirits on a cloth.
- Place white vinegar on a cloth and wring tightly so it's damp but not wet. Blot over the mark.
- For a brown stain, wipe with 2 drops of glycerine on a toothbrush. Leave for 90 minutes. Tightly wring a cloth in white vinegar, fold the cloth flat and polish out the glycerine without pushing it into the back of the carpet or upholstery.
- Absorb moisture by covering the area with paper towel. Place a book on top of the paper towel to assist with absorption.

On cotton/fabric

- Remove excess under the tap using cold water.
- Wipe with methylated spirits on a cloth.
- Blot with or soak in white vinegar.
- For a brown stain, wipe with glycerine. Leave for 90 minutes.
- Wash according to the fabric. Dry on the clothesline or clothes airer.

RICE

On carpet/upholstery

- Remove excess by lifting with a plastic comb or by blotting with paper towel.
- Scribble with a cake of bathroom soap run under cold water.
- Blot with a damp cloth.
- Absorb moisture by covering the area with paper towel. Place a book on top of the paper towel to assist with absorption.

In pot or pan

- Add white vinegar 1 cm deep to the burnt pot or pan.
- Place in the freezer.
- When the vinegar freezes, remove and allow to thaw.
- Sprinkle with bicarb and, while fizzing, scrub with a nylon brush.
- If the pot won't fit in the freezer, sprinkle with bicarb followed by white vinegar and scrub with a nylon brush. Repeat until clean.

TIP

To pick up wet rice or other gluggy food from the floor, turn on the vacuum cleaner and suck up one leg of a pair of pantyhose before wrapping the end of the pantyhose around the vacuum cleaner head. Secure tightly. Suck up paper towel. Then suck up the food. It will stick to the paper towel at the end of the pantyhose leg. Turn off the vacuum cleaner and remove the pantyhose.

ROCKMELON

On carpet/upholstery

- Remove excess by lifting with a plastic comb or by blotting with paper towel.
- Place white vinegar on a cloth and wring tightly so it's damp but not wet. Blot over the mark.
- Wipe with a damp cloth.
- Absorb moisture by covering the area with paper towel. Place a book on top of the paper towel to assist with absorption.

On cotton/fabric

- Remove excess under the tap using cold water.
- Blot with or soak in white vinegar until the stain is removed.
- Wash according to the fabric. Dry on the clothesline or clothes airer.

On hard surfaces

- Remove excess and sprinkle surface with bicarb.
- Spray with white vinegar.
- While fizzing, scrub with a nylon brush.

- Wipe with a damp cloth.
- For marble, wipe with a cake of bathroom soap and cold water on pantyhose. Do not use white vinegar on marble.

ROSE OIL

(see 'Essential Oils')

RUBBER

For perishing

- Scrub with uniodised salt.
- Mix equal parts talcum powder and glycerine and wipe over the rubber. This slows the perishing process. It's great for windscreen wiper blades.

TIP

Don't leave anything made of rubber sitting in sunshine. It will accelerate the perishing process.

RUBBER MARK

On carpet/upholstery

- Remove excess by wiping with a damp cloth.
- Sprinkle with uniodised salt and rub with pantyhose.
- Wipe with a damp cloth.
- Vacuum.

On concrete/timber

- Sprinkle with coarse uniodised salt.
- Sweep with a stiff broom.
- Rinse with a hose.

On cotton/fabric

- Wipe with a damp pencil eraser.
- Scrub with uniodised salt on a brush.
- Wash according to the fabric. Dry on the clothesline or clothes airer.

On stone

- Wipe with acetone on a cloth.

RUST

In cake tins

- Fill with 1 teaspoon of white vinegar mixed with water and stand overnight.
- Rinse in water.

In cast-iron cooking pot

- Add enough cooking oil to cover the base of the pot.
- Place the pot over low heat. When the oil starts to fume, turn off the heat and allow to cool. This seasons the pan and prevents further rust.
- When cool, rub with paper towel.

In toilet

- Hard water fur is crystalline mineral growth from water. It's often prickly, black deposits, but the colour can vary depending on the water and pipes. Hard water fur can cause rust.

- To clean hard water fur from the cistern, put ton disposable rubber gloves, then put ½ cap of *CLR* or *Ranex* into the cistern and leave for 1 hour. Flush the toilet.
- For heavy staining, put on disposable rubber gloves and wipe the toilet bowl with *CLR* or *Ranex* on a cloth. Don't use *CLR* or *Ranex* as a regular cleaner – it only removes calcium, lime or rust.

⚠ WARNING

Don't use CLR *or* Ranex *on your skin because it can cause irritation.*

On aluminium

- Cut a potato in half and dip one of the cut surfaces in bicarb.
- Rub the bicarb end over the rust.
- Rinse with water.

On carpet/upholstery

- Place a small mountain of uniodised salt over each rust mark.
- Squeeze drops of fresh lemon juice over each mountain of salt until it's moist but doesn't collapse. Stop squeezing before the juice hits the bottom of the salt.
- Expose to sunlight or ultraviolet light for at least 4 hours. The rust will be absorbed into the salt.
- Vacuum.

On cotton/fabric (not wool)

- Place a small mountain of uniodised salt over each rust mark.

- Squeeze drops of fresh lemon juice over each mountain of salt until it's moist but doesn't collapse. Stop squeezing before the juice hits the bottom of the salt.
- Leave in sunshine for at least 4 hours. The rust will be absorbed into the salt. It could take a few attempts before the rust shifts.
- Wash according to the fabric. Dry on the clothesline or clothes airer.

On cutlery

- Polish the cutlery by hand with a paste of bicarb and white vinegar.
- Rinse with water.

On fibreglass

- Sprinkle with bicarb followed by white vinegar.
- While fizzing, scrub with a toothbrush.
- For a stubborn stain, mix equal parts glycerine and *Gumption* and scrub with a toothbrush.
- Rinse with water.

On marble

- Mix plaster of Paris and water to the consistency of peanut butter.
- Spread 5 mm to 1 cm thick over the stain.
- Allow to dry completely. If it feels cold on the back of your hand, it's not dry.
- When dry, brush off with a stiff brush.
- You may need to repeat this several times.

On painted wrought iron

- Rub with rust converter on a paintbrush or rag.

On plastic

- Wipe with a paste of glycerine and talcum powder on a cloth.

On shower tiles

- Sprinkle uniodised salt over one of the ends of a cut lemon and use it over the tiles. Repeat.
- Rub grout with the salted lemon end. Leave for 10 minutes before wiping with a damp cloth.

On stainless steel

- Sprinkle uniodised salt over the mark, add fresh lemon juice and scrub with pantyhose.
- Alternatively, sprinkle uniodised salt over the end of a cut lemon and rub with the lemon.

On wool

- Place a small mountain of uniodised salt over each mark.
- Squeeze drops of fresh lemon juice over each mountain of salt until it's moist but doesn't collapse. Stop squeezing before the juice hits the bottom of the salt.
- Leave in sunshine for at least 4 hours.
- Hand wash in 1 teaspoon of cheap shampoo and blood-heat (body temperature) water.
- Rinse in 1 teaspoon of cheap hair conditioner and blood-heat water.
- Gently wring and dry flat on a towel in the shade.

S

SAFFRON

On carpet/upholstery

- Remove excess by lifting with a plastic comb or by blotting with paper towel.
- Blot with 2 drops of lavender oil on a cloth until removed.
- Absorb moisture by covering the area with paper towel. Place a book on top of the paper towel to assist with absorption.

On cotton/fabric

- Remove excess under the tap using cold water.
- Blot with lavender oil on a cloth.
- Wash according to the fabric. Dry on the clothesline or clothes airer.

On hard surfaces

- Mix 1 teaspoon of lavender oil and 1 litre of water in a spray pack.
- Spray the solution and wipe with a cloth.

SALAD DRESSING

On carpet/upholstery

- Remove excess by blotting with paper towel.
- Massage with a couple of drops of dishwashing liquid on your fingertips until the liquid feels like jelly.
- Wipe with a damp cloth until the dishwashing liquid is removed.
- Absorb moisture by covering the area with paper towel. Place a book on top of the paper towel to assist with absorption.

- If the dressing contains sugar, the stain may reappear in a couple of weeks. If so, repeat.

On cotton/fabric

- Remove excess under the tap using cold water.
- Massage with a couple of drops of dishwashing liquid on your fingertips until the liquid feels like jelly.
- Wash according to the fabric. Dry on the clothesline or clothes airer.
- If the dressing contains sugar, the stain may reappear in a couple of weeks. If so, repeat.

On timber

- Mix plaster of Paris and water to the consistency of peanut butter.
- To each cup of mixture, add 1 teaspoon of dishwashing liquid.
- Spread 5 mm to 1 cm thick over the stain.
- Allow to dry completely. If it feels cold on the back of your hand, it's not dry.
- When dry, brush off with a broom.
- If the timber needs re-oiling, restore tannins by wiping with cold black tea on a cloth and allow to dry. Then re-oil.

SALSA

On carpet/upholstery

- Remove excess by lifting with a plastic comb or by blotting with paper towel.
- For red salsa, massage with a couple of drops of dishwashing liquid on your fingertips until the liquid feels like jelly.

- Wipe with a damp cloth until the dishwashing liquid is removed.
- Place white vinegar on a cloth and wring tightly so it's damp but not wet. Blot over the mark.
- For green salsa, massage with a couple of drops of dishwashing liquid on your fingertips until the liquid feels like jelly, then wipe with white spirits on a cloth. Remove with a damp cloth.
- In both cases, absorb moisture by covering the area with paper towel. Place a book on top of the paper towel to assist with absorption.

On cotton/fabric

- Remove excess by lifting with a plastic comb.
- For red salsa, massage with a couple of drops of dishwashing liquid on your fingertips until the liquid feels like jelly.
- Rinse under blood-heat (body temperature) water.
- Blot with or soak in white vinegar.
- For green salsa, massage with a couple of drops of dishwashing liquid on your fingertips until the liquid feels like jelly, then wipe with white spirits.
- In both cases, wash according to the fabric. Dry on the clothesline or clothes airer.

SAP

On carpet/upholstery

- Remove excess by lifting with a plastic comb or by blotting with paper towel.

- For white or clear sap, scrub with 2 drops of tea tree oil on a toothbrush. Wipe with a damp cloth.
- For red or honey-coloured sap, scrub with equal parts tea tree oil and glycerine on a toothbrush. Leave for 20 minutes. Remove with a damp cloth.
- In all cases, absorb moisture by covering the area with paper towel. Place a book on top of the paper towel to assist with absorption.

On cotton/fabric

- Remove excess by lifting with a plastic comb.
- For white or clear sap, blot with tea tree oil.
- For red or honey-coloured sap, rub with equal parts tea tree oil and glycerine. Leave for 20 minutes.
- In all cases, wash according to the fabric. Dry on the clothesline or clothes airer.

On pavers/sandstone

- Scrub with 2 drops of eucalyptus oil on a toothbrush.
- Mix 1 teaspoon of dishwashing liquid in a 9-litre bucket of water.
- Scrub the mixture with a deck scrubber or stiff brush. Repeat, if needed.

On timber

- Wipe with glycerine. Leave for 90 minutes.
- Mix 1 teaspoon of dishwashing liquid in a 9-litre bucket of water.
- Scrub the mixture with a deck scrubber or stiff brush. Repeat, if needed.

TIP

To remove sap and dirt from secateurs, rub the blades with lemon juice and 1 drop of tea tree oil on an old cork coated in coarse uniodised salt.

SATAY SAUCE

On carpet/upholstery

- Remove excess by lifting with a plastic comb or by blotting with paper towel.
- Massage with a couple of drops of dishwashing liquid on your fingertips until the liquid feels like jelly.
- Wipe with a damp cloth until dishwashing liquid is removed.
- Place white vinegar on a cloth and wring tightly so it's damp but not wet. Blot over the mark.
- Absorb moisture by covering the area with paper towel. Place a book on top of the paper towel to assist with absorption.

On cotton/fabric

- Remove excess under the tap using cold water.
- Scribble with a cake of bathroom soap run under cold water.
- Massage with a couple of drops of dishwashing liquid on your fingertips until the liquid feels like jelly.
- Blot with or soak in white vinegar.
- Wash according to the fabric. Dry on the clothesline or clothes airer.

SAUCEPAN

(see 'Pot or Pan')

SCORCH MARKS

(see 'Burn Marks')

SCRATCH

On Bakelite/*glassware*

- Wipe with a little sweet almond oil on a cloth.
- For deep scratches, mix ½ teaspoon of whiting with 2 tablespoons of glycerine to the consistency of runny cream.
- Rub the mixture in circles with a cloth until the scratches are removed.
- Wipe with a damp cloth.
- Alternatively, apply jewellers rouge with a rotary tool or electric buff.

On fibreglass

- Place 2 drops of glycerine on *No-Fil* sandpaper.
- Sand over the scratch.

On leather

- For brown leather, cut a walnut (the nut, not the shell) in half and rub one of the cut surfaces over the scratch. Leave for 1 hour for the colour to cure.
- For other leather, use coloured shoe cream (not shoe polish or wax). Apply with a cloth over the scratched area only.

- Rub the scratches with the back of a warm stainless steel spoon (dip the spoon in a glass of boiling water and dry with a tea towel) to set the shoe cream.
- Wipe with leather conditioner. Make your own – see **Household formulas**.

On plastic

- Wipe with 1 part glycerine to 5 parts blood-heat (body temperature) water on a cloth.

On polyurethane

- Wipe with a small amount of *Brasso* on a cloth using speed rather than pressure. It will look worse before it looks better.

On shower screen

- Glass cancer is the haze on glass that looks like soap scum or water marks. It's caused by chemical residue and the damage is permanent. Don't use harsh abrasives on glass (including commercial glass cleaners).
- To clean glass and alleviate cancer, wipe with white vinegar on a cloth. Then firmly wipe over the glass with 1 teaspoon of sweet almond oil on a cloth.

On silver

- Using your fingertips, rub with unprocessed wheat bran slightly moistened with sweet almond oil.

On splashback (ceramic/glass/tile)

- Wipe with bicarb on a cloth followed by white vinegar on a cloth.

- For deep scratches, mix ½ teaspoon of whiting with 2 tablespoons of glycerine to the consistency of runny cream.
- Rub the mixture in circles with a cloth until the scratches are removed.
- Alternatively, apply jewellers rouge with a rotary tool or electric buff.

On stainless steel

- Wipe with a dab of *Gumption* on a cloth.
- Sprinkle with bicarb and spray with white vinegar.
- While fizzing, scrub with a damp cloth.
- Polish with a dry cloth.
- For deep scratches, apply jewellers rouge using a rotary tool with a felt buff.

On timber

- Wipe with tinted beeswax on a cloth.
- Alternatively, wipe with baby oil on a cloth.
- Alternatively, scribble with a crayon in a matching colour. Aim a hair dryer over the top to gently melt the crayon into the scratch and buff with rolled up pantyhose.

TIP

Don't use scratched ceramic plates because bacteria can get into the scratches. Recycle them as pot-plant saucers.

SCUBA GEAR

(see 'Wetsuit')

SCUFF MARK

On carpet/upholstery

- Wipe with methylated spirits or white spirits on a cotton ball.
- Sprinkle with talcum powder.
- When dry, vacuum.

On cotton/fabric

- Place a dry cotton ball on the back of the stain. Wipe the front of the stain with methylated spirits on a cotton ball.
- Alternatively, place a dry cotton ball on the back of the stain. Wipe the front of the stain with white spirits on a cotton ball.
- Wash according to the fabric. Dry on the clothesline or clothes airer.

On linoleum/vinyl

- Rub with a pencil eraser.
- Alternatively, wipe with coarse uniodised salt on a cloth dampened with a little glycerine.
- For linoleum, buff with a little kerosene on rolled up pantyhose.

On timber

- Rub with a pencil eraser.

SEAFOOD

On carpet/upholstery

- Remove excess by lifting with a plastic comb or by blotting with paper towel.

- Scribble with a cake of bathroom soap run under cold water.
- Wipe with a damp cloth.
- For a greasy residue, massage with a couple of drops of dishwashing liquid on your fingertips until the liquid feels like jelly. Wipe with a damp cloth until the dishwashing liquid is removed.
- For an old stain, clean an area twice the size of the stain because seafood stains spread during decomposition.
- In all cases, absorb moisture by covering the area with paper towel. Place a book on top of the paper towel to assist with absorption.

On cotton/fabric

- Remove excess under the tap using cold water.
- Scribble with a cake of bathroom soap run under cold water.
- For a greasy residue, massage with a couple of drops of dishwashing liquid on your fingertips until the liquid feels like jelly.
- Wash according to the fabric. Dry on the clothesline or clothes airer.

TIP

To remove a fishy odour in the fridge, after cleaning, mix equal parts dry mustard and bicarb on a tray. Leave in the fridge until the odour is absorbed.

SELF-TANNING LOTION

On carpet/upholstery

- Remove excess by blotting with paper towel.
- Massage with a couple of drops of dishwashing liquid on your fingertips until the liquid feels like jelly.
- Wipe with a damp cloth until the dishwashing liquid is removed.
- Scrub with 2 drops of lavender oil on a toothbrush. Leave for 90 minutes.
- Tightly wring a cloth in white vinegar, fold the cloth flat and polish out the lavender oil without pushing it into the back of the carpet or upholstery.
- Absorb moisture by covering the area with paper towel. Place a book on top of the paper towel to assist with absorption.

On cotton/fabric

- Remove excess under the tap using blood-heat (body temperature) water.
- Massage with a couple of drops of dishwashing liquid on your fingertips until the liquid feels like jelly.
- Wipe with 2 drops of lavender oil. Leave for 90 minutes.
- Alternatively, remove excess then soak in ½ lid of *Vanish NapiSan Oxi Action* and 9 litres of water for 20 minutes. Don't use on wool, silk or leather.
- In both cases, wash according to the fabric. Dry on the clothesline or clothes airer.

On stone

- Massage with a couple of drops of dishwashing liquid on your fingertips until the liquid feels like jelly.

- Wipe with a damp cloth.
- Spray with 1 teaspoon of lavender oil per litre of water.
- Wipe with a damp cloth.

SEMEN

On carpet/upholstery

- Remove excess by blotting with paper towel.
- For old stains, place ice cubes in a zip-lock bag and place over the stain first.
- Scribble with a cake of bathroom soap run under cold water, then leave for 2 minutes.
- Wipe with a damp cloth.
- Absorb moisture by covering the area with paper towel. Place a book on top of the paper towel to assist with absorption.

On cotton/fabric

- Remove excess under the tap using cold water.
- Scribble with a cake of bathroom soap run under cold water.
- Leave for 2 minutes.
- Wash according to the fabric. Dry on the clothesline or clothes airer.

On mattress

- Scribble with a cake of bathroom soap run under cold water.
- Scrub with a nylon brush until the soap becomes foamy.
- Sprinkle with talcum powder and leave until absorbed.
- Whack with a tennis racquet or cricket bat, or equivalent.
- When dry, vacuum.

SHEEPSKIN

To clean

- Mix 1 teaspoon of cheap shampoo in a tub of blood-heat (body temperature) water.
- Immerse the sheepskin.
- Gently massage with your hands as though washing your hair.
- Rinse in blood-heat water.
- To prevent stiffening, dry slowly in the shade. Brush regularly with a hairbrush as it's drying.

SHOE POLISH

On carpet/upholstery

- Remove excess by lifting with a plastic comb or by blotting with paper towel.
- For liquid shoe wax, wipe with white spirits on a cloth. Massage with equal parts tea tree oil and dishwashing liquid on your fingertips until the liquid feels like jelly. Wipe with a damp cloth until removed.
- For shoe polish cream (water-based), wipe with methylated spirits on a cotton ball. Massage with a couple of drops of dishwashing liquid on your fingertips until the liquid feels like jelly. Wipe with a damp cloth until the dishwashing liquid is removed.
- For shoe polish paste, wipe with tea tree oil on a cotton ball. Wipe with a damp cloth.
- In all cases, absorb moisture by covering the area with paper towel. Place a book on top of the paper towel to assist with absorption.

On cotton/fabric

- Remove excess by blotting with paper towel.
- For liquid shoe wax, wipe with white spirits. Massage with equal parts tea tree oil and dishwashing liquid on your fingertips until the liquid feels like jelly.
- For shoe polish cream (water-based), wipe with methylated spirits on a cotton ball. Massage with a couple of drops of dishwashing liquid on your fingertips until the liquid feels like jelly.
- For shoe polish paste, wipe with tea tree oil on a cotton ball.
- In all cases, wash according to the fabric. Dry on the clothesline or clothes airer.

On stone

- For shoe polish wax, wipe with white spirits on a cloth.
- For liquid shoe polish, wipe with tea tree oil on a cloth.
- For shoe polish cream, wipe with methylated spirits on a cloth.
- In all cases, if stubborn, mix plaster of Paris and water to the consistency of peanut butter.
- To each cup of mixture, add 1 teaspoon of the appropriate solvent.
- Spread 5 mm to 1 cm thick over the stain.
- Allow to dry completely. If it feels cold on the back of your hand, it's not dry.
- When dry, brush away.

SHOWER SCREEN

For scratch marks

- Glass cancer is the haze on glass that looks like soap scum or water marks. It's caused by chemical residue and the damage is permanent. Don't use harsh abrasives on glass (including commercial glass cleaners).
- To clean glass and alleviate cancer, wipe with white vinegar on a cloth. Then wipe firmly over the glass with 1 teaspoon of sweet almond oil on a cloth to temporarily remove the haze.

To clean

- For glass, clean with white vinegar or methylated spirits on a cloth.
- For polycarbonate screens, clean with white vinegar.

SHUTTERS

(see 'Timber Shutters')

SILK

For bleaching/yellowing

- Mix 2 tablespoons of 3 per cent hydrogen peroxide in a 9-litre bucket of blood-heat (body temperature) water.
- Immerse silk with a dinner plate on top to keep it fully in the solution. Leave for 6 hours.
- Remove from the bucket and place in a tub of blood-heat water with 1 cup of white vinegar.
- Hand wash in 1 teaspoon of cheap shampoo and blood-heat water.
- Rinse in blood-heat water.

- Gently wring and dry flat on a towel in the shade out of the wind, so the fibres don't tangle and leave a dusty look.

For creasing

- Mix 2 drops of glycerine and 1 teaspoon of cheap shampoo and add to blood-heat (body temperature) water. Hand wash the item.
- Rinse in 1 teaspoon of cheap hair conditioner and blood-heat water.
- Gently wring and lay flat on a towel in the shade out of the wind, so the fibres don't tangle and leave a dusty look.
- When almost dry, iron on a cool setting with a cloth covering the silk so it doesn't contact the surface of the iron.

To clean

- Hand wash in 1 teaspoon of cheap shampoo and blood-heat (body temperature) water.
- Rinse in 1 teaspoon of cheap hair conditioner and blood-heat water.
- Gently wring and dry flat on a towel in the shade out of the wind, so the fibres don't tangle and leave a dusty look.

TIP

Silk can develop watermarks from spot removal so dry slowly in the shade. If you have watermarks, wring a cloth in equal parts white vinegar and water so it's just damp. Wipe over the stain, pressing heavily in the centre and easing the pressure as you move towards the outside. Dry flat in the shade away from the wind.

SILVER

For tarnish

- Sprinkle with bicarb followed by a little white vinegar.
- While fizzing, polish with a clean cloth.

TIP

To prevent tarnish, rub silver with a couple of drops of sweet almond oil on a cloth.

To clean

- Sprinkle with bicarb and spray with white vinegar. Rub with pantyhose while the mixture is fizzing.
- For shadow marks, wipe with non-gel toothpaste on a cloth. Then wipe with bicarb and white vinegar on a cloth.

SILVERFISH

To deter

- Place 1 camphor ball, 4 cloves, 2 drops of lavender oil and 2 drops of eucalyptus oil in a small muslin bag. (You could also use 6 cedar chips in place of the cloves or eucalyptus oil.) Tie it off and hang in your wardrobe. Replace eucalyptus and lavender oils every 2 months. Replace the rest yearly. This also deters moths and mould.

SINK

To clean

- For stainless steel, porcelain, glass and brass, sprinkle with a little bicarb and splash with a little white vinegar.
- If heavily stained, wipe with *Gumption* on a cloth.
- For polycarbonate or composite, wipe with equal parts glycerine and talcum powder on a cloth. Leave for 5 minutes then polish off.

SKI WAX

(see 'Wax')

SLUGS

To deter

- Crush a whole clove of garlic in 1 litre of water in a spray pack. Leave for 2 hours. Spray over the garden.
- Alternatively, wipe petroleum jelly on the edges of garden beds.
- Renew every couple of months.

SMOKE

On carpet/upholstery

- Sprinkle with bicarb. If you like scent, add a couple of drops of lavender oil.
- Sweep backwards and forwards over the surface with a brush.
- Leave for 20 minutes.
- Vacuum.

On glass

- Mix 2 tablespoons of cigarette ash, 2 tablespoons of white vinegar and 2 tablespoons of bicarb to form a slurry.
- Apply the mixture and leave for 5 minutes until the edges start to dry.
- Rub off with pantyhose.

On walls

- For light stains, mix 2 tablespoons of cigarette ash with 2 tablespoons of *Gumption* and wipe with a cloth.
- For heavy stains, mix 2 tablespoons of cigarette ash, 2 tablespoons of bicarb and 2 tablespoons of white vinegar in a bowl. Leave for 5 minutes.
- Put on rubber gloves and wipe the mixture over the walls using rolled up pantyhose. Leave for 5 minutes.
- Remove with damp pantyhose.
- To clean wallpaper, rub with a slice of stale bread.

SNAILS

To eradicate

- To make a trap for snails, cut an orange in half, remove the flesh and half-fill the two orange skins with beer. The snails will be attracted by the beer, will climb in and won't be able to get out.

TIP

If snails are eating the mail in your letterbox, wipe under the outside rim with petroleum jelly. The snails won't cross it. Renew every couple of months.

SOAP SCUM

On ceramic

- Scrub with pantyhose and blood-heat (body temperature) water.

On glassware

- Mix 1 tablespoon of white vinegar with 1 cup of water.
- Place the glass in the mixture.
- Polish with a cloth.

On shower screen

- Wipe with bicarb and white vinegar on a cloth.
- If scratched, wipe with sweet almond oil on a cloth.

SOFA

(see 'Couch')

SOFT DRINK

On carpet/upholstery

- Remove excess by blotting with paper towel.
- Mix equal parts white vinegar and blood-heat (body temperature) water.
- Scrub the mixture with a toothbrush or pantyhose in all directions – north, south, east and west.
- Absorb moisture by covering the area with paper towel. Place a book on top of the paper towel to assist with absorption.

- If there's colour, wipe with white vinegar and expose to sunlight or ultraviolet light. (If using ultraviolet light, protect areas around the stain with cardboard.) Check every 2 hours.
- If a shadow returns in a couple of weeks, repeat.

On cotton/fabric

- Remove excess under the tap using cold water.
- Blot with or soak in white vinegar and hang in sunshine before washing.
- Wash according to the fabric. Dry in sunshine.

On stone

- Blot with white vinegar.
- If stubborn, mix plaster of Paris and water to the consistency of peanut butter.
- To each cup of mixture, add 2 teaspoons of white vinegar.
- Spread 5 mm to 1 cm thick over the stain.
- Allow to dry completely. If it feels cold on the back of your hand, it's not dry.
- When dry, brush away.

SOIL

(see 'Dirt')

SOOT

On carpet/upholstery

- Remove excess by vacuuming.
- Cut a cake of bathroom soap in half lengthways and round the edges. Dampen it under cold water and use like a rolling pin across the soot. The soot will stick to the soap. Remove the soot from the soap using water as you go.

- Absorb moisture by covering the area with paper towel. Place a book on top of the paper towel to assist with absorption.

On cotton/fabric

- Wash under the tap using cold water.
- If soot remains, cut a cake of bathroom soap in half lengthways and round the edges. Dampen it in water and use like a rolling pin across the soot. The soot will stick to the soap. Clear the soot from the soap with water as you go.
- Wash according to the fabric. Dry on the clothesline or clothes airer.

On timber

- Vacuum any loose particles.
- Wipe with 2 drops of dishwashing liquid on pantyhose.
- Rinse with a damp cloth.

On walls

- For light stains, mix 2 tablespoons of cigarette ash with 2 tablespoons of *Gumption* and wipe with a cloth.
- For heavy stains, mix 2 tablespoons of cigarette ash, 2 tablespoons of white vinegar and 2 tablespoons of bicarb to form a slurry. Wear disposable rubber gloves (because this mixture can burn skin) and scrub the mixture with a stiff brush. Leave for 5 minutes. Remove with blood-heat (body temperature) water on a soft broom.

SORBOLENE CREAM

On carpet/upholstery

- Remove excess by lifting with a plastic comb or by blotting with paper towel.
- Massage with a couple of drops of dishwashing liquid on your fingertips until the liquid feels like jelly.
- Wipe with a damp cloth until the dishwashing liquid is removed.
- If a shadow remains, wipe with a cake of bathroom soap run under cold water.
- Wipe with a damp cloth.
- Absorb moisture by covering the area with paper towel. Place a book on top of the paper towel to assist with absorption.

On cotton/fabric

- Remove excess under the tap using cold water.
- Massage with a couple of drops of dishwashing liquid on your fingertips until the liquid feels like jelly.
- If a shadow remains, wipe with 2 drops of tea tree oil.
- Wash according to the fabric. Dry on the clothesline or clothes airer.

SOUP

On carpet/upholstery

- Remove excess by lifting with a plastic comb or by blotting with paper towel.
- For vegetable soup, wipe with white vinegar on a cloth. If high in vegetable dye (tomato, pumpkin etc.), place white vinegar on a cloth and wring tightly before blotting over

the mark. Expose to sunlight or ultraviolet light. (If using ultraviolet light, protect areas around the stain with cardboard.) Check every 2 hours.

- For meat soup, scribble with a cake of bathroom soap run under cold water. Wipe with a damp cloth. If high in fats and oil, massage with a little dishwashing liquid on your fingertips until the liquid feels like jelly, then wipe with a damp cloth until the dishwashing liquid is removed.
- If there's chilli or red colourant in any soup, place white vinegar on a cloth and wring tightly before blotting over the mark. Expose to sunlight or ultraviolet light. (If using ultraviolet light, protect areas around the stain with cardboard.) Check every 2 hours.
- In all cases, absorb moisture by covering the area with paper towel. Place a book on top of the paper towel to assist with absorption.

On cotton/fabric

- Remove excess under the tap using cold water.
- For vegetable soup, blot with or soak in white vinegar and hang in sunshine.
- For meat soup, scribble with a cake of bathroom soap run under cold water. Rub the fabric against itself using your hands.
- For greasy marks, massage with a couple of drops of dishwashing liquid on your fingertips until the liquid feels like jelly.
- In all cases, wash according to the fabric. Dry in sunshine.

SOUR CREAM

On carpet/upholstery

- Remove excess by blotting with paper towel.
- Massage with a couple of drops of dishwashing liquid on your fingertips until the liquid feels like jelly.
- Wipe with a damp cloth until the dishwashing liquid is removed.
- Absorb moisture by covering the area with paper towel. Place a book on top of the paper towel to assist with absorption.

On cotton/fabric

- Remove excess under the tap using cold water.
- Massage with a couple of drops of dishwashing liquid on your fingertips until the liquid feels like jelly.
- Wash according to the fabric. Dry on the clothesline or clothes airer.

SOY SAUCE

On carpet/upholstery

- Remove excess by blotting with paper towel.
- Place white vinegar on a cloth and wring tightly before blotting over the mark.
- Place the vinegar cloth in one hand and a dry cloth in the other and wipe hand over hand, as though stroking a cat.
- Absorb moisture by covering the area with paper towel. Place a book on top of the paper towel to assist with absorption.

On cotton/fabric

- Rinse the stain with white vinegar.
- If stubborn, heat white vinegar in the microwave until it's steaming. Pour through the stain until removed.
- Wash according to the fabric. Dry on the clothesline or clothes airer.

On silk tie

- Soak entire tie in white vinegar overnight.
- Rinse in blood-heat (body temperature) water.
- Dry flat on a towel in the shade out of the wind. If it starts to pucker, lay another towel on top as it dries.

On stone

- Wipe with white vinegar on a cloth.
- If stubborn, mix plaster of Paris and water to the consistency of peanut butter.
- To each cup of mixture, add 2 teaspoons of white vinegar.
- Spread 5 mm to 1 cm thick over the stain.
- Allow to dry completely. If it feels cold on the back of your hand, it's not dry.
- When dry, brush away.

SPA BATH

To clean

- Place 1 cup of bicarb in a full tub of water.
- Run the spa bath for 5 minutes.
- Add 2 cups of white vinegar and run for a further 5 minutes.
- Drain and rinse with clean water.
- Remove chalk deposits with white vinegar.

SPAGHETTI BOLOGNESE

(see 'Bolognese Sauce')

SPIDERS

To deter

- Rub lemon skin or sprinkle 1–2 drops of lemon oil (not lemon essence) along the bristles of a clean broom.
- Wipe the broom over the areas spiders like – collect the old webs as you go.
- If you're not able to use a broom, mix 5 drops of lemon oil with 1 drop of dishwashing liquid in a 1-litre spray pack of water. Lightly spray over the area every 3 months.

TIP

Make your own lemon oil. Place lemon zest (grate the peel) on plastic wrap and leave on a sunny windowsill. The oil will leach from the peel onto the plastic. Store in a small vial.

SPINACH

On carpet/upholstery

- Remove excess by lifting with a plastic comb or by blotting with paper towel.
- Place white vinegar on a cloth and wring tightly so it's damp but not wet. Blot over the mark.
- Absorb moisture by covering the area with paper towel. Place a book on top of the paper towel to assist with absorption.

- For a green stain, expose to sunlight or ultraviolet light. (If using ultraviolet light, protect areas around the stain with cardboard.) Check every 2 hours.

On cotton/fabric

- Remove excess with cold water.
- Blot with or soak in white vinegar.
- Alternatively, remove excess then make a paste of *Vanish NapiSan Oxi Action* and water the consistency of spreadable butter. Don't use on wool, silk or leather. Place over the stain for 30 minutes.
- In both cases, wash according to the fabric. Dry in sunshine.

SPORT DRINK

(see 'Energy Drink')

SPORTSWEAR

To clean

- Rinse in 1 cup of white vinegar per 9-litre bucket of water.
- Wash according to the fabric. Dry in sunshine.

SQUID INK

On carpet/upholstery

- Remove excess by blotting with paper towel.
- Rot some full cream milk in the sun until it forms solids.
- Place the solids on the ink stain.
- When the ink is absorbed, remove with a plastic comb.
- Wipe with a damp cloth.

- Remove smell by wiping with lemon oil on a cloth.
- Absorb moisture by covering the area with paper towel. Place a book on top of the paper towel to assist with absorption.

On cotton/fabric

- Rot some full cream milk in the sun until it forms solids.
- Place the solids on the stain.
- When the squid ink is absorbed, rinse in water.
- Wash according to the fabric. Dry on the clothesline or clothes airer.

STEAK SAUCE

(see also 'Barbecue Sauce')

On carpet/upholstery

- Remove excess by lifting with a plastic comb or by blotting with paper towel.
- Scribble with a cake of bathroom soap run under cold water.
- Wipe with white vinegar on a cloth.
- Absorb moisture by covering the area with paper towel. Place a book on top of the paper towel to assist with absorption.
- To remove food colouring, expose to sunlight or ultraviolet light. (If using ultraviolet light, protect areas around the stain with cardboard.) Check every 2 hours.

On cotton/fabric

- Remove excess under the tap using cold water.
- Scribble with a cake of bathroom soap run under cold water. Rub the fabric against itself using your hands.

- Blot with or soak in white vinegar until the stain is removed.
- Alternatively, remove excess then soak in ½ lid of *Vanish NapiSan Oxi Action* and 9 litres of water for 30 minutes. Don't use on wool, silk or leather.
- In both cases, wash according to the fabric. Dry in sunshine.

STICKER RESIDUE

On carpet/upholstery

- Wring a cloth in white vinegar and place over the residue. Leave for 30 minutes.
- Remove and wipe stain with tea tree oil on a cotton ball.
- If stubborn, wipe with eucalyptus oil on a cotton ball.
- Absorb moisture by covering the area with paper towel. Place a book on top of the paper towel to assist with absorption.

On cotton/fabric (not silk)

- Soak in white vinegar to loosen the residue.
- Wipe with tea tree oil.
- If stubborn, wipe with eucalyptus oil on a cloth.
- If residue is yellow, wipe with lavender oil on a cloth.
- Wash according to the fabric. Don't put in the dryer until the residue is completely removed, as the heat from the dryer will set the sticker glue.

On silk

- Wipe with tea tree oil.
- Wipe with lavender oil.
- Wipe with white vinegar.

- Massage with 1 teaspoon of cheap shampoo using your fingertips.
- Rinse entire garment in blood-heat (body temperature) water.
- Gently wring and dry flat on a towel in the shade away from the wind, so the fibres don't tangle and leave a dusty look.

STICKY LABEL

On glass jar

- Fill the jar with hot water and put the lid on. Leave for 5 minutes. The label should peel off. To remove residue, wipe with tea tree oil.
- Alternatively, mix 1 drop of dishwashing liquid and a little water on plastic wrap. Place the plastic wrap over the label. Leave for 10 minutes. Remove the plastic wrap – the sticker should come away.
- Alternatively, run a hair dryer backwards and forwards over the label to melt the glue.
- For stickier labels, apply 2 drops of tea tree oil along the top edge of the label. Leave for about 15 minutes. Peel off.
- Stronger still is eucalyptus oil applied with a cotton ball. Use sparingly because it can remove paint.

STICKY TAPE RESIDUE

On carpet/upholstery

- Mix ½ teaspoon of tea tree oil and 2 cups of blood-heat (body temperature) water.
- Wipe on the solution with pantyhose until the residue is removed. Allow to dry.

- Alternatively, cover the residue with a damp cloth, then place plastic wrap on top. Leave for 5 minutes.
- Remove the plastic and wipe tea tree oil over the adhesive gum. Roll the adhesive gum off with tissues.

TIP

Everything – from sticky tape to scissors – should have a designated spot. Putting items in a special place will not only speed up your cleaning, but life inside the house will also be easier because you won't be searching high and low for whatever you need.

STRAWBERRY

(see 'Berry')

SUNSCREEN

On carpet/upholstery (not leather)

- Remove excess by blotting with paper towel.
- Massage with a couple of drops of dishwashing liquid on your fingertips until the liquid feels like jelly.
- Wipe with a damp cloth until the dishwashing liquid is removed.
- Wipe with 2 drops of glycerine on a toothbrush. Leave for 90 minutes.
- Tightly wring a cloth in white vinegar, fold the cloth flat and polish out the glycerine without pushing it into the back of the carpet or upholstery.
- Absorb moisture by covering the area with paper towel. Place a book on top of the paper towel to assist with absorption.

On cotton/fabric

- Remove excess under the tap using cold water.
- Massage with a couple of drops of dishwashing liquid on your fingertips until the liquid feels like jelly.
- Wipe with 2 drops of glycerine on a toothbrush. Leave for 90 minutes.
- Blot with or soak in white vinegar.
- Wash according to the fabric. Dry on the clothesline or clothes airer.

On leather

- Wipe with saddle soap on pantyhose.
- Remove with paper towel.
- Wipe with leather conditioner. Make your own – see **Household formulas**.

On plastic in car interior

- Wipe with equal parts glycerine and dishwashing liquid on a cloth.
- Remove with a warm, damp cloth.

SUPERGLUE

On carpet/upholstery

- Wedge a metal comb underneath the superglue to protect the surface. Wipe only over the superglue with superglue remover or acetone (not nail polish remover) on a cotton bud. The superglue will melt.
- Alternatively, apply steam to the superglue and rub with pantyhose.
- In both cases, neutralise the smell by wiping with white vinegar on a cloth.

On quartz/stone benchtops

- Wring a cloth in boiling water, place the cloth over the stain for 30 seconds, then remove the glue with either a credit card or a single-sided razor blade held at a low angle.
- Wipe with superglue remover or acetone on a cloth.
- Neutralise with white vinegar on a cloth.

SUSHI

On carpet/upholstery

- Remove excess by lifting with a plastic comb or blotting with paper towel.
- Place white vinegar on a cloth and wring tightly so it's damp but not wet. Blot over the mark.
- Scribble with a cake of bathroom soap run under cold water.
- Wipe with a damp cloth.
- Absorb moisture by covering the area with paper towel. Place a book on top of the paper towel to assist with absorption.

On cotton/fabric

- Remove excess under the tap using cold water.
- Blot with or soak in white vinegar.
- Scribble with a cake of bathroom soap run under cold water. Rub the fabric against itself using your hands.
- Wash according to the fabric. Dry on the clothesline or clothes airer.

SWEAT MARKS

(see 'Body Odour/Perspiration')

SWEET CHILLI SAUCE

On carpet/upholstery

- Remove excess by blotting with paper towel.
- Place white vinegar on a cloth and wring tightly so it's damp but not wet. Blot over the mark.
- Massage with a couple of drops of dishwashing liquid on your fingertips until the liquid feels like jelly.
- Wipe with a damp cloth until the dishwashing liquid is removed.
- Alternatively, remove excess, wipe with lemon juice on a cloth, then massage with dishwashing liquid until the liquid feels like jelly.
- In both cases, absorb moisture by covering the area with paper towel. Place a book on top of the paper towel to assist with absorption.

On cotton/fabric

- Rinse the stain with white vinegar.
- If stubborn, heat white vinegar in the microwave until it's steaming. Pour through the stain until removed.
- To remove oils, massage with a couple of drops of dishwashing liquid on your fingertips until the liquid feels like jelly.
- Wash according to the fabric. Dry in sunshine.

SWEET POTATO

On carpet/upholstery

- For cooked sweet potato, remove excess by lifting with a plastic comb. For raw sweet potato, wipe with equal parts glycerine and white vinegar on a cloth first.

- Scribble with a cake of bathroom soap run under cold water.
- Wipe with a damp cloth.
- Absorb moisture by covering the area with paper towel. Place a book on top of the paper towel to assist with absorption.

On cotton/fabric

- For cooked sweet potato, remove excess under the tap using cold water. For raw sweet potato, wipe with equal parts glycerine and white vinegar on a cloth first.
- Scribble with a cake of bathroom soap. Rub the fabric against itself using your hands.
- Wash according to the fabric. Dry on the clothesline or clothes airer.

SWIMMING COSTUME

To clean

- Never wash with laundry detergent. Laundry detergent breaks down latex and elastane, making them perish, pucker and lose elasticity.
- Rinse in 1 cup of white vinegar per 9-litre bucket of water. If you rinse right after swimming, your swimming costume will last for longer.
- Dry in sunshine.

T

TABASCO SAUCE

On carpet/upholstery

- Remove excess by blotting with paper towel.
- Place white vinegar on a cloth and wring tightly so it's damp but not wet. Blot over the mark.
- Absorb moisture by covering the area with paper towel. Place a book on top of the paper towel to assist with absorption.

On cotton/fabric

- Rinse the stain with white vinegar.
- If stubborn, heat white vinegar in the microwave until it's steaming. Pour through the stain until removed.
- Wash according to the fabric. Dry in sunshine.

TANDOORI

(see also 'Vindaloo')

On carpet/upholstery

- Remove excess by lifting with a plastic comb or by blotting with paper towel.
- Massage with a little dishwashing liquid on your fingertips until the liquid feels like jelly.
- Wipe with a damp cloth until the dishwashing liquid is removed.
- Place white vinegar on a cloth and wring tightly so it's damp but not wet. Blot over the mark.
- Wipe with 2 drops of lavender oil on a cloth.
- To remove food colouring, expose to sunlight or ultraviolet light. (If using ultraviolet light, protect areas around the stain with cardboard.) Check every 2 hours.

- Absorb moisture by covering the area with paper towel. Place a book on top of the paper towel to assist with absorption.

On chopping board

- Wipe with 2 drops of lavender oil on a cloth.
- Scrub with dishwashing liquid and water.

On cotton/fabric

- Remove excess under the tap using cold water.
- Massage with a couple of drops of dishwashing liquid on your fingertips until the liquid feels like jelly.
- Rinse under blood-heat (body temperature) water.
- Place a dry cotton ball behind the stain. Working in circles from the outside to the inside, wipe the front of the stain with 2 drops of lavender oil on a cotton ball.
- Wash according to the fabric. Dry in sunshine.

TAR

On carpet/upholstery

- Remove excess by lifting with a plastic comb.
- Wipe with 2 drops of baby oil and 2 drops of tea tree oil on a cloth or pantyhose.
- When the tar softens, sprinkle with talcum powder.
- Rub with tissues. The tar will come away in little balls.
- Vacuum.
- Alternatively, remove excess then wipe with kerosene on pantyhose.
- Rinse with a damp cloth.
- Scribble with a cake of bathroom soap run under cold water.

- Wipe with a damp cloth.
- Absorb moisture by covering the area with paper towel. Place a book on top of the paper towel to assist with absorption.

On cotton/fabric

- If you can, place the fabric in the freezer.
- When frozen, cut off as much tar as possible with scissors or a blade.
- Dampen the back of the stain with baby oil and tea tree oil on a cotton ball.
- Working from the outside to the inside, rub the front of the stain with white spirits on a cotton ball.
- Massage with a couple of drops of dishwashing liquid on your fingertips until the liquid feels like jelly.
- Alternatively, remove excess then wipe with kerosene on pantyhose. Rinse with water.
- Wash according to the fabric. Dry on the clothesline or clothes airer.

On stone

- Remove excess by scraping with a single-sided razor blade.
- Wipe with baby oil and tea tree oil on a cloth. Alternatively, wipe with kerosene on pantyhose.
- If stubborn, mix plaster of Paris and water to the consistency of peanut butter.
- To each cup of mixture, add 1 teaspoon of dishwashing liquid.
- Spread 5 mm to 1 cm thick over the stain.
- Allow to dry completely. If it feels cold on the back of your hand, it's not dry.
- When dry, brush away.

TARTARE SAUCE

On carpet/upholstery

- Remove excess by lifting with a plastic comb or by blotting with paper towel.
- Massage with a couple of drops of dishwashing liquid on your fingertips until the liquid feels like jelly.
- Wipe with a damp cloth until the dishwashing liquid is removed.
- Absorb moisture by covering the area with paper towel. Place a book on top of the paper towel to assist with absorption.

On cotton/fabric

- Remove excess under the tap using cold water.
- Massage with a couple of drops of dishwashing liquid on your fingertips until the liquid feels like jelly.
- Wash according to the fabric. Dry on the clothesline or clothes airer.

TEA

(see also 'Green Tea')

On carpet/upholstery

- For fresh spills, remove excess by blotting with paper towel.
- Lightly brush with 2 drops of glycerine on a toothbrush. Work from the outside to the inside of the stain.
- Tightly wring a cloth in white vinegar, fold the cloth flat and polish out the glycerine without pushing it into the back of the carpet or upholstery.

- For old spills, wipe with 2 drops of glycerine on a cloth. Leave for 90 minutes, then wipe with white vinegar.
- To remove milk, massage with a couple of drops of dishwashing liquid on your fingertips until the liquid feels like jelly. Wipe with a damp cloth until the dishwashing liquid is removed.
- Absorb moisture by covering the area with paper towel. Place a book on top of the paper towel to assist with absorption.

On cotton/fabric (not wool)

- If old, wipe with 2 drops of glycerine and leave for 90 minutes first.
- Blot with or soak in white vinegar.
- Wash according to the fabric. Dry on the clothesline or clothes airer.

On laminate

- Wipe with equal parts *Gumption* and glycerine on rolled up pantyhose.
- Wipe again with a damp cloth.

On marble/stone

- Mix plaster of Paris and water to the consistency of peanut butter.
- To each cup of mixture, add ½ teaspoon of glycerine.
- Spread 5 mm to 1 cm thick over the stain.
- Allow to dry completely. If it feels cold on the back of your hand, it's not dry.
- When dry, remove with a plastic scraper.

On wool

- Massage with equal parts glycerine and cheap shampoo on your fingertips.
- Leave for 30 minutes.
- Rinse in blood-heat (body temperature) water.
- Rinse in 1 teaspoon of cheap hair conditioner and blood-heat water.
- Gently wring and dry flat on a towel in the shade.

TEAPOT

To clean ceramic

- Sprinkle with bicarb followed by white vinegar.
- When the mixture fizzes, scrub with a nylon brush or pantyhose.
- Wipe with a damp cloth.

To clean silver

- Place 1 cup of unprocessed wheat bran in a large bowl. Add drops of white vinegar one at a time, stirring as you go, until the mixture resembles breadcrumbs. It shouldn't be wet. Place into the toe of pantyhose, tie off and rub over the teapot.
- Alternatively, apply the mixture directly wearing old cotton socks on your hands to prevent sweat from tarnishing the silver. Wipe with a damp cloth.
- For shadow marks, wipe with non-gel toothpaste, then wipe with bicarb and white vinegar on a cloth. Wipe with a damp cloth.

TELEVISION

Television screens are very sensitive and should be cleaned with care.

To clean LCD and plasma

- First, turn off the TV.
- Wipe the screen with one damp and one dry pair of pantyhose. Lightly rub with the damp pair and then with the dry pair.

THERMOS

To clean

- Put 2 tablespoons of bicarb, 2 tablespoons of white vinegar and 2 tablespoons of uncooked rice inside the thermos.
- Put your hands on top and shake, but not for too long. Don't put the lid on or it will explode.
- Let it sit for 30 minutes.
- Shake again and rinse.

TIGER BALM

On carpet/upholstery

- Remove excess by lifting with a plastic comb or by blotting with paper towel.
- Scribble with a cake of bathroom soap run under blood-heat (body temperature) water.
- Wipe with a damp cloth.
- Wipe again with 2 drops of tea tree oil on a cotton ball.
- Absorb moisture by covering the area with paper towel. Place a book on top of the paper towel to assist with absorption.

On cotton/fabric

- Scribble with a cake of bathroom soap run under blood-heat (body temperature) water.
- Rinse in blood-heat water.
- Wipe with 2 drops of tea tree oil.
- Wash according to the fabric. Dry on the clothesline or clothes airer.

TILE

(Indoor/outdoor)

To clean

- Sprinkle with a little bicarb. Spray with white vinegar.
- While fizzing, sweep with a broom or wipe with a cloth.
- To finish, wipe with a damp cloth.
- To clean grout, scrub with a plastic (not metal) scourer while bicarb and white vinegar is fizzing.

TIMBER SHUTTERS

To clean

- For heavier soiling, cut a kitchen sponge in half. Place each half sponge on one inside of a pair of tongs. Secure with rubber bands.
- Place one sponged tong end on the top and the other on the bottom of each slat, pinch the ends together and run along each slat.
- If very dirty, dip the sponges in a solution of black tea and hot water and run along the slats.
- For lighter soiling, put on white gloves and run your fingers along the slats.

TIP

Have a peg handy in case the front doorbell rings while you're cleaning the shutters. That way you know where to resume cleaning.

TISSUE

In washing machine

- To remove tissue fluff, put your hand inside the toe of pantyhose and wipe over the drum of the washing machine. The tissue will stick to the pantyhose.
- For garments covered in tissue, wash in the washing machine and add pantyhose. The tissue will stick to the pantyhose.
- For remaining fluff, put on disposable rubber gloves and wash your gloved hands with a cake of bathroom soap and water. Shake your hands dry. Stroke over the fabric and the tissue will attach to the rubber gloves.

TOBACCO

(see 'Cigarette Ash' or 'Cigarette Staining')

TOFFEE

On carpet/upholstery

- Remove excess by lifting with a plastic comb or by blotting with paper towel.
- Scribble with a cake of bathroom soap run under blood-heat (body temperature) water.
- Scrub with a toothbrush or pantyhose in all directions – north, south, east and west.

- Blot with equal parts white vinegar and water on a cloth.
- Absorb moisture by covering the area with paper towel. Place a book on top of the paper towel to assist with absorption.
- When almost dry, repeat.
- If a shadow returns in a couple of weeks, repeat again.

On cotton/fabric

- Soak in cold water first.
- Scribble with a cake of bathroom soap and blood-heat (body temperature) water. Rub the fabric against itself using your hands.
- Rinse in equal parts white vinegar and water.
- Wash according to the fabric. Dry on the clothesline or clothes airer.

On stone

- Wipe with a cake of bathroom soap run under blood-heat (body temperature) water on a cloth.
- Mix plaster of Paris and water to the consistency of peanut butter.
- To each cup of mixture, add 1 teaspoon of dishwashing liquid.
- Spread 5 mm to 1 cm thick over the stain.
- Allow to dry completely. If it feels cold on the back of your hand, it's not dry.
- When dry, brush away.

TOILET

To clean

- Flush the toilet to wet the inside of the bowl.
- Sprinkle bicarb over the inside of the bowl.

- Wipe the top of the cistern with bicarb and white vinegar on a cloth.
- Wipe the top of the toilet lid, under the lid, the top of the seat and under the seat with the same cloth.
- Splash white vinegar over the bicarb in the bowl and use a toilet brush to scrub, including under and around the rim.
- Wipe the top of the rim with a cloth.
- Rinse the cloth under hot water and wipe again.
- Flush.
- Rinse the cloth and wipe the outside of the toilet bowl right to the floor, including the plumbing at the back.
- For stubborn stains, leave 2 denture tablets in the bowl for 1 hour. Then flush.

TIP

To save on cleaning, place 2 denture tablets in the toilet cistern once a week.

TOMATO

On carpet/upholstery

- Remove excess by lifting with a plastic comb or by blotting with paper towel.
- Place white vinegar on a cloth and wring tightly so it's damp but not wet. Blot over the mark.
- For a red stain, expose to sunlight or ultraviolet light. (If using ultraviolet light, protect areas around the stain with cardboard.) Check every 2 hours.
- Absorb moisture by covering the area with paper towel. Place a book on top of the paper towel to assist with absorption.

On cotton/fabric

- Remove excess under the tap using cold water.
- Blot with or soak in white vinegar until the stain is removed.
- Wash according to the fabric. Dry in sunshine.

On stone

- Wipe with white vinegar on a cloth.
- If stubborn, mix plaster of Paris and water to the consistency of peanut butter.
- To each cup of mixture, add 2 teaspoons of white vinegar.
- Spread 5 mm to 1 cm thick over the stain.
- Allow to dry completely. If it feels cold on the back of your hand, it's not dry.
- When dry, brush away.

TOMATO SAUCE

On carpet/upholstery

- Remove excess by lifting with a plastic comb or by blotting with paper towel.
- Place white vinegar on a cloth and wring tightly so it's damp but not wet. Blot over the mark.
- Absorb moisture by covering the area with paper towel. Place a book on top of the paper towel to assist with absorption.
- For a red stain, expose to sunlight or ultraviolet light. (If using ultraviolet light, protect areas around the stain with cardboard.) Check every 2 hours.

On cotton/fabric

- Remove excess under the tap using cold water.
- Blot with or soak in white vinegar. For a red stain, hang in sunshine before washing.
- Wash according to the fabric. Dry in sunshine.

On plastic

- Mix 2 drops of glycerine and talcum powder until it forms a paste.
- Wipe on the mixture with a cloth.
- Alternatively, rub uniodised salt and lemon juice into the plastic and leave in sunshine.

On stone

- Remove excess by blotting with paper towel.
- Place white vinegar on a cloth and wring tightly so it's damp but not wet. Blot over the mark.
- If stubborn, mix plaster of Paris and water to the consistency of peanut butter.
- To each cup of mixture, add 2 teaspoons of white vinegar.
- Spread 5 mm to 1 cm thick over the stain.
- Allow to dry completely. If it feels cold on the back of your hand, it's not dry.
- When dry, brush away.

TONER

On carpet/upholstery

- Rot some full cream milk in the sun until it forms solids.
- Place the solids over the stain.
- When the ink is absorbed, remove the rotten milk solids by lifting with a plastic comb.

- Scribble with a cake of bathroom soap run under cold water.
- Wipe with a damp cloth.
- Absorb moisture by covering the area with paper towel. Place a book on top of the paper towel to assist with absorption.

On cotton/fabric

- Rot some full cream milk in the sun until it forms solids.
- Place the solids over the stain.
- When the ink is absorbed, wash off the rotten milk solids.
- Wash according to the fabric. Dry on the clothesline or clothes airer.

TOOTHPASTE

Remove as soon as possible because it can bleach surfaces.

On carpet/upholstery

- Remove excess by lifting with a plastic comb or by blotting with paper towel.
- Place white vinegar on a cloth and wring tightly so it's damp but not wet. Blot over the mark.
- Absorb moisture by covering the area with paper towel. Place a book on top of the paper towel to assist with absorption.

On timber

- Wipe with water on rolled up pantyhose.
- If the toothpaste has bleached the timber, wipe with a damp tea bag. The tannins in tea draw out the tannins in the timber and replace the colour.

On wool

- Remove excess under the tap using blood-heat (body temperature) water.
- Blot with equal parts white vinegar and water on a cloth.
- Soak in 1 teaspoon of cheap shampoo and blood-heat water for 30 minutes.
- Rinse in blood-heat water.
- Gently wring and dry flat on a towel in the shade.

TOY

To clean hard toy

- Mix ¼ teaspoon of tea tree oil and 1 litre of water in a spray pack. Tea tree oil is a great disinfectant and is non-toxic.
- Spray over the toy and wipe with a cloth.
- To clean a mouldy rubber toy, add ¼ teaspoon of oil of cloves to a 4-litre bucket of blood-heat (body temperature) water.
- Place the toy in the bucket, squeeze so water gets inside and leave for 2 hours.
- Remove, squeeze out the water and set aside to dry.

To clean soft toy

- Place in the freezer to kill microscopic bugs and dust mites.
- Check the label. Most can be washed in the washing machine on a gentle cycle. Instead of detergent, use 1 tablespoon of cheap shampoo. Place in a delicates bag or pillowcase.
- Don't use the dryer but hang the toys to dry in sunshine.

- Alternatively, after removing from the freezer, mix 1 kg of unprocessed wheat bran and drops of white vinegar until the mixture resembles breadcrumbs. Place inside a pillowcase and add the soft toy. Tie off and shake well.
- Remove toy and brush with a scrubbing brush.

TREACLE

(see 'Maple Syrup')

TREE SAP

(see 'Sap')

TRUFFLE OIL

(see 'Cooking Oil')

TULLE

For glue

- Boil the kettle to generate steam.
- Hold the affected area over the steam for 1 minute.
- Rub over the glue with pantyhose. The glue will be pulled off.

To smooth

- To stiffen or smooth tulle, mix 1 tablespoon of pure soap flakes with 1 litre of water in a spray pack.
- Shake the mixture until the soap flakes are completely dissolved.
- Spray over the tulle.

- Pull the tulle straight and dry with a hair dryer. Don't hold the hair dryer too close or the heat will melt the tulle.

TUNA

(Tinned with oil)

On cotton/fabric

- Remove excess under the tap using cold water.
- Scribble with a cake of bathroom soap run under cold water.
- Massage with a couple of drops of dishwashing liquid on your fingertips until the liquid feels like jelly.
- Rinse using cold water.
- Wash according to the fabric. Dry on the clothesline or clothes airer.

TURMERIC

On carpet/upholstery

- Remove excess by blotting with paper towel.
- Blot with 2 drops of lavender oil on a cloth until removed.
- Absorb moisture by covering the area with paper towel. Place a book on top of the paper towel to assist with absorption.

On cotton/fabric

- Remove excess under the tap using cold water.
- Place a dry cotton ball behind the stain. Blot the front of the stain with 2 drops of lavender oil on a cotton ball.
- Wash according to the fabric. Dry on the clothesline or clothes airer.

On stone

- Massage with a couple of drops of dishwashing liquid on your fingertips until the liquid feels like jelly.
- Wipe with a damp cloth.
- If stubborn, mix plaster of Paris and water to the consistency of peanut butter.
- To each cup of mixture, add 1 teaspoon of lavender oil.
- Spread 5 mm to 1 cm thick over the stain.
- Allow to dry completely. If it feels cold on the back of your hand, it's not dry.
- When dry, brush away.

TYRE MARK

On concrete

- Dampen concrete with water.
- Sprinkle with uniodised salt.
- Sweep backwards and forwards with a stiff broom.
- Rinse with a hose.

On cotton/fabric/vinyl flooring

- Mix 2 tablespoons of uniodised salt, 2 tablespoons of talcum powder and 1 tablespoon of glycerine to a paste.
- Place over the mark. Leave for 90 minutes.
- Rinse using cold water.
- For vinyl flooring, wipe with a damp cloth.
- For others, wash according to the fabric. Dry on the clothesline or clothes airer.

On stone

- Wipe with uniodised salt on a scrubbing brush.
- If stubborn, mix plaster of Paris and water to the consistency of peanut butter.
- To each cup of mixture, add 1 teaspoon of white spirits.
- Spread 5 mm to 1 cm thick over the stain.
- Allow to dry completely. If it feels cold on the back of your hand, it's not dry.
- When dry, brush away.

U

UGG BOOTS

To clean

- Pour 1 teaspoon of cheap shampoo into each boot and place in a pillowcase.
- Wash in the washing machine with cold water on the gentle cycle.
- When drying, stuff old towels inside each boot and dry in the shade.

UMBRELLA

(Patio/handheld)

To clean canvas

- Mix 2 cups of uniodised salt in a small bucket of water.
- Apply the mixture with a brush or broom.
- Leave to dry.
- Rinse the salt off with water.

To clean plastic

- Clean with water.
- If very dirty, add 1 teaspoon of dishwashing liquid to the water.
- Wipe plastic attachments with 2 drops of glycerine on a cloth.

To clean raffia

- Raffia attracts bugs, so hose or wash regularly.
- Mix 2 tablespoons of uniodised salt in 1 cup of water. Allow to dissolve.
- Wipe the salt solution across the surface with rolled up pantyhose.

- When dry, brush off the salt.
- Spray with surface insecticide spray.

URINE

On carpet/upholstery

- For fresh stains, remove excess by blotting with paper towel.
- Place white vinegar on a cloth and wring tightly so it's damp but not wet. Blot over the mark.
- For old stains, turn on an ultraviolet light in a darkened room and the urine stains will show up yellow.
- Mark around the stains with a piece of white chalk.
- Blot inside the chalk marks with white vinegar on a cloth.
- Alternatively, for fresh and old stains, fill a bucket with cold water and enough dishwashing liquid to generate a sudsy mix.
- Scrub with only the suds on a toothbrush using as little water as possible.
- Wipe with a damp cloth.
- In all cases, absorb moisture by covering the area with paper towel. Place a book on top of the paper towel to assist with absorption.
- Never soak urine stains because it pushes the stain further into the fibres.

On cotton/fabric

- Remove excess under the tap using cold water.
- Blot with or soak in white vinegar.
- Wash according to the fabric. Dry on the clothesline or clothes airer.

On mattress

- Place white vinegar on a cloth and wring tightly so it's damp but not wet. Blot over the mark.
- Alternatively, add a little dishwashing liquid to water to generate a sudsy mix. Scrub only the suds into the stain with a cloth.
- In both cases, put the mattress in the sun if possible. If not, use paper towel with a book on top to absorb moisture and dry with a hair dryer.
- Neutralise the smell by wiping with lemon juice on a cloth.

On stone/timber

- If the urine has penetrated, mix plaster of Paris and water to the consistency of peanut butter.
- To each cup of mixture, add 2 teaspoons of white vinegar.
- Spread 5 mm to 1 cm thick over the stain.
- Allow to dry completely. If it feels cold on the back of your hand, it's not dry.
- When dry, brush off with a broom.

V

VANILLA ESSENCE

On carpet/upholstery

- Remove excess by blotting with paper towel.
- For a new stain, place white vinegar on a cloth and wring tightly so it's damp but not wet. Blot over the mark.
- For an old stain, wipe with 2 drops of glycerine on a toothbrush or cloth. Leave for 90 minutes. Tightly wring a cloth in white vinegar, fold the cloth flat and polish out the glycerine without pushing it into the back of the carpet or upholstery.
- For imitation vanilla, use previous steps and then leave for 24 hours. Then wipe with white vinegar on a cloth.
- Absorb moisture by covering the area with paper towel. Place a book on top of the paper towel to assist with absorption.

On cotton/fabric

- Remove excess under the tap using blood-heat (body temperature) water.
- For an old stain, wipe with 2 drops of glycerine on a cloth. Leave for 90 minutes.
- For a new stain, blot with or soak in white vinegar.
- Alternatively, for an old or new stain, soak in ½ lid of *Vanish NapiSan Oxi Action* and 9 litres of blood-heat water for 30 minutes. Don't use on wool, silk or leather.
- Wash according to the fabric. Dry on the clothesline or clothes airer.

On timber

- Vanilla can eat through varnish and paint.
- For a sealed surface, wipe with 2 drops of dishwashing liquid and water on a cloth. You may need to replace the paint or varnish.

VANILLA EXTRACT

On carpet/upholstery

- Remove excess by blotting with paper towel.
- Mix equal parts white vinegar and blood-heat (body temperature) water.
- Scrub the mixture with a toothbrush or pantyhose in all directions – north, south, east and west – until removed.
- Absorb moisture by covering the area with paper towel. Place a book on top of the paper towel to assist with absorption.
- When the carpet appears to be almost dry, repeat.
- If a shadow returns in a couple of weeks, repeat again.

On cotton/fabric

- Remove excess under the tap using cold water.
- Blot with or soak in white vinegar.
- Wash according to the fabric. Dry on the clothesline or clothes airer.

VARNISH

To clean

- For oily or grimy patches on varnished surfaces, scatter damp tea leaves over the stain and allow the tannins to break down and absorb the grime.
- Polish with beeswax on a cloth.

To remove

- Wipe with white spirits on a cloth.
- On painted surfaces, wipe with white spirits on a cloth, then wipe with a damp cloth and allow to dry.

VASELINE

(see 'Petroleum Jelly')

VASE

To clean

- Wash with a couple of drops of dishwashing liquid and water.
- Coat stains in baby oil and leave for 2 hours.
- Remove the oil with a paintbrush (cover the metal part with sticky tape) or a bamboo skewer with chewed ends.
- To access hard-to-reach areas, create a curl in the end of a bamboo skewer and work it into the area.

VEGEMITE

On carpet/upholstery

- Remove excess by lifting with a plastic comb or by blotting with paper towel.
- Massage with a couple of drops of dishwashing liquid on your fingertips until the liquid feels like jelly.
- Wipe with a damp cloth until the dishwashing liquid is removed.
- Absorb moisture by covering the area with paper towel. Place a book on top of the paper towel to assist with absorption.

On cotton/fabric

- Remove excess under the tap using blood-heat (body temperature) water.
- Massage with a couple of drops of dishwashing liquid on your fingertips until the liquid feels like jelly.
- Wash according to the fabric. Dry on the clothesline or clothes airer.

TIP

To remove a splinter from skin, apply ¼ teaspoon of Vegemite *and cover with a* Band-Aid. *The splinter will rise to the surface.*

VEGETABLE DYE

On carpet/upholstery

- Remove excess by blotting with paper towel.
- Place white vinegar on a cloth and wring tightly so it's damp but not wet. Blot over the mark.
- Expose to sunlight or ultraviolet light. (If using ultraviolet light, protect areas around the stain with cardboard.) Check every 2 hours.
- Absorb moisture by covering the area with paper towel. Place a book on top of the paper towel to assist with absorption.

On wool

- Blot with 2 drops of lavender oil on a cloth. Leave for 20 minutes.
- Wash in 1 teaspoon of cheap shampoo and blood-heat (body temperature) water.

- Rinse in blood-heat water.
- Gently wring and dry flat on a towel in the shade.

VENETIAN BLINDS

To clean

- Cut a kitchen sponge in half. Place each sponge half on one inside end of a pair of tongs and secure with rubber bands.
- Place the sponged tongs over the top and bottom of each slat, pinch together and run along the slat.
- If very dirty, wipe slats with black tea and hot water on the tongs.
- Alternatively, make a bran ball. Place 1 cup of unprocessed wheat bran in a large bowl. Add drops of white vinegar one at a time, stirring as you go, until the mixture resembles breadcrumbs. It shouldn't be wet. Place the mixture into the toe of pantyhose and tie off tightly. It will be the size of a tennis ball.
- Wipe the bran ball over the dirty slats as though using an eraser.
- When finished, store the bran ball in a zip-lock bag in the freezer to use again.
- Alternatively, put on white gloves and run your fingers along the slats.

TIP

Have a peg handy in case the front doorbell rings while you're cleaning the blinds. That way you know where to resume cleaning.

VINAIGRETTE

(see 'Salad Dressing')

VICKS VAPORUB

(see 'Ointment')

VINDALOO

(see also 'Tandoori')

On carpet/upholstery

- Remove excess by lifting with a plastic comb or by blotting with paper towel.
- Massage with a couple of drops of dishwashing liquid on your fingertips until the liquid feels like jelly.
- Wipe with a damp cloth until the dishwashing liquid is removed.
- Place white vinegar on a cloth and wring tightly so it's damp but not wet. Blot over the mark.
- Wipe with 2 drops of lavender oil on a cloth.
- To remove food colouring, expose to sunlight or ultraviolet light. (If using ultraviolet light, protect areas around the stain with cardboard.) Check every 2 hours.
- Absorb moisture by covering the area with paper towel. Place a book on top of the paper towel to assist with absorption.

On chopping board

- Wipe with 2 drops of lavender oil on a cloth.
- Scrub with dishwashing liquid and water.

On cotton/fabric

- Remove excess under the tap using cold water.
- Massage with a couple of drops of dishwashing liquid on your fingertips until the liquid feels like jelly.
- Rinse under blood-heat (body temperature) water.
- Place a dry cotton ball behind the stain. Wipe the front of the stain with 2 drops of lavender oil on a cloth.
- Wash according to the fabric. Dry in sunshine.

VOMIT

On carpet/upholstery

- Remove excess by lifting with a plastic comb or by blotting with paper towel.
- Scribble with a cake of bathroom soap run under cold water.
- Massage with a couple of drops of dishwashing liquid on your fingertips until the liquid feels like jelly.
- Wipe with a damp cloth until the dishwashing liquid is removed.
- If the vomit contains bile (pale lime green colour), wipe with equal parts glycerine and dishwashing liquid on a cloth. Wipe with a damp cloth until the dishwashing liquid is removed.
- To get rid of the smell, mix 1 tablespoon of lemon juice with 1 litre of water in a spray pack and spray over the area.
- Absorb moisture by covering the area with paper towel. Place a book on top of the paper towel to assist with absorption.

On cotton/fabric

- Remove excess under the tap using cold water.
- Soak in ½ lid of *Vanish NapiSan Oxi Action* and 9 litres of hot water for 30 minutes. Don't use on wool or silk. For wool and silk, rinse in 1 teaspoon of cheap shampoo and blood-heat (body temperature) water.
- If it contains bile (pale lime green colour), wipe with equal parts glycerine and dishwashing liquid.
- Wash according to the fabric. Dry in sunshine.

On mattress

- Remove excess by lifting with a plastic comb or by blotting with paper towel.
- Wipe with a damp cloth.
- To get rid of the smell, mix 1 tablespoon of lemon juice with 1 litre of water in a spray pack and spray over the mattress.
- If you can, put the mattress in the sun to dry it out and to kill bacteria.
- If you can't get it in sunshine, dry with a hair dryer.

W

WARDROBE

For mould

- Wipe interior walls with 1/4 teaspoon of oil of cloves in a 250-ml bottle of baby oil on a cloth. Relabel bottle.
- To absorb moisture, tie 6 sticks of white blackboard chalk together with string or ribbon and leave inside the wardrobe to absorb moisture. When the chalk sticks are wet, place them in the sun until they dry out. You can use them over and over again.
- For serious continuous damp, seek professional advice.

For mustiness

- Place 2 drops of oil of cloves on a tissue. Place the tissue on top of an opened packet of loose-leaf tea. Leave in the wardrobe.

For nasties

- Mix 2 bay leaves (which deter moths), 5 whole cloves (which kill mould spores and deter silverfish), 1 tea bag (which kills dust mites), 1–2 heads of lavender (which add fragrance and deter flying insects), 2 cedar chips (which deter moths) and 1 tablespoon of bicarb (which absorbs moisture and helps prevent mould) in a bowl. Place the mixture in the centre of a small piece of muslin or cotton voile and tie up with string or ribbon. Place inside the wardrobe.

To clean timber

- Wipe with furniture polish. Make your own – see **Household formulas**.

WASABI PASTE

On carpet/upholstery

- Remove excess by lifting with a plastic comb or by blotting with paper towel.
- Place white vinegar on a cloth and wring tightly so it's damp but not wet. Blot over the mark.
- Place the vinegar cloth in one hand and a dry cloth in the other and wipe hand over hand, as though stroking a cat, until the stain is removed.
- Absorb moisture by covering the area with paper towel. Place a book on top of the paper towel to assist with absorption.

On cotton/fabric

- Remove excess under the tap using cold water.
- Blot with or soak in white vinegar.
- Wash according to the fabric. Dry on the clothesline or clothes airer.

WASHING MACHINE

For mould on rubber seals

- Mix 1/4 teaspoon of oil of cloves with 1 litre of water in a spray pack.
- Lightly spray over the area.
- Leave for 24 hours.
- Rub with pantyhose dipped in damp, uniodised salt.
- Respray with the oil of cloves solution and leave to dry.

To clean

- On a quick cycle, run an empty load with ½ cup of bicarb in the washing detergent slot and ½ cup of white vinegar in the fabric conditioner slot.
- To clean the seals, wrap an old tea towel around a plastic knife, dip in white vinegar and work under and around the seals.
- Wipe hinges with 2 drops of machine oil and clear away any fluff and dirt.
- For top-loader machines, each quarter, take out the agitator and remove lint and gunk with a plastic comb. Don't remove the grease. The instruction manual will explain how to remove the agitator.

WASPS

To deter

- Remove all nests.
- Mix 4 teaspoons of dried mint or 8 teaspoons of freshly chopped mint with 1 litre of boiling water in a spray pack. Let the solution sit for 15 minutes.
- Lightly spray over the affected area, including old nests.

WATER FILTER

To clean

- When changing a water filter cartridge, add ½ cup of uniodised salt to 1 litre of water, pour it into the top reservoir and allow it to work through the filter.
- When the salt water has worked its way through, fill the top reservoir with clean water and replace the cartridge.

- For stand-alone water containers, add a pinch of uniodised salt and ½ teaspoon of white vinegar when refilling with water. This stops the water from becoming brackish but won't affect the taste.
- In all cases, wipe the outside with uniodised salt and water on a tightly wrung cloth.

WATER MARK

On carpet/upholstery

- Place 1 cup of unprocessed wheat bran in a large bowl. Add drops of white vinegar one at a time, stirring as you go, until the mixture resembles breadcrumbs. It shouldn't be wet. Place in the toe of pantyhose and tie off.
- Use like an eraser in every direction – north, south, east and west.
- Vacuum.

On French-polished timber

- Warm beeswax in the microwave in 10-second bursts.
- Cut a lemon into wedges and remove the flesh from one wedge – don't get juice on the skin of the wedge.
- Apply the warm beeswax to the yellow side of the lemon peel.
- Rub over the mark in the direction of the grain using speed, not pressure.

On polyurethane-sealed surface

- Rub with a little *Brasso* on a cloth. It will look worse before it looks better.

On shower screen

- Glass cancer is the haze on glass that looks like soap scum or water marks. It's caused by chemical residue and the damage is permanent. Don't use harsh abrasives on glass (including commercial glass cleaners).
- To clean glass and alleviate cancer, wipe with white vinegar on a cloth. Then wipe with 1 teaspoon of sweet almond oil on a cloth. Wipe firmly over the glass.

On silk

- Gently rub with a clean white silk square across and down the grain of the silk. Don't rub diagonally.
- If persistent, sprinkle silk with talcum powder, then rub with silk square.
- Alternatively, blot with equal parts white vinegar and water on a cloth. Press heavily in the centre and ease the pressure as you move to the outside.
- Dry flat on a towel in the shade, away from the wind so the fibres don't tangle and leave a dusty look.

On timber

- Wipe with cold black tea.
- Polish with a fine coating of beeswax or carnauba wax – you only need 1 teaspoon for every 4 metres of timber.

On toilet

- Sprinkle with talcum powder and allow to dry.
- Put on rubber gloves and apply *CLR* or *Ranex* to the talcum powder and allow to soak in. Don't get *CLR* or *Ranex* on your skin because it can cause irritation.
- Still wearing gloves, neutralise the chemicals by wiping with white vinegar on a cloth.

WATERMELON

On carpet/upholstery

- Remove excess by lifting with a plastic comb or by blotting with paper towel.
- Place white vinegar on a cloth and wring tightly so it's damp but not wet. Blot over the mark.
- Sprinkle with a little bicarb. Allow to dry.
- Vacuum.

On cotton/fabric

- Remove excess under the tap using cold water.
- Blot with or soak in white vinegar.
- Wash according to the fabric. Dry in sunshine.

On timber

- Wipe with dishwashing liquid on a cloth and allow to dry.
- The timber will have a silvery look. Leave a tea bag over the timber until the colour is restored.

WAX

(Beeswax, candle, surfboard, ski; see also 'Paraffin Wax')

On cardboard

- Place a piece of clean, unbleached calico over the cardboard.
- Warm the calico with a hair dryer on a warm (not hot) setting.
- Place the cardboard and calico in a plastic bag and leave in the freezer for 20 minutes.
- Remove from the freezer and place on a hard, flat surface.

- If too big for the freezer, put ice cubes in a zip-lock bag and place over the calico until hard.
- Gently pull the calico away. The wax should crack off.
- Repeat if there's any remaining wax.

On carpet/upholstery

- Put ice cubes in a zip-lock bag and place over the wax.
- When the wax is chilled, remove excess by lifting with a plastic comb. Vacuum.
- When you've removed as much wax as possible, blot with 2 drops of tea tree oil on a cotton ball or cloth.
- Wipe with a damp cloth until removed.
- Absorb moisture by covering the area with paper towel. Place a book on top of the paper towel to assist with absorption.

On cooktop

- Put ice cubes in a zip-lock bag and place on top of the wax.
- When the wax is chilled, scrape away as much as possible with a dull knife. If removing wax from an enamel stovetop, use a plastic or wooden spatula.
- Rub with 2 drops of tea tree oil on pantyhose.
- If removing the chilled wax from a glass cooktop, do not scrape but use tea tree oil only.

On cotton/fabric

- If possible, place in the freezer for 15 minutes. If not, place ice cubes on top of the wax.
- When the wax is chilled, remove as much as possible by rubbing the fabric with the wax on it against itself or scraping off the wax with a plastic comb.

- Rub 2 drops of tea tree oil over the wax residue.
- Wash according to the fabric. Dry on the clothesline or clothes airer.

On granite

- Scrub with 2 drops of tea tree oil on pantyhose. Repeat if the wax returns to the surface. (Because granite is porous, the wax can penetrate.)
- For watermarks, rub with a little *Brasso* on a cloth. It will look worse before it looks better.

On timber

- Rub with 2 drops of tea tree oil on a cloth.
- Alternatively, rub with a piece of damp silk in the direction of the grain. This cuts through the wax without damaging the surface. If a greasy stain remains, rub with a little tea tree oil on a cloth.
- For coloured wax, wipe with a small amount of white vinegar or lemon juice, and expose to either sunlight or ultraviolet light. Protect the surrounding area with cardboard. Check every 2 hours.

WEEVILS

To deter

- Place dried (they must be dried) bay leaves at 50-cm intervals along your pantry shelves and inside containers. Always keep flour and grains in airtight containers.
- Alternatively, place 1 tablespoon of salt in a square of plastic wrap and shape into a ball. Make a few pin holes in the plastic wrap. Place inside containers.

TIP

Turn fresh bay leaves upside down to dry so the essential oils work their way to the tips of the leaves.

WETSUIT

After swimming

- After swimming in chlorine or salt water, rinse wetsuit in a 9-litre bucket of water containing 1 cup of white vinegar and dry in the shade.

For wax

- Place in the freezer or put ice cubes over the wax.
- When the wax is chilled, remove as much as possible by rubbing the fabric against itself.
- To remove wax residue, wipe with 2 drops of tea tree oil.

To clean

- Place the wetsuit in a bathtub with blood-heat (body temperature) water, 1 teaspoon of glycerine, 1 cup of white vinegar and 1 cup of uniodised salt.
- Stomp up and down on it with clean feet.
- Rinse in blood-heat water.
- Dry in the shade.
- Store flat or with fabric between the folds so the surface doesn't come into contact with itself.

WHITE MARK

On café blinds (polypropylene)

- Wipe with sweet almond oil on a cloth.
- To prevent marks, wipe with sunscreen on a cloth.

On glass

- Wipe with sweet almond oil on a cloth.

On plastic

- Polish with equal parts glycerine and talcum powder on a cloth.
- If this doesn't work, the plastic is damaged.

On tiles

- For salt or lime scale, wash with white vinegar on a broom.
- If this doesn't work, it's glass cancer, which means the surface is permanently damaged. Clean and alleviate by wiping with sweet almond oil on a stiff broom and polishing with a cloth. Seal with a good-quality tile sealer.

On timber

- Wipe with equal parts mayonnaise and bicarb on pantyhose.
- Aim a hair dryer on a warm (not hot) setting at the timber.
- Wipe with a damp cloth.
- Alternatively, wipe with *Brasso* on a cloth. It will look worse before it looks better.

WITE-OUT

(see 'Correction Fluid')

WHITE WINE

(see 'Wine')

WHITEBOARD MARKER

(see 'Pen')

WINDOWS

(see 'Glass')

WINDSCREEN

For stone chips/hazing

- Wipe with sweet almond oil on a cloth after washing.

For wax build-up

- Rub with equal parts glycerine and tea tree oil on pantyhose.
- Remove residue with a couple of drops of dishwashing liquid and water on a cloth. Remove dishwashing liquid with water.

WINE

On carpet/upholstery

- Remove excess by blotting with paper towel. Don't apply salt or soda water.
- Sprinkle with a little bicarb and tap with your fingers. Red wine will change colour from red to pale grey.
- Wring a cloth in white vinegar and wipe out the bicarb. Repeat until the colour is removed.
- Leave to dry.
- Vacuum. Repeat, if needed.
- For old stains, wipe with 2 drops of glycerine on a toothbrush. Leave for 90 minutes. Then follow the instructions above.

On cotton/fabric

- Rinse under blood-heat (body temperature) water.
- Blot with or soak in white vinegar until the stain is removed.
- For old stains, wipe with 2 drops of glycerine. Leave for 90 minutes. Then blot with or soak in white vinegar.
- Wash according to the fabric. Dry on the clothesline or clothes airer.

On stone

- Wipe with white vinegar on a cloth.
- If stubborn, mix plaster of Paris and water to the consistency of peanut butter.
- To each cup of mixture, add 2 teaspoons of white vinegar.
- Spread 5 mm to 1 cm thick over the stain.
- Allow to dry completely. If it feels cold on the back of your hand, it's not dry.
- When dry, brush away.

WOOD BORER

(see 'Furniture Beetle')

WOOL

Jumpers need different treatment – see 'Jumper'.

DIY dryclean

- Sprinkle with uniodised salt.
- Rub with a clean handkerchief or piece of linen. Don't go in circles but up and down with the grain of the fabric.
- When clean, shake vigorously and brush with a bristle brush.

For shrinkage/stretching

- For dark-coloured jumpers, mix 2 tablespoons of Fuller's earth or Epsom salts in a 15-litre bucket of blood-heat (body temperature) water.
- For light-coloured jumpers, mix 4 tablespoons of Fuller's earth or Epsom salts in a 15-litre bucket of blood-heat water.
- Immerse the item and gently agitate with your hands until it's thoroughly wet.
- Leave for 10–15 minutes. Don't leave it longer or it will bleach.
- Rinse item in blood-heat water.
- Gently wring and dry flat in the shade on a clean towel.
- Gently stretch it back into shape as it's drying. Pin the outline to a towel. To make the stretch even, hold a wide-toothed comb on each inside edge of the jumper and stretch outwards using the combs.

For yellowing

- Soak with 1 teaspoon of cheap shampoo and 1 tablespoon of 3 per cent hydrogen peroxide in 9 litres of blood-heat (body temperature) water for 20 minutes. Place a dinner plate on top to keep item immersed.
- Rinse in blood-heat water.
- Gently wring and dry flat on a towel in the shade.

To clean most woollens

- Wash in 1 teaspoon of cheap shampoo and blood-heat (body temperature) water.
- Rinse in 1 teaspoon of cheap hair conditioner and blood-heat water.
- Gently wring and dry flat on a towel in the shade.

To clean suits, coats and jackets

- Put 1 kg of unprocessed wheat bran in a bowl and add white vinegar until the mixture resembles breadcrumbs – it should be clumping but not wet.
- Fill a pillowcase with the mixture and place the garment inside.
- Close the top of the pillowcase and shake vigorously. Alternatively, sit on the closed pillowcase for an hour a day for a week.
- Remove the item and shake until the bran is removed (best done outside). Remove residue with a stiff brush.

To deter moths

- Mix 2 large cedar chips, 2 bay leaves and 1 teaspoon of camphor flakes. Store in the tied-off toe of pantyhose.

To deter silverfish

- Mix 2 whole cloves with 2 large cedar chips, 2 bay leaves and 1 teaspoon of camphor flakes. Store in the tied-off toe of pantyhose.

TIP

If you need to hang woollens, put pantyhose through the sleeves and peg the pantyhose to the clothesline.

WORCESTERSHIRE SAUCE

On carpet/upholstery

- Remove excess by blotting with paper towel.
- Place white vinegar on a cloth and wring tightly so it's damp but not wet. Blot over the mark.

- Absorb moisture by covering the area with paper towel. Place a book on top of the paper towel to assist with absorption.

On cotton/fabric

- Rinse the stain with white vinegar.
- If stubborn, heat white vinegar in the microwave until it's steaming. Pour through the stain until removed.
- Wash according to the fabric. Dry on the clothesline or clothes airer.

On stone

- Wipe with white vinegar on a cloth.
- If stubborn, mix plaster of Paris and water to the consistency of peanut butter.
- To each cup of mixture, add 2 teaspoons of white vinegar.
- Spread 5 mm to 1 cm thick over the stain.
- Allow to dry completely. If it feels cold on the back of your hand, it's not dry.
- When dry, brush away.

Y

YELLOWING

On antique fabric

- If the fabric is synthetic, wipe with methylated spirits on a cloth and rinse in cold water before following the instructions below.
- Place a small mountain of uniodised salt over each mark.
- Squeeze drops of fresh lemon juice over each mountain of salt until it's moist but doesn't collapse. Stop squeezing before the juice hits the bottom of the salt. Leave in the sun to dry.
- Remove the salt when dry. Repeat, if needed.
- If yellowing is from contact with plastic, mix bicarb and cold water to the consistency of peanut butter.
- Apply to the stain and allow to dry. Then brush off.
- If the fabric is sturdy, wipe with a dab of *CLR* or *Ranex* on a cloth. Don't get *CLR* or *Ranex* on your skin because it can cause irritation.
- As soon as the yellow mark bleeds, rinse under cold water.
- Wipe with white vinegar on a cloth.
- If the yellowing is from timber shelving, wipe with 2 drops of glycerine on a cloth. Leave for 90 minutes.
- In all cases, wash according to the fabric. Dry on the clothesline or clothes airer.

On ceramic

- Wipe with glycerine, then sprinkle with talcum powder and allow to dry.
- Put on rubber gloves and apply *CLR* or *Ranex* to the talcum powder and allow to soak in. Don't get *CLR* or *Ranex* on your skin because it can cause irritation.
- Rinse with water. Dry in sunshine.

- Alternatively, add 4 denture tablets to a sink of hot water, immerse item and leave overnight. Dry in sunshine.

On cotton/fabric (not antique/silk/wool)

- For synthetic fibres, dip in methylated spirits and wring out tightly.
- For natural fibres, soak overnight in ½ lid of *Vanish NapiSan Oxi Action* and 9 litres of blood-heat (body temperature) to hot water. Don't use on wool or silk.
- In both cases, wash according to the fabric. Dry in sunshine.

On ivory

- Ivory yellows with age and you can't make it white again.
- Clean by mixing sweet almond oil and talcum powder to the consistency of runny cream.
- Apply the mixture with a cotton bud.
- Polish off immediately with a damp cotton bud.

On plastic

- Make a paste of glycerine and talcum powder.
- Gently rub the mixture onto the marks with a cloth.
- If the plastic has already perished (looks burnt), it can't be salvaged.

On silk/wool

- Mix 2 teaspoons of 3 per cent hydrogen peroxide in a 9-litre bucket of blood-heat (body temperature) water.
- Immerse the item and put a dinner plate on top to keep it fully in the solution. Leave for 6 hours.
- Remove and hand wash in a bucket of blood-heat water with 1 cup of white vinegar.

- Rinse in 1 teaspoon of cheap shampoo and blood-heat water.
- Gently wring and dry flat on a towel in the shade away from the wind.

YOGHURT

On carpet/upholstery

- Remove excess by lifting with a plastic comb or by blotting with paper towel.
- Scribble with a cake of bathroom soap run under cold water.
- Wipe with a damp cloth.
- Absorb moisture by covering the area with paper towel. Place a book on top of the paper towel to assist with absorption.

On cotton/fabric

- Remove excess under the tap using cold water.
- Scribble with a cake of bathroom soap run under cold water. Rub the fabric against itself using your hands.
- Wash according to the fabric. Dry on the clothesline or clothes airer.

Z

ZINC CREAM

On carpet/upholstery

- Remove excess by lifting with a plastic comb or by blotting with paper towel.
- Wipe with equal parts baby oil and tea tree oil on a cloth.
- Sprinkle with a little talcum powder.
- Scrub with pantyhose.
- For remaining stains, massage with a little dishwashing liquid on your fingertips until the liquid feels like jelly.
- Wipe with a damp cloth until the dishwashing liquid is removed.
- Absorb moisture by covering the area with paper towel. Place a book on top of the paper towel to assist with absorption.

On cotton/fabric

- Remove excess under the tap using cold water.
- Wipe with equal parts baby oil and tea tree oil on a cloth.
- Massage with a little dishwashing liquid on your fingertips until the liquid feels like jelly.
- Rinse under blood-heat (body temperature) water.
- Wash according to the fabric. Dry on the clothesline or clothes airer.

ZIPPER

For looseness

- Sprinkle a little salt on the teeth of the zipper. Work up and down.

For encrusted salt

- This is a common problem for sailors.
- Wipe with white vinegar on a cloth.
- For metal zippers, rub over the zipper with a lead pencil or graphite powder. Work the zipper up and down.
- For nylon zippers, wipe with equal parts glycerine and talcum powder and work the zipper up and down to loosen. Rinse with a damp cloth.

For stickiness

- For metal zippers, wipe with white vinegar on a cloth.
- Rub over the zipper with a lead pencil or graphite powder. Work the zipper up and down.
- For nylon zippers, apply 2 drops of glycerine and work the zipper up and down.
- Sprinkle with talcum powder. Work the zipper up and down.

HOUSEHOLD FORMULAS

ACID-FREE DRAWER LINERS

- Fill a spray pack with warm water, add 1 tea bag and allow to sit for 3 minutes. Remove the tea bag and add 2 drops of oil of cloves and your favourite perfume or essential oil to the bottle.
- Spray over acid-free paper (available from newsagencies and removalists).
- Allow the paper to dry, cut to size and place in drawers and cupboards. Replace each year.

BRAN BALL

(Can be used on upholstery, fabric, suede)

- Put 1 cup of unprocessed wheat bran in a bowl and add white vinegar, 1 drop at a time, until the mixture resembles breadcrumbs – it should be clumping but not wet.
- Place the mixture into the toe of pantyhose and tie tightly. Rub the pantyhose across a surface like an eraser.
- The bran ball can be reused again and again. Store in a zip-lock bag in the freezer. Add drops of white vinegar to re-moisten.

CAR WASH SOLUTION

- Mix 3 cups of strong black tea, 1 teaspoon of tea tree oil and 1 teaspoon of dishwashing liquid in a 9-litre bucket of warm water.
- Use a sponge to apply, then rinse with a hose.

CARPET CLEANER

(For steam cleaning)

- Carpet steam-cleaning machines can be hired at supermarkets. They come with a bottle of cleaning chemicals.
- Use only half the amount the manufacturer suggests and top up with 2 tablespoons of bicarb, 2 tablespoons of white vinegar, 2 tablespoons of methylated spirits, 2 teaspoons of glycerine and 2 teaspoons of eucalyptus oil.
- This solution is also a great multi-purpose spot cleaner. Leave it in a 1-litre spray pack and use as needed.

FURNITURE POLISH/LEATHER CONDITIONER

- Place 1 teaspoon of beeswax, 1 teaspoon of lavender oil and 1 teaspoon of lemon oil on a cotton cloth, such as an old T-shirt.
- Place in the microwave in a microwave-safe dish. Microwave on high in 10-second bursts until the beeswax melts.
- When it cools, use it over leather and timber.
- After using it, place the cloth in a zip-lock bag and store in the freezer ready to use again.

GENERAL CLEANER FOR CARPET

- Mix 2 tablespoons of bicarb, 2 tablespoons of white vinegar, 2 tablespoons of methylated spirits, 2 teaspoons of glycerine, 2 teaspoons of eucalyptus oil, 2 teaspoons of dishwashing liquid and 1 litre of water in a spray pack. Lightly spray over carpet, then wipe with a damp cloth.

GLYCERINE SOLUTION

(To remove tannin stains)

- Mix 2 tablespoons of glycerine with 2 cups of water and place in a 1-litre spray pack.
- Lightly mist over areas. Leave for 90 minutes. Wipe off with a damp cloth.

HARD SURFACE CLEANER

- Combine 1 teaspoon of lavender oil, 1 cup of white vinegar and 1 litre of water in a spray pack. Shake well before use.
- Lightly mist over hard surfaces, then wipe surfaces with a clean cloth.
- Don't use this on marble because white vinegar is an acid and will eat into marble.

INSECTICIDE SPRAY

- Mix 4 teaspoons of dried mint or 8 teaspoons of freshly chopped mint with 1 litre of boiling water in a spray pack.
- Let it sit for 15 minutes. Spray as needed.

LAUNDRY DETERGENT FOR DELICATES AND SOFT WOOLLENS

- Mix ½ cup of pure soap flakes, ¼ cup of cheap shampoo, 2 teaspoons of bicarb and 2 teaspoons of white vinegar in a clean, appropriately labelled detergent bottle. Add 2 litres of water, shake and it's ready to use.
- Add fragrance if desired, such as 2 teaspoons of lavender oil, but be careful adding eucalyptus oil because it strips colour and oils from fabric.

- Adding ½ teaspoon of tea tree oil is a good disinfectant and antiviral.
- For a regular-size, lightly soiled load, use 1 tablespoon of detergent for a top loader and ½ tablespoon for a front loader.

LAUNDRY DETERGENT FOR SENSITIVE SKIN

- Combine 1 tablespoon of pure soap flakes, the juice of 1 lemon and 2 tablespoons of bicarb in a large jar. Add 2 cups of warm water, mix well and label the jar.
- For a regular-size, lightly soiled load, use 1 tablespoon of detergent for a top loader and ½ tablespoon for a front loader.

LEMON OIL

- Place lemon zest (grate the peel) on plastic wrap and leave on a sunny windowsill. The oil will leach from the peel onto the plastic. Store in a small vial.

MOULD REMOVER FOR HARD SURFACES

- Mix ¼ teaspoon of oil of cloves in a 1-litre spray pack of water.
- Spray and leave for 24 hours before respraying. Wipe surfaces with a clean cloth.

PRE-WASH LAUNDRY SPRAY

- Mix 2 tablespoons of methylated spirits, 2 teaspoons of lavender oil, 1 teaspoon of tea tree oil, 2 teaspoons of glycerine, 1 teaspoon of dishwashing liquid and 500 ml of warm water in a spray pack.
- Shake and lightly mist as needed.

SURFACE SPRAY

- Mix 1 teaspoon of lavender oil with 1 litre of water in a spray pack. Use on hard surfaces.

TIMBER SEALANT

- Timber surfaces can be sealed with varnish, polyurethane, shellac or wax. To work out the sealant, take a pin or needle, hold it in a pair of pliers and heat it on the stove. Touch the pin or needle to an inconspicuous part of the item and work out what smell it creates. If it smells like burnt plastic, it's coated in polyurethane. If it smells like an electrical fire, it's an oil-based varnish. If it smells like burnt hair, it's shellac. If it smells like a snuffed candle, it's wax. If it smells like burnt fries, it's tung oil.
- To repair polyurethane, apply a little *Brasso* with a lint-free cloth and rub swiftly over the mark in the direction of the grain. It will look worse before it looks better. *Brasso* partially melts polyurethane and allows it to refill the tiny air holes that leave white water marks.
- Shellac, varnish and wax are repaired with beeswax. Warm beeswax in a bowl in the microwave until just softened, then apply with the skin side of a piece of lemon peel. Don't get any lemon juice on the peel because the acid in the juice will neutralise the oils and they won't work. Rub in the direction of the grain using speed, not pressure.
- To repair tung oil, clean the surface and reapply tung oil according to instructions.